MW01385529

NAIS

Journal of the NATIVE AMERICAN *and*
INDIGENOUS STUDIES ASSOCIATION

VOLUME 6.1

2019

NAIS (ISSN 2332-1261) is published two times a year in spring and fall (Northern hemisphere) by the University of Minnesota Press, 111 Third Avenue South, Suite 290, Minneapolis, MN 55401-2520. http://www.upress.umn.edu

Copyright 2019 by the Regents of the University of Minnesota

All rights reserved. With the exception of fair use, no part of this publication may be reproduced, stored in a retrieval system, or transmitted, in any form or by any means, electronic, mechanical, photocopying, recording, or otherwise, without a license or authorization from the Copyright Clearance Center (CCC), or the prior written permission of the University of Minnesota Press.

Postmaster: Send address changes to *NAIS,* University of Minnesota Press, 111 Third Avenue South, Suite 290, Minneapolis, MN 55401-2520.

Information about manuscript submissions can be found at naisa.org, or inquiries can be sent to journal@naisa.org.

Books for review should be addressed to
NAIS, The University of Texas at Austin, 150 W. 21st Street, Stop B3700, Austin, TX, 78712-1155.

Address subscription orders, changes of address, and business correspondence (including requests for permission and advertising orders) to *NAIS,* University of Minnesota Press, 111 Third Avenue South, Suite 290, Minneapolis, MN 55401-2520.

SUBSCRIPTIONS

- **Individual subscriptions to *NAIS*** are a benefit of membership in the Native American and Indigenous Studies Association. To become a member, visit http://naisa .org/. NAISA has four membership categories with annual dues that range from $25 to $100 and run on a calendar year.
- **Institutional subscriptions to *NAIS*** are $108 inside the U.S., $113 outside the U.S. Checks should be made payable to the University of Minnesota Press and sent to *NAIS,* University of Minnesota Press, 111 Third Avenue South, Suite 290, Minneapolis, MN 55401-2520.
- **Back issues of *NAIS*** are $27 for individuals (plus $6.00 shipping for the first copy, $1.25 for each additional copy inside the U.S.A.; $9.50 shipping for the first copy, $6 for each additional copy, outside the U.S.A.).
- **Digital subscriptions to *NAIS* for institutions** are available online through the JSTOR Current Scholarship Program at http://www.jstor.org/r/umnpress.

JEAN M. O'BRIEN COEDITOR
(*White Earth Ojibwe*) University of Minnesota
ROBERT WARRIOR COEDITOR
(*Osage*) University of Kansas
SIERRA WATT MANAGING EDITOR
(*Pechanga Band of Luiseño*) University of Kansas
SASHA M. SUAREZ MANAGING EDITOR
(*White Earth Ojibwe*) University of Minnesota

EDITORIAL BOARD

JENNIFER ADESE
(*Otipemisiwak/Métis*)
University of Toronto, Mississauga
LOURDES ALBERTO
(*Zapotec*)
University of Utah
CHRIS ANDERSEN
(*Métis*)
University of Alberta
ERIC CHEYFITZ
Cornell University
ALEJANDRA DUBCOVSKY
University of California, Riverside
ALYOSHA GOLDSTEIN
University of New Mexico
JOANNA HEARNE
University of Missouri
BRENDAN HOKOWHITU
(Ngāti Pukenga [*Māori*])
University of Waikato
DANIEL HEATH JUSTICE
(*Cherokee Nation of Oklahoma*)
University of British Columbia
BRIAN KLOPOTEK
(*Choctaw*)
University of Oregon
AILEEN MORETON-ROBINSON
(*Goenpul*)
Queensland University of Technology

CHRISTOPHER PEXA
(*Spirit Lake Dakota*)
University of Minnesota
KEITH RICHOTTE
(*Turtle Mountain Band of Chippewa Indians*)
University of North Carolina—Chapel Hill
DANIEL RIVERS
(*Cherokee Nation of Oklahoma*)
Ohio State University
DAVID DELGADO SHORTER
University of California, Los Angeles
NOENOE SILVA
(*Kanaka Maoli*)
University of Hawaiʻi, Mānoa
ROSE STREMLAU
Davidson College
JOHN TROUTMAN
National Museum of American History, Smithsonian
EVE TUCK
(*Aleut Community of St. Paul Island*)
University of Toronto
RENAE WATCHMAN
(*Diné*)
Mount Royal University

NAIS

Journal of the NATIVE AMERICAN *and*
INDIGENOUS STUDIES ASSOCIATION

CONTENTS

VOLUME 6 ● ISSUE 1

2019

Articles

Interventions

Reviews

JASON R. SELLERS

An "Indyan Called Nangenutch or Will": Indian Identity and Identification in a 1668 Long Island Rape Trial

ON MARCH 19, 1667/68, in the town of East Hampton on the southeastern tip of Long Island, Nangenutch, a Montauk Indian also known to the English as Will, met Mary and John Miller as he approached their home. A bound laborer delivering a bag of corn for grinding, Nangenutch accompanied Mary back to the house while John continued onward to visit a neighbor. Once inside "the Indian came and pulled her down into the floore, and pulled up her Coates, and stopped her mouth with his hand, and thrust her against a block, and being too strong for her, against her will hee committed the act of uncleannesse upon her body" amid her continued protests before eventually desisting. Fleeing her home, Mary encountered a neighbor, to whom she related the attack, and by the following day local magistrates had indicted Nangenutch and deposed Mary and two previous victims. They referred the case to a higher court, which examined Nangenutch on March 28. He largely confirmed Mary's account, and the case proceeded to trial the following month. Despite concluding unanimously that the defendant had not committed the capital crime of rape because he had not ejaculated, the court found him guilty of attempted rape, ordering him publicly whipped and sold into slavery in the Leeward Islands "that all Indyans may bee deterred to attempt the like." However, Nangenutch evaded his punishment by escaping his Manhattan jail and rejoining his natal community at Montauk. Frustrated by their inability to apprehend the fugitive as he occasionally appeared near East Hampton over the next two years, English officials issued orders barring him from entering the town and levied a fine on the Montaukett that was later used to extract land concessions from the struggling community.[1]

A rare instance of documented Indian sexual assault on an English woman, this episode provides a unique opportunity to consider the fate of Native individuals and communities forced to grapple with a shifting matrix of social relations as a succession of colonial regimes undermined Native

American economic independence, political and legal sovereignty, and cultural autonomy. As Nangenutch tried to negotiate the new colonial order, his attack was shaped by dramatic upheavals in the world around him. Moreover, the persistent ties between Nangenutch and his natal community and the consequences of his actions for the Montauketts as a whole reinforce the impression that his experience was indeed more than simply personal. By the late seventeenth century, the Montauketts—like other Natives in England's growing North American colonies—struggled to define the relationship between themselves and the newer colonial communities as they positioned themselves in a developing regional social landscape.[2]

None of these considerations excuse the violence Nangenutch inflicted on Mary and at least two previous victims, and it is certainly reasonable to view him as a sexual predator and serial offender. But to so simplify his story would be to dismiss—to borrow a phrase from Wendy Warren—a "life in need of reconstruction" and to neglect an opportunity to carefully consider the influence of complex forces on a historical actor. The result would caricature an individual who appears in the documentary record only in relation to this single incident and thus frame his historical experience entirely in European American legal terms that obscure other aspects of his fuller life. Ashley Glassburn Falzetti has argued that archival absences erase the complex identities and histories of Native individuals in order to explain and justify settler colonialism; Nangenutch's subsequent disappearance from the historical record reflects not just his individual erasure but also the diminished stature of the Montauketts on English Long Island. Nangenutch's case, then, offers a chance to examine rather than reproduce the historical forces that largely silenced Nangenutch himself and ultimately the Montaukett as well.[3]

The documentary record produced by English colonial authorities most transparently reflects their concerns about governing Indian subjects and English legal procedures and standards of evidence surrounding the crime of rape. A series of legal records details the sequence of events that spanned just over a month from attack to indictment to trial to verdict. That the documents are dated from only five days and that Nangenutch's master served as "Interpreter betweene the prisoner and the prosecutor" remind us that this is a limited and mediated account. A second body of sources complements the trial records but treats the incident only intermittently, as a series of letters and court orders stretching into 1670 addresses Nangenutch's escape and subsequent reappearance, as well as the fine levied against his community.[4]

Despite these limitations, a pattern of behavior on Nangenutch's part, as well as something of the larger story of Montaukett-English relations in colonial New York, emerges in the documentary record. Individual experiences, like that of Nangenutch, inevitably occurred within the larger context of English colonialism in North America and, in this instance, New York in particular. To date, John Strong has provided both the most thorough examination of this case and the most complete study of the Montaukett Indians. He has argued that, following a period of tenuous colonial claims during which the Montauketts were able to negotiate first with the Dutch and then the English on an eastern Long Island middle ground, Nangenutch's trial and its aftermath from 1668 to 1670 reinforced emerging patterns of dependence that left the Montauketts subject to English colonial domination. More broadly, Susanah Shaw Romney has argued that even though networks of personal relationships constituted the basis of political and economic systems in both the Native Hudson Valley and New Netherland, the failure to establish intimate connections between Native and colonial communities led to the escalating intercultural violence of the seventeenth century.[5]

While historians studying Native American responses to colonial regimes have considered the extension of English legal jurisdiction a crucial part of the erosion of Native sovereignty, others have turned to cultural considerations to explore the logic employed in empire building and the subjugation of Native peoples. In particular, a number of scholars have considered sexuality in the context of larger imperialist projects, arguing that legal and social proscriptions created and enforced racial boundaries and therefore structured power relations in colonial America.[6] Sharon Block has identified the ways in which white men used patriarchal privileges derived from their social and economic positions to imbue sexual coercion with the appearance of consent and described how legal processes protected the prerogatives of these men while denying Black and Native men the ability to claim such power. John Wood Sweet has joined Block and Cornelia Hughes Dayton in concluding that such practices "placed much heavier weight on the social identities of the perpetrators and their victims" than on the physical actions that had occurred.[7] But Jennifer Morgan and Kirsten Fischer's caution about some scholars' tendency to overlook personal agency and the desires of individuals is a crucial one. A decade ago, they noted that most scholarship on colonial American sexuality addresses white men, including their fear that cross-cultural sex could overturn the racial order, rather than how others experienced sexual relations. Interested explicitly in Native and African American women, Fischer and Morgan remind us that exploring the motives and experiences of individuals can provide additional insight into the negotiation of power and status in early America.[8]

Considering Nangenutch's individual experiences in East Hampton and the ramifications of his trial and its aftermath for a Montaukett community grappling with English colonialism, this article explores the intersection of individual lived experience with the forces of European colonialism. Applying Morgan and Fischer's reminder more broadly, this essay considers the intensely personal nature of Nangenutch's attacks on three women, with particular attention to his attack on Mary, doing so from the perspectives of both the victims and the perpetrator. However, it necessarily approaches their experiences through a heavily mediated legal record that frames the episode in terms of patriarchal rights and a larger set of colonial relations. Strong's and Romney's work thus informs this article's sense that the very fact that individual experiences were subsumed by a legal process designed to defend English institutions reflected existing inequalities in colonial New York and furthered the systemic oppression of Native peoples. A personal crime became inevitably political because Nangenutch and Mary were inextricably entwined in a larger set of colonial relations that made their social identities and individual experiences emblematic of a larger struggle between the Montauketts and their English neighbors.

As colonialism recast formerly mutually beneficial economic exchange and upset the relative political and social equality of Long Island's neighboring peoples to the benefit of European settlers, it limited Native access to economic and social resources. Nangenutch's own ties to the settler community failed to provide access to the burgeoning English society's social and economic capital; instead, they subordinated him in ways that made what were likely personal attacks on three English women appear to endanger the social relations, property regime, and legal standing from which he was excluded. Colonial officials responded to Nangenutch's assault on Mary as an explicit threat to the power of English patriarchs rather than simply a personal crime, giving it a symbolic importance that made it part of a larger ideological project of colonizing Native peoples. By extending legal jurisdiction over a man the English community identified as an Indian, colonial officials denied Montaukett sovereignty while simultaneously solidifying the boundaries that distinguished Montauk Indians and their English neighbors on Long Island. Because of his marginalization in East Hampton, stemming from his people's struggles with colonization, Nangenutch's individual experience reverberated upon the entire Montaukett community, which saw its marginal political status reinforced by the racial identification and declining social status the trial made abundantly clear.[9]

———

The Montauketts had been a tributary of the powerful Pequots until the New England colonies and Native allies resentful of Pequot power decimated the latter's population in the 1630s. Having escaped one oppressive relationship, the Montauketts subsequently found themselves caught between Narragansett attempts to fill the void left in Native New England by subjecting smaller groups to their own power, Dutch efforts to secure their hold on Long Island, and the aspirations of New Englanders hoping to subsume the Dutch colony. Grappling with increasing material dependence, the Montauketts in 1648 sold English men from Connecticut the land on which the buyers would eventually establish East Hampton on the southeastern fork of Long Island. The move also appeared to be an attempt to counter both Dutch and Narragansett efforts to subjugate the Montauketts by installing an English trade partner and military ally nearby, one part of the sachem Wyandanch's efforts to strengthen his people by building a network of connections with nearby Native and colonial communities.[10]

By the time an English government replaced the Dutch regime in 1664, epidemic disease and escalating Niantic efforts to reduce them to tributary status had diminished Montaukett numbers, forcing them to largely abandon their own lands to take refuge near or within English towns. Thus by 1668 English jurisdiction was solidifying over the whole of Long Island, reinforcing the economic dominance and cultural pressures English settlers had begun to exert on the Montauketts over the previous two decades. Nangenutch personally experienced firsthand both these increasingly unbalanced power relations and Montaukett strategies of creating new ties with their neighbors, assuming the name Will while living as a bound laborer in the home of East Hampton's Richard Shaw. His experience was not unique on Long Island, nor would it have been unusual in New England or the Chesapeake, where recent wars between colonial and Native populations had left Native Americans diminished in numbers and resources and power, displaced from their lands, and either confined to small reserves or isolated and absorbed into colonial settlements.[11]

These developments also disrupted social ties that bound together members of Native communities. During Nangenutch's trial, officials inquired "if hee did the same to her as he used to do to his squaw." Although the court compared his attack on Mary to the sexual prerogatives of English patriarchs, Native notions of marriage prioritized the resulting social connections and kinship structures in which they embedded individuals. The question's phrasing indicated that Nangenutch had been separated from a partner; the couple may have simply lived apart at this time, or his wife may have been a victim of the series of epidemics that between 1659 and 1664 killed an estimated two-thirds of the remaining Montaukett population. More than simply depriving him of a sexual partner, though, the conditions surrounding his residence in East Hampton left Nangenutch socially isolated by stretching, if not permanently sundering, the personal ties that positioned him within the Montaukett community.[12]

Nangenutch thus acted in a historical moment at which English hegemony impeded more familiar means of performing Native ethnic, gender, and status identities. Material dependence on English settlers whose colonial government projected legal authority over Long Island's Natives and an inability to defend themselves against mainland Native powers like the Niantic dramatically circumscribed expressions of Montaukett masculinity that a generation earlier had allowed men to build status and extend kin relations based on their effectiveness as hunters and warriors. Nangenutch's assault on Mary Miller, then, was influenced by the ways in which the changing status of his community curtailed individual expressions of Native identity.[13]

But his attack was also conditioned by Montaukett strategies for combatting isolation by fostering new connections, strategies that could reconstitute social ties and markers of identity. Writing about Dutch New Netherland, Romney has described Native strategies of leveraging connections created by the fur trade and less formal food exchanges to solidify social and political relationships with European newcomers. Similarly, Daniel Mandell has argued that New England Indians responding to colonization embraced "flexible social and cultural boundaries," maintaining ties to their communities of origin while also partaking of "behavioral and symbolic norms" to create new social, political, and economic connections to colonial society. Accordingly, by the time Nangenutch found himself laboring in East Hampton in 1668, he was part of a larger effort by Long Island's Montauketts to construct new ties with their English neighbors to secure their place in the colonial landscape.[14]

As Nangenutch took up residence within an English home, labored in the local economy, and socialized with English colonists, he established connections with English men and women. Embedded within an English household that served as the fundamental unit of English society, he would have observed the social relations that allowed English men to control the personal property and dependent labor that supported their own status and secured the position of other family members within English society. Embracing elements of English identity therefore appeared empowering to people living, like Nangenutch, in a colonial world in which Indians struggled to secure a place. In contrast to his roots in a Montaukett community increasingly marked by material poverty and social isolation, his ties to English East Hamptonites provided potential avenues for accessing the material and social resources of the burgeoning English community on Long Island.

Immersed in English East Hampton, Nangenutch demonstrably developed new personal connections via his economic and social activities and invoked those ties in the course of his trial. During his examination in court, he initially deflected a query about whether he had attacked Mary inside her home by insisting he did not remember, "having beene drinking Liquor at Mr. Backers." Nangenutch's drinking may have been a coping mechanism or excuse for his behavior, but, more subtly, the comment claimed a degree of integration into East Hampton society. The Duke of York had prohibited conveying alcohol to New York's Indians since 1665, reprising similar measures instituted during the Dutch era. Nangenutch thus tried to highlight a relationship based on mutual trust that neither he nor Backer would betray the other as they both flaunted the law. Peter Mancall has argued that Indians consciously incorporated alcohol into religious rituals designed to mobilize spiritual power. Although Backer could just as easily have been motivated by profit rather than a sense of social equality, drinking as a social ritual solidified Nangenutch's new ties to English men, potentially empowering him amid what Mancall describes as "the enormous frustrations and angers that understandably built up among peoples who witnessed their world always on the defensive," as the Montauketts had on seventeenth-century Long Island.[15]

Nangenutch's social drinking, then, demonstrated a degree of familiarity with—and perhaps acceptance by—East Hamptonites, and court records show that he was also well-known to the specific individuals involved in his case. Acting on their existing knowledge of Nangenutch's history in the town, local magistrates responding to his assault on Mary Miller immediately deposed two more women, including a second woman named Mary Miller, wife of George. Earlier, Nangenutch had assaulted Mary (George) following a wheat delivery; in the most recent incident, Mary reported that on meeting Nangenutch her husband "sent his wife back to open the doore that the Indian might set in the corne." Although court records treated the offenses as discrete episodes, the attacks on Mary and Mary (George) both derived from preexisting relationships, as a routine delivery became the pretext for Nangenutch's assault. That Mary (George) told him "I would have him com no more" indicates he had been in her home in a similar capacity before, and John Miller's apparent comfort asking his wife to supervise the delivery alone confirms the impression that Nangenutch's residence and employment in the neighborhood made him a familiar presence in the daily life of East Hampton.[16]

Moreover, Nangenutch surely recognized that the families with which he interacted on business constituted attractive social connections. Several related Millers owned land and held political positions in the town;

meanwhile, the second woman deposed in the aftermath of Nangenutch's assault on Mary, nineteen-year-old Annah Chatfield, belonged to one of East Hampton's most prominent households. Romney points out that Native men and women living in settler towns encountered numerous opportunities to establish intimate relationships, whether sexual or simply personal. Hailing from a culture that did not observe clear distinctions between economic and social exchange, Nangenutch could initially have hoped that his regular interactions with these families would more firmly entwine him in the empowering web of social relations to which his economic role introduced him.[17]

These developing connections left Nangenutch inhabiting a complex cultural position reflected in the ways he was described in the archival record. The indictment described him as "an Indyan commonly called and knowne by the name of Nangenutch amongst the Indyans, and by the name of Will amongst the English," and the deponents referred to him as "Will the Indian."[18] While both descriptions continued to associate him with the Native community, they also acknowledged his English name. Native and English identities were not necessarily incompatible and certainly were not mutually exclusive. Performing different elements of a multifaceted identity could even be an asset, and Nangenutch drew from a variety of cultural practices as he navigated daily life in a colonial community. Indeed, Native cultures often assigned individuals new names when they assumed new political or social responsibilities, and here the widespread use of his English name reflected his developing role in East Hampton. Because Nangenutch's English name, like his economic role and residence in East Hampton, captured a fluid identity that increasingly tied him to the English community, he had reason to embrace it.[19]

What the new name suggested about Nangenutch's identity, however, may not have been consistent with how colonists understood his social position, as his liminality subjected him to varying interpretations by Montauketts, English, and Nangenutch himself. Barbara J. Fields and Karen E. Fields have noted that as part of a process they call "racecraft," individuals may be identified in ways inconsistent with their own identities. Their marginal social status exposes them to that imposed understanding, which in turn reinforces their alienation and subjection.[20] In Nangenutch's case, naming as an act of power signaled the dominance of an ascendant English culture that did not need to cater to Native cultures or accommodate Native identities—at least not those of the Montauketts. English colonists who identified Nangenutch as "Will the Indian" marked him as a member of a diminished outside community occupying a subordinate position in an English village, lacking even the surname that would link him to other English people.

Socially isolated, economically dependent, and culturally alien, he remained primarily an Indian, his transition into East Hampton society eroding his personal autonomy and undermining familiar avenues to social mobility, as well as imposing a new name on him. He found himself in East Hampton exactly because years of interactions between Montauketts and colonists had failed to create the close ties that would have empowered the Montauketts enough to preserve their independence. Court records ratified that loss of power when they justified the extension of English jurisdiction over Nangenutch by reproducing East Hampton residents' identification of him as "Will the Indian."[21]

It is in light of this tension between Nangenutch's identity and identification that we should read his behavior in the assaults on Mary and two other women, as well as the English community's response. Nangenutch almost certainly recognized the disparity between his own position and that of English patriarchs among whom he moved. Although his archival trail hints at his latent ties with East Hampton's English residents, it ultimately far more visibly demonstrates the limitations of those connections' power to incorporate him into colonial society. Those connections were powerful; they proved not truly empowering. Even if his adoption of English cultural elements and economic roles signaled Nangenutch's fluid identity and strengthened his social connections, English East Hamptonites consistently identified him as an Indian only tenuously associated with English society, encapsulating their attitude by calling him "Will the Indian."

The long history of Natives' failed efforts to leverage exchange and physical proximity to create empowering social connections with colonists first in New Netherland and then in New York, as well as the attendant loss of power they experienced as a result, left Nangenutch displaced and marginalized in East Hampton. Consequently, the English people with whom he interacted held very clear notions of Nangenutch's standing and therefore possessed expectations for how their own relative status structured interactions with him. All three women expressed personal desires when they reacted against his unwanted sexual advances. But Annah, Mary (George), and Mary also lived within English households where the patriarchal rights of their husbands or fathers protected them from attack. Additionally, they participated in the local economy through a set of transactional relationships, including when Nangenutch in his role as a laborer temporarily entered domestic spaces they controlled. Accordingly, they engaged Nangenutch in modes of interaction familiar from previous encounters with him but found their security disrupted when he betrayed their expectations by pursuing sexual contact. Nangenutch's unexpected actions transformed once-familiar economic exchanges into a violent attack on the women themselves and on the English social and cultural norms that protected them.

Confident in both the inviolability of their own positions and the transgressive nature of Nangenutch's behavior, all three women immediately and repeatedly rejected his advances. In their depositions, Mary (George) told the Court of Assizes for the Colony of New York that she had "thrust him from me" after he followed her, and Annah reported that Nangenutch ignored her warnings but left after "she strooke him with the stoole," both women's resistance halting the attacks short of what Mary experienced. During his trial, Nangenutch told the court that Mary "cryde out all the while, and often bad him Leave off or lett her alone, Thereupon being afraid some body hearing the Noyse shee made, might come in . . . hee left off."[22] Prevailing English notions of normative sex as a battle in which virtuous women resisted men's initial advances easily accommodated physical force as an acceptable means of persuasion while downgrading women's words and actions and assigning men responsibility for determining consent. As a result, English courts skeptical of rape claims looked for evidence of sustained physical and verbal resistance when they examined victims. That Annah and Mary (George) thwarted Nangenutch's pursuit provided evidence enough of their resistance, but Nangenutch's own explanation of why he eventually stopped his attack on Mary acknowledged her sustained resistance as well.

All three women's resistance was predicated upon their expectations for appropriate interactions with Nangenutch and their clear understanding that they had been wronged as he tried to violate their bodies. Possessed of multiple reasons to reject Nangenutch's advances, none of these women appear to have experienced any confusion about the inappropriate nature of his conduct. Women often hesitated to report sexual attacks, uncertain whether they would be judged complicit, since English cultural norms and legal practices sometimes made coercive and consensual sexual relations difficult to distinguish and put the burden of proof on women. But local officials were obviously aware of Nangenutch's earlier offenses, and Mary testified that as soon as Nangenutch had gone, "shee shut the door[e and] shee went to Rich: Shaws and the first person she[e saw] was Rich: Shaws wife [Remember]; and shee told R: Shaws wife what the Indian had done, and Richards wife came in and told it to John Miller." She first told another woman, who could evaluate Mary's claims before seeking further action, mediate between Mary and her husband, and perhaps lend emotional support. But by immediately departing for Shaw's home, where she knew her husband had gone, Mary also acted within the parameters of a marriage that made her sexually unavailable to men other than her husband and reliant on her husband as her protector. Mary (George), too, was married, while the younger Annah remained under the protection of her father as a patriarch regulating sexual access to his dependents. That these three women reported Nangenutch indicates their clear understanding that he had violated normative English social structures.[23]

Part of what placed Nangenutch clearly and permanently outside those networks of intimate social and kinship relations was his race. While being deposed, Mary repeatedly referred to "the Indian," employing a racial identifier rather than Nangenutch's name, and the depositions of Annah and Mary (George) described him as "Will the Indian." Although that identification set Nangenutch apart, it was only after his initial advances that Mary (George) perceived him as "ill minded," while Annah related that it was after she rejected his advances that he "talked baudily in Indian which she did not well understand." In the sequence of both accounts it was Nangenutch's sexual advances that conveyed his harmful intent rather than prior assumptions that he was dangerous because he was an Indian. None of the women indicated they were wary of Nangenutch at the outset of their encounters, but once his intentions were clear they read less transparent parts of their encounters as similarly menacing. In particular, Annah's comment that he "talked baudily in Indian" implicitly linked his status as an Indian to his illicit behavior, presuming his speech constituted a verbal extension of his physical assault despite her admitted inability to fully understand the language. Nangenutch's identification as an Indian did not make him inherently suspect to these women, but it apparently reinforced other evidence of his harmful intentions.[24]

All three women likely saw in this latest incident an opportunity to seek justice for Nangenutch's attacks, and invoking racial language helped them do so. Annah and Mary (George) shared with Mary the initial trauma of an attack, and all three revisited their experiences while testifying in relation to the trial. But as earlier victims, Annah and Mary (George) also had to cope with a lingering insecurity as their assailant returned to the neighborhood, conducting business and continuing his assaults. English cultural narratives that normalized force in sexual relations, assigned men responsibility for determining consent, and upheld patriarchal relations men could use to maneuver women into vulnerable positions frequently enabled English men to blur the lines between coercive and consensual sexual relations. Highlighting Nangenutch's status as an Indian who by definition lacked the status and privileges of English men, the women rejected any ambiguity surrounding his behavior. Moreover, they portrayed him as anomalous within English East Hampton, suggesting that the threat he posed to English people and institutions could be removed from the community. For them, Nangenutch's racial identification negated any ability to shape sexual contact between himself and English women to appear consensual, denying him the sexual power inherent in English masculinity.

The women's reactions to Nangenutch were based on and reinforced the English colonialism that marginalized Native individuals. At a historical moment in which, based on his own individual experiences and the struggles of his people, optimism about his incorporation into English society was so clearly unwarranted, Mary presumed Nangenutch knew his behavior was inappropriate. Mary told the neighbor to whom she first reported the assault that she had "said if hee would let har goe she would not tell what he had done," a promise that would have appealed to Nangenutch only if he anticipated punishment for his actions. Had he been an English man capable of manufacturing the appearance of consent—simply "Will" rather than "Will the Indian"—he might have construed this offer as ex post facto complicity in covert sexual intercourse. But Nangenutch's own actions support Mary's assumption that he understood the transgressive nature of these encounters.[25]

Nangenutch chose in each incident to escalate his pursuit of sexual contact rather than accept the woman's resistance as a message his advances were unwanted. Persistent attempts to initiate sexual contact marked his encounter with Mary (George), Nangenutch following her from house to barn and laying "his hands on [her] in an unsimly manner" after she told him to leave and turned her back on him. Similarly, Annah reported that even after she declined to follow him to another room and "toke upp A stoole and said she would kill him if he did not let her alone," he "put his hand into her bosome." Nangenutch's quick resort to physical violence when he met verbal resistance in these earlier episodes demonstrated that he was unconcerned with the women's consent. Mary (George) and Annah ultimately drove him away, but his more sustained assault on Mary took a slightly different course. He confessed that he surprised her, "took up her Coates and threw her Downe backwards upon the floore that then she crying out being afraid, hee stopt her mouth with his hand." Perhaps anticipating rejection, he relied on physical violence from the outset and then stifled Mary's verbal protests. Although sexual contact was clearly contested, Nangenutch tried to overcome his victims' various forms of sustained resistance. Each woman's reactions communicated to Nangenutch that his actions were inappropriate, but the larger pattern of behavior exhibited in a series of attacks in which he quickly resorted to force and ignored repeated protests demonstrates that the women's desires were incidental to his purpose.[26]

Nangenutch did, however, try at different moments in these attacks to lend them the appearance of normal social relations. Juxtaposed with his victims' continuous resistance, Nangenutch's use of these strategies implicitly acknowledged that his behavior was transgressive. Annah reported that on entering the Chatfield home, Nangenutch "toke her by the hand and asked her to goe into the other rome." Reproducing courting behaviors to initiate the sexual contact Annah subsequently rejected, Nangenutch preemptively tried to mask the appearance of coercion even as he proceeded to follow and grope his victim.[27] Nangenutch also tried to obscure Mary's resistance during both his attack and the trial that ensued. Although he had previously testified he was "afraid some body hearing the Noyse shee made, might come in . . . hee left off," trial minutes noted that he "denyes that shee cryde out or made any resistance or that hee laid his hands on her mouth." He first tried to literally block her cries and then figuratively silence her by denying that such literal silencing had been necessary at all. The varying testimony suggests Mary did cry out, and her perceived silence was a product of the assault taking place in an isolated location where no one could hear her. Moreover, upon ceasing this most recent attack, Nangenutch demurred when Mary told him to leave the house and "said he must light his pipe." In different circumstances, that apparent lack of urgency might be the mark of an innocent man, but Nangenutch had already admitted his fears of being caught assaulting Mary. In this instance, such a mundane action perhaps was a deliberate attempt to act unconcerned. That strategy could minimize the offense Nangenutch realized he had committed and perhaps offer a chance to de-escalate a conflict and restore amicable relations. At the least, he momentarily delayed the inevitable report of his behavior.[28]

Nangenutch tried to normalize these assaults by obscuring signs of resistance, but as Block has pointed out, only accepted community members possessed the social capital to successfully replicate consensual amorous relations. If Nangenutch had learned from observing colonists that English men were entitled to overpower women's resistance and determine their consent or that English men's testimony would be privileged over women's, he had also learned from his experiences in East Hampton that his marginal status as an outsider made him ineligible to claim the rights of English men. Even if Nangenutch truly expected his efforts to overcome or silence the women's resistance to work, his ineffectual use of strategies available to English men to blur the line between consensual and coercive sexual relations highlights the social arrangements and privileges from which he was excluded in East Hampton.[29]

While Nangenutch's precise motives in these three incidents are unclear, sexual desire remains the simplest explanation for Nangenutch's approaches to all three women and for his persistence in pursuing sexual contact. On first being asked whether he had attacked Mary, he insisted that "hee doth not remember hee did any such thing hee having beene drinking Liquor." Since Natives sometimes exonerated individuals who committed crimes under the disruption of alcohol, and drunkenness sometimes stood as a successful defense in colonial courts, Nangenutch could have been trying to excuse his behavior. Intoxication could also have truly impeded his memory and so contributed to what court records describe as his "divers tales." More importantly, being under the influence of alcohol could have lowered inhibitions that governed Nangenutch's typical interactions with Mary and perhaps contributed to the earlier assaults on Annah and Mary (George). That the explanation he offered focused so narrowly on a particular incident rather than his pattern of behavior suggests he conceived of his attack as a discrete offense involving only himself and Mary.[30]

The inequalities that structured colonial society positioned Nangenutch to carry out attacks that violated social hierarchies, but it seems unlikely he deliberately reacted against those inequalities. His role as an economic subordinate connected him to the English women he attacked in the places where those attacks occurred, both of which were associated with English men. Nangenutch's explanation that "hee began to have such an Intent" when "hee saw [Mary] goe home alone" suggested the attack was more opportunistic than considered. More tellingly, when "the Sentence and Decree of the Court was read and interpreted to the Indyan . . . upon his knees likewise hee begd pardon and forgivenesse of Mary Miller for the Injury hee had done her" rather than addressing her husband or the court. Nangenutch had been born into a matrilineal Montaukett community in which women continued to exercise political power and occupy leadership roles, and previous friendly encounters with Mary might have established a personal relationship that reinforced his sense of her personal autonomy. Nangenutch apologized directly to Mary for what he recognized as an affront to Mary herself, casting his attack as personal more than political.[31]

By neglecting to address his actions' import for the larger social order that John, Mary's husband, represented, Nangenutch subverted a legal framework that presented John as the person wronged in the attack. Given this circumstance and because rape and other sexual crimes are frequently about power, I want to explore a compatible, but more speculative, explanation hinted at above. Although Nangenutch could not present himself as an acceptable sexual partner for English women nor claim the privileges inherent in English patriarchy, his attacks could nonetheless assert his manhood in a colonial social order that increasingly stripped Native men of components of their status and identity. Romney has argued that whereas intimate ties connecting Native groups in the Hudson Valley eased conflict among them, the failure of physical proximity and economic exchange to produce similar connections between Native and European communities led to a series of wars in New Netherland's later years. Among combatants in eastern Algonquian warfare, according to Alice Nash, captive taking challenged an enemy's ability to protect his family at a moment of attack, pitting the martial prowess of groups of men against each other. With Native cultural practices shaping intercultural warfare, we might read Nangenutch's assaults in terms of a contest over masculine prestige; his alienation from English society positioned its members as antagonists, and his attacks challenged English men's ability to protect their homes and families. In this interpretation, Annah, Mary (George), and Mary became proxies for a struggle between English and Montaukett masculinity carried out via attacks on female kin, and Nangenutch ignored their protests precisely because his objective was to attack the very power structures that underpinned their resistance.[32]

Given the Montauketts' diminished numbers, shrinking land base, and economic and military dependence on the colonial communities surrounding them, Montaukett men as a group were less able to build status through open warfare by 1668. However, understanding warfare more broadly as a contest for power allows for the possibility that some men may have sought other avenues to individually express masculine identities, a possibility that with Nangenutch was most apparent in his attack on Mary. Recalling the assault, Mary testified that after "he came in, shee bad him set the bagg on the stoole, and she sate downe by the fire." Nangenutch at that moment faced in Mary a woman to whom he had no legitimate sexual access, a member of an English kin group and larger community from which he was excluded, an economic partner to whom he was subordinate, and a person controlling the kind of secure domestic space that he as a bound laborer did not possess. More, several of those characteristics rested on her marriage to a man who represented the elements of English patriarchy—sexual access, property, dependents, social ties, economic and institutional power—Nangenutch was denied in East Hampton. When Nangenutch "came and pulled her down onto the floore, and pulled up her Coates," he sought to empower himself at his victim's—and perhaps her husband's—expense by challenging the restrictions East Hampton's colonial society imposed upon him as a member of a colonized community. Thus, his attack on Mary threatened the circles of social and economic standing from which he was excluded, operating as an attack both on her personally and on the larger colonial order she represented.[33]

Nangenutch himself may not have intended to threaten colonial institutions and social relations or recognized the full ideological significance of his attacks, but colonists reacted to the larger implications of what they understood as a veiled attack on the English community. The indictment of Nangenutch noted that it was "John Miller of Easthampton in the East Ryding of Yorkshire upon Long Island Husbandman" who presented the case, and the verdict pointedly responded to "an Indictment brought into the court by John Miller of Easthampton upon Long Island Husbandman." Since his own power entailed the ability to define his wife's consent, John immediately understood the assault as rape and so pursued legal action. Invested in protecting John's status and the rights over his wife's body that status conferred, English officials identified him in legal documents as a "Husbandman," the term encompassing the combined social and economic roles that cohered in John's person and that Nangenutch had violated. What Mary, Mary (George), and Annah experienced as violations of their bodies and personal security in their homes, their husbands and fathers experienced as violations of patriarchal prerogatives. Accordingly, colonial officials were concerned with the danger Nangenutch posed to the property and rights underpinning those men's social capital rather than with the emotional distress of his victims.[34]

Given the clear challenge to John's authority Nangenutch's attack on Mary presented, it seems surprising that he remained at liberty when he had similarly accosted English women in two earlier incidents. That Annah and Mary (George) were promptly deposed demonstrates that the events they recounted had entered the historical memory of the community, even if they do not explicitly appear elsewhere in the documentary record. Surely, then, the incidents had been addressed in some fashion, given the sense of violation the women and their male relations must have felt. Moreover, each woman belonged to a prominent family for whom legal or even informal recourse was available and desirable. These earlier incidents could have been dealt with out of court by Nangenutch's master, but English courts sometimes charged sexual assailants with lesser crimes, and trial records do indicate that Nangenutch had previously run afoul of the law.[35]

The trial transcripts noted, "The said Indyan when he lived with Richard Shaw was twice guilty of Theft; prove of which faults hee was publickely whip't by the Magistrates order." Lacking further detail, the simplest explanation is that Nangenutch in fact stole property. Access to shared resources helped define Native communities' boundaries, so an Indian recently relocated to East Hampton and adjusting to English notions of private property could easily have committed what the courts regarded as theft. A second explanation is that a more culturally conversant Nangenutch aware of English property norms retaliated against more powerful members of East Hampton society by attacking their property or trying to appropriate it for himself. Whether or not he completely understood that his relocation into

English society involved a property regime incompatible with his own exist-ing notions of what constituted personal and community property, Nange-nutch seemed to recognize that controlling property was a means to power in the society in which he found himself. When colonists who understood the incidents as attacks on English property punished Nangenutch to enforce the proper behavior of a subject in a colonial society, they communicated his exclusion from an English property regime and society at large.[36]

Other than as evidence of the defendant's character and background, the pair of thefts at first glance has no clear connection to a later sexual assault, but that court officials noted the incidents suggests they found them per-tinent to the rape trial. Because all three assaults Nangenutch committed occurred in domestic spaces belonging to English men, they also violated the sanctity of private property. Mary had been attacked near the hearth, while Mary (George) had retreated from house to barn. Similarly, Annah testified that "she beinge in her fathers house that Will the Indian came into the house and . . . asked her to goe into the other rome . . . and her boddis was of and he put his hand into her bosome." According to Annah's testimony, Nangenutch caught her unprepared when he entered the house uninvited, violating pri-vate domestic space before violating her body. Because New England Puri-tans who "metaphorically fused" houses and bodies linked their individual lives to a larger social and political structure, Nangenutch's assaults consti-tuted attacks on the larger domestic order, including patriarchal preroga-tives that governed homes and sexual access to dependents. These incidents thus involved simultaneous violations of "the interlaced English norms of patriarchy and private property," aligning instances of sexual assault with property crimes. It is possible that the thefts were separate incidents men-tioned to further establish Nangenutch's criminal history, but given the close association between patriarchy and private property, the incidents identi-fied as "Theft" may actually have been the assaults on Mary (George) and Annah. If this was the case, the legal framing that decentered the victims' experiences downgraded Nangenutch's offenses while trying unsuccessfully to correct his behavior. Regardless of whether the earlier instances of "theft" were actual property crimes or indicated the previous assaults, they helped establish Nangenutch as a persistent and unrepentant danger to an English social order based on private property and patriarchal rights.[37]

Whether the earlier incidents had been dealt with informally or tried as property crimes, only with the third incident was Nangenutch prosecuted for a sexual crime. Accounts of the earlier episodes served now to document a clear pattern of behavior that culminated in Nangenutch's attack on Mary. The rape trial provided Annah and Mary (George) a measure of vindication as Nangenutch was finally tried for a sexual crime with the possibility of capital punishment. Neither of the earlier assaults involved penetration, and neither deposition indicated the involvement of a witness equivalent to Remember Shaw or physical contact that would have produced material evidence on the bodies of Nangenutch, Mary (George), or Annah. The final attack, then, prompted legal action because it was the only one that approximated the strict legal definition of rape to which the court eventually adhered in its verdict.[38]

What distinguished the most recent assault was that Mary had been unable to fight off Nangenutch's attack. That sexual contact had occurred was not disputed, Mary testifying that Nangenutch "did penetrate her body a Thumbs breadth or thereabouts" and court minutes reporting that upon examination "the Indyan confesses that hee . . . did enter her body a litle way." Instead, it was the nature of that contact that was in question, since Nangenutch pleaded not guilty to the rape charge, arguing that "hee desisted upon her intreaty." The court seemed to accept that defense but, more importantly, explained that in addition to "some contradictions in the Informacion," it found "no appearan[ce] of any resistance . . . prooved either by Markes upon her body or upon the Indyans." Based partly on its inability to determine the extent to which Nangenutch had used force in the assault, the Court of Assizes concluded that "there is not Cause of Death in the fact with the Circumstances thereof," declining to convict Nangenutch of the capital crime of rape.[39]

However, in rendering its verdict, the court had actually reached a more complicated conclusion via a legal sleight of hand, transforming the indictment's accusation that Nangenutch "did commit a Rape" into the question of whether "Will: did . . . by force and strength attempt and compasse the carnall knowledge of the body of Mary Miller." This new formulation compelled the court to consider several related but distinct issues: whether Nangenutch had intended to rape Mary, whether he had used force to pursue that aim, and, if so, whether he had succeeded. Testimony clearly established that penile penetration had occurred, proving that sex had been the immediate objective of the encounter. Lacking physical evidence, the court relied on "the testimonies remitted to the Court of the civill and good behavior of the said Mary Miller" to inform its interpretation of the sexual contact as nonconsensual and conclude that she would not have encouraged Nangenutch. Accepting that Mary had been "surpriz'd in the matter, whereby the said Indyan was encouraged to the first part of the attempt," the court determined it was only due to her surprise that Mary had not immediately mounted an effective resistance. Mary and Nangenutch agreed that he had penetrated her, but Mary's declaration that "hee did not spend [ejaculate] in her" further undermined the rape charges.[40]

Some British legal scholars contended that emission was a necessary criterion in determining rape, but others disagreed and insisted that penetration was the sole precondition. In practice, colonial American courts rarely based decisions on emission, but Mary's admission may have reinforced the Court of Assizes' misgivings about convicting Nangenutch of rape. Concluding that he had not succeeded, the court instead referred four separate times to Nangenutch's "attempt" before sentencing him to a public whipping and sale into the Leeward Islands. In ruling that Nangenutch had attempted to rape Mary, the court could adhere to strict evidentiary requirements while still finding and punishing wrongdoing. The logic of that conclusion accommodated both Nangenutch's contention that he had not raped Mary and her experience of a violent assault that violated her body, home, and marriage.[41]

Beyond those pragmatic considerations, the verdict also contributed to a larger ideological project. Scholars considering the role of sexuality and intimate relations in colonialism have argued that images of Indian women comprised one component of an ideology of conquest that combined "European fantasies of territorial and sexual domination." Depictions of "the sexually appealing Indian 'maiden' and the overworked 'squaw drudge'" implied that Native women would abandon Native men and embrace cultural assimilation, Native peoples and lands being subsumed into European empires. In this context, Nangenutch's attack on an English woman threatened to upend an ideology that naturalized colonial domination, upsetting arguments that Native men posed neither a sexual threat to English women nor a military threat to English colonization.[42]

That larger ideological import contributed to what English colonists understood as the "haynousnesse of the attempt" and no doubt influenced the court's determination to make an example of Nangenutch "that all Indyans may bee deterred to attempt the like upon any Christians hereafter." Convicting and punishing Nangenutch allowed the colonial government to discourage challenges to its power and English social dominance, as well as the underlying ideology that supported them. The Court of Assizes' need to discipline his behavior stemmed less from the personal trauma Nangenutch's attacks inflicted on his victims than from its need to control a member of a distinct ethnic community transplanted into English East Hampton. In preserving his life while condemning him to slavery in the Leeward Islands, the court exerted the English government's power to treat Nangenutch as a colonial subject. Unable to reform his behavior with punishments stemming from earlier incidents, it instead transformed his value as a bound laborer into value as a saleable commodity, a move that served empire symbolically and financially. Moreover, by redefining the assault as *attempted* rape and by revising Mary's earlier assertion that "hee did not spend in her" into the verdict's language that "the Indyan did not make any masculine Ejection in her body," the verdict symbolically undercut Nangenutch's masculinity. Annah and Mary (George) had fended off Nangenutch's advances, and even Mary stopped him short of orgasm, the three women's defenses thwarting his personal attack on English patriarchal power and, supported by the court's actions, protecting English social and economic arrangements. The court thus reacted to Nangenutch's perceived capacity to challenge English social structures by denigrating the threat he—and, by extension, other Indian men—actually posed while simultaneously subordinating Native men to colonial power structures.[43]

Despite Nangenutch's alias, physical residence, economic role, and social connections, town residents and colonial officials identified him not as a community member but as a cultural outsider with no claim to the material and social resources that defined their community. His personal status and social mobility diminished in Montaukett society and tightly circumscribed by English society, Nangenutch channeled his frustrations through the same channels that might once have promised integration into a new community. English colonial officials responding to his latest attack on Mary interpreted his actions as threats to English institutions and colonial power relations. Whether his assault on English cultural norms was deliberate or accidental, it further justified the marginalization that had shaped his actions in the first place. In its final verdict, New York's Court of Assizes confirmed Mary's, Mary (George)'s, and Annah's identification of their assailant not primarily as an English man "by the name of Will" but as "Nangenutch an Indyan of Montauke." He was simultaneously denied full participation in colonial society and subjected to the colonial regime's legal apparatus, his personal experience emblematic of the Montauketts' declining status and power in colonial New York.[44]

The diminishing stature of Long Island's Indians subjected them to English legal jurisdiction, which Nangenutch experienced as the culmination of his ongoing alienation in East Hampton and his victims experienced as an opportunity to eventually realize some form of redress. But the assault, trial, and conviction had larger ramifications beyond those personal experiences; it also reverberated onto Nangenutch's natal community, with consequences for the Montauketts as a whole. The mere fact that the trial proceeded through New York's legal system presumed that the colonial government could claim legal jurisdiction over Montaukett individuals, one piece of an ongoing effort to subjugate Long Island's Native communities to English colonial structures. Though the Montauketts' declining status and power were apparent by 1668, they remained a sizeable community with their own land base and Native leadership, retaining some independence and an ability to influence colonial affairs. Their potential to ally with powerful mainland tribes or even assist in a Dutch return to New York could threaten the tenuous English control of the island. That leverage motivated New York's recently installed English administration to maintain a stable relationship with its Native neighbors, a goal aided by the 1665 introduction of a series of reforms known collectively as the Duke's Laws. The laws attempted to standardize legal codes and procedures across New York, guaranteeing due process to all the colony's inhabitants and codifying evidentiary standards. The laws simultaneously laid out a series of provisions specific to Indian relations, these competing imperatives perhaps muddling the status of Indians.[45]

With Nangenutch's case, New York officials found an opportunity to simplify the ambiguous—even contradictory—status of Nangenutch and the Montauketts. Faced with a complex individual linked to two communities that could both claim jurisdiction over his actions and armed with a set of laws that offered the option to treat Indians as equal members of the colonial populace, the Court of Assizes chose to privilege Nangenutch's fundamental Indianness in defining him while also extending its jurisdiction over an inhabitant. Rather than acknowledge competing Native and colonial notions of justice and overlapping claims to jurisdiction, the court imposed English legal norms across eastern Long Island. The circumstances of Nangenutch's subsequent escape and then the transformation of his individual punishment into one borne by his entire community reinforced the links between the racialized identities and legal subjugation of the Montauk Indians. Ultimately, English officials used legal mechanisms to define the social and physical boundaries around English New York, creating first Nangenutch and then the entire Montaukett people as aliens despite their familiarity and proximity.[46]

Apparently, at least a portion of the Montaukett community concurred with English colonists who identified Nangenutch as first and foremost an Indian still integrated into the Native community via his personal connections. Four Montaukett men reportedly helped Nangenutch escape as he awaited sale and transport out of the colony. A successful jailbreak indicated the remaining strength and resources of the Montaukett Indians and the degree to which they continued to consider Nangenutch one of them even while he physically resided in the English town. This scenario assumes that the Montauketts were dissatisfied with the trial's outcome, whether because they believed Nangenutch not guilty, felt the verdict imposed an alien form of justice on an individual they claimed as a community member, judged the punishment meted out to be unfair, or even saw Nangenutch's actions as acceptable responses to the disadvantages he faced in East Hampton. In ruling that "there is not Cause of Death," the Court of Assizes had adhered to strict legal definitions of rape and observed requirements that two eyewitnesses were necessary for conviction in capital crimes cases. But by unilaterally reframing the question of wrongdoing in terms of intent in order to impose a punishment—sale out of the colony—to which white defendants would have been immune, the court ignored the stipulation of the Duke's Laws to treat trials involving Indians "as if the Case had been betwixt Christian and Christian." In convicting Nangenutch of attempted rape and sentencing him to whipping and sale, the court endorsed a version of events that identified him as an outsider excluded from English social and economic resources but nonetheless subject to English laws. His subsequent escape reinforced that his strongest ties were to those outside the English community and confirmed definitions of Indians in general as outsiders by marking him and his four accomplices as fugitives antagonistic to a legal system that helped define East Hampton, Long Island, and greater New York as English societies.[47]

However, citing the security of New York's city jail, John Strong has suggested that English officials allowed the escape either to avoid provoking a hostile response from the Montauketts—more in keeping with the spirit of the duke's imperative and an acknowledgment that they yet retained some influence—or to create leverage in land dealings with them. This scenario, in which colonists hoped to extract concessions from the Montauketts as a whole, rests on subsequent developments that certainly proved fortuitous for English East Hampton. Although there is no proof of a deliberate plot to use the trial to dispossess the Montauketts of land, colonial responses to Nangenutch's escape did extend his marginal status to his entire community, with consequences for its territorial base.

Inheriting the case when he replaced Richard Nicolls as governor just a month after Nangenutch's trial, Francis Lovelace lamented that by escaping, "the Indian . . . hath left a considerable Charge upon the Country occasioned by his miscarriage." His escape constituted another form of attack on the logic of English colonialism by transforming Nangenutch from an asset to the colony—first a bound laborer, then a saleable slave—into a liability, as the costs for his prosecution and imprisonment devolved to the government. Lovelace hoped to recapture the fugitive or arrest the four men who had helped him and "make them pay the Charges" for Nangenutch's trial and imprisonment, which Strong has estimated at about four pounds, but New York's Commission on Indian Affairs instead levied a fine on the Montaukett community as a whole. Variously described as four hundred bushels of corn or forty pounds, the fine was roughly equivalent to four years of agricultural production for ten Montaukett households, a heavy burden for a community whose material well-being was deteriorating due to a diminished land base and limited physical mobility. When the Montauketts were unable to pay the entire fine by April 1669 "in regard of [their] great poverty," Lovelace granted "another yeare for the payment of the whole summe," though by June of the same year he had already "thought fitt to repeale the former order." Likely anticipating that the Montauketts would default, several enterprising East Hampton residents put up a bond guaranteeing the payment, effectively purchasing the Montaukett debt in court, and in concert with the commission they soon began pressuring the Montauketts to give them land in payment.[48]

The fine again contradicted the Duke's Laws standardizing the legal treatment of all New York residents by assigning the Montauketts as a whole responsibility for Nangenutch's guilt and transforming his individual punishment into a burden placed upon his entire community. There was some logic to this action, since Nangenutch and his associates continued to evade colonial authorities despite their known identities, presumably supported by other sympathetic community members. That fact implicated a larger network of Montauketts in which Nangenutch was enmeshed in ways he had never been in English East Hampton, although it remains possible that only a small subset of Montauketts was complicit in Nangenutch's escape and continued evasion of authorities. By assigning responsibility to all the Montauketts, colonial authorities further created them as a group of New York residents distinct from the colony's English citizens, imagining Nangenutch as representative of an entire racial group not entitled to the rights of English New Yorkers rather than as an individual acting only on his own behalf.

Having succeeded in socially alienating Nangenutch by defining him simply as an Indian despite his more complex identity and the Montauk Indians as a group by ignoring the ostensible protections of the Duke's Laws to punish them collectively for an individual's actions, New Yorkers proceeded next to physical alienation. Under mounting pressure from East Hampton proprietors and the Commission on Indian Affairs, accommodationist Montauketts agreed to grant a section of land in payment of the fine, and Lovelace confirmed the arrangement in May 1671. Surrendering one-third of their remaining land base further reduced the Montauketts' economic independence and thus their ability to maintain distance from an English society that disadvantaged them. The English obtained official title to additional lands over which they could exercise exclusive jurisdiction at the expense of the Montauketts, who, though not completely displaced by the cession, were increasingly subject to treatment as social and legal outsiders on their former territory. The aftermath of Nangenutch's trial thus had significant symbolic and material consequences for the Montaukett Indians, continued land loss reinforcing their deteriorating status in the English colony.[49]

Nangenutch's trial had demonstrated the treatment the Montauketts could expect under the English colonial regime. However, like the larger community, Nangenutch apparently remained visible around East Hampton, his presence raising concerns, because Mary, "being married wife and living in ye Towne of East Hampton[,] into ye Towne if ye said Indyan should bee permitted to come it may breed ill bloud and cause some disturbance." In June 1669 Governor Lovelace instructed that "Will ye Indyan bee Ordered not to come into East Hampton or any of ye Townes at ye East end of Long Island; ffor the wch an Order is to bee made, & hee to bee acquainted therewith," though the final version of the order actually specified only that "ye said Will: ye Indyan doe not presume to come into or very neare the said Towne of East Hampton." That the instructions presumed the order could be delivered to Nangenutch suggested he was a regular presence in the area. However, having already been identified by his victims and the Court of Assizes as an Indian excluded from East Hampton's English society and patriarchal status, Nangenutch was now physically barred from a delineated space he had continued to frequent—and a space that soon expanded when the Montauketts relinquished land to cover the fine derived from his trial. Long since denied access to English economic and social resources and recently denied equality under English law, Nangenutch now found himself denied a legitimate physical presence on the lands contiguous with that expanding society. His constrained physical mobility echoed his stunted social mobility, a tangible reminder of the diminishing status of the Montaukett people of eastern Long Island.[50]

The social status imposed on the Montauketts assumed physical form in segregated spaces for members of a community marked as distinct and became tangible in the records that documented their lives. Nangenutch's life is visible mostly in court records that clearly treated him as a colonial subject but not a citizen, records framed by the very colonial ideologies that shaped his actions and English responses. Nangenutch's case vividly illustrates the opportunity scholars have to read creatively against the archive to examine the experiences of historical actors negotiating colonialism. Individuals like Nangenutch who appear only momentarily in the documentary record not only operated within a larger matrix of cultural influences but also responded to those circumstances as individuals with their own personal histories and motivations.

By the time Nangenutch attacked Mary in 1668, a half-century of Dutch and English colonization had combined with the ongoing power struggles between Native polities to erode the Montauketts' subsistence base and political autonomy. But while the dynamics of the region's balance of power were upset by seventeenth-century developments, earlier patterns of forging relationships between individuals and communities to secure material prosperity and peace offered hope for potentially constructing new relationships and networks in the early years of English dominion in New York. Indians adapting to changed circumstances pursued new roles in and alongside English communities; Nangenutch, as one example, took up residence as a laborer identified by an English name, his daily life initiating him into English culture and establishing personal connections that formerly would have helped integrate him into a new community.

But even as Nangenutch exhibited a complex mix of cultural traits influenced by both Native and settler societies, the social and material resources to which he aspired in light of his natal community's declining fortunes remained beyond his reach. When those traits failed to fully integrate him into English East Hampton, the connections he had formed instead operated as channels through which he threatened colonial society. If Annah, Mary (George), and Mary experienced the assaults as traumatic personal affronts, the women also represented the larger networks of power and resources from which Nangenutch remained excluded. Whether Nangenutch deliberately targeted English social arrangements or, more likely, inadvertently threatened them in a series of personal encounters, his attacks on these women challenged English East Hampton's racial boundaries, segregated physical spaces, patriarchal privileges, and property regime, all of which limited Nangenutch's social mobility and material security.

Nangenutch thus responded as an individual to the larger historical forces he confronted. Conversely, colonists reacted to his attacks in light of their broader ideological concerns and the challenge he posed to the colonial project. More than just providing a chance to force Natives to relinquish land or submit to colonial jurisdiction, Nangenutch's attack on Mary seemed to colonists to exhibit the real danger Indians posed to the institutions and relations underlying colonial society. When the Court of Assizes elected to treat Nangenutch primarily as an Indian, the decision in turn helped resolve the ambiguous status of Long Island's Montauketts not as an integrated community of rights-bearing English citizens but as an increasingly subjugated population relegated to a diminishing territory. Court procedures and documents that consistently paired the names Nangenutch and Will appeared to tacitly accept his multifaceted identity. But by nearly always appending the designation "Indian" or "Indyan," English residents and officials signaled their understanding that his assigned social status superseded whatever identity he might express. That label conferred upon him a subordinate status within an explicitly English East Hampton society. Moreover, it did so by associating him with a separate and physically removed community that, when its members were later implicated in his escape, could be punished collectively for Nangenutch's ability to evade colonial authorities. The 1668 trial and its aftermath thus transformed Nangenutch's personal guilt for raping Mary into a burden borne by the entire Montaukett people. The message to Nangenutch and to the Montauketts was clear: Long Island's English newcomers would identify any Native inhabitants as "Indian" or "Indyan" inferior colonial subjects, discounting their political, economic, and social ties to Native and European neighbors, as well as the complex identities they expressed as they tried to position themselves in a colonial world.

JASON R. SELLERS is an assistant professor in the Department of History and American Studies at the University of Mary Washington.

Notes

I would like to thank John Strong and Sharon Block for their thoughtful comments on multiple versions of this article and the anonymous reviewers whose critical feedback helped me rethink my central argument and strengthen the essay as a whole. Participants at NAISA's 2015 annual meeting and the NEH's 2015 Summer Institute, *On Native Grounds: Studies of Native American Histories and the Land*, also shaped my thinking in the early stages of this project. The quotation in the title is from Peter R. Christoph, ed., *Administrative Papers of Governors Richard Nicolls and Francis Lovelace, 1664–1673*, New York Historical Manuscripts: English, vol. 22 (Baltimore, MD: Genealogical Publishing Co., 1980), 71.

1. Christoph, *Administrative Papers*, 63–64, 71. I have followed John Strong in using "Montauk Indians" (members of the Native community living in the area the Dutch and then English recognized as Montauk) and "Montaukett" (the name preferred by the community today) rather than "a Montauk" or "a Montaukett Indian." John A. Strong, *The Montaukett Indians of Eastern Long Island* (Syracuse, NY: Syracuse University Press, 2001), xiv, 3, 9; Bruce G. Trigger, ed., *Northeast*, vol. 15 of *Handbook of North American Indians*, ed. William C. Sturtevant (Washington, DC: Smithsonian Institution Press, 1984), 174. I have chosen to use "Nangenutch" rather than "Will" to reinforce his Native identity and status, especially since "the Indyan" was consistently appended to his English name anyway. This name was also rendered "Nangenuge" in at least one document; see Christoph, *Administrative Papers*, 225n22:45a.2.

2. Christoph, *Administrative Papers,* 68. On the rarity of rape cases involving Native American men and English women, see David Baker, "American

Indian Executions in Historical Context," *Criminal Justice Studies: A Critical Journal of Crime, Law and Society* 20, no. 4 (2007): 327; Yasuhide Kawashima, *Puritan Justice and the Indian: White Man's Law in Massachusetts, 1630–1763* (Middletown, CT: Wesleyan University Press, 1986), 163–64; Richard Godbeer, *Sexual Revolution in Early America* (Baltimore, MD: Johns Hopkins University Press, 2002), 167–68.

3. Wendy Anne Warren, "'The Cause of Her Grief': The Rape of a Slave in Early New England," *Journal of American History* 93, no. 4 (2007): 1032, 1049; Ashley Glassburn Falzetti, "Archival Absence: The Burden of History," *Settler Colonial Studies* 5, no. 2 (2015): 5, 12–13.

4. Christoph, *Administrative Papers*, 69.

5. John A. Strong, "The Imposition of Colonial Jurisdiction over the Montauk Indians of Long Island," *Ethnohistory* 41, no. 4 (Fall 1994): 561–90; Strong, *Montaukett Indians*; Susanah Shaw Romney, *New Netherland Connections: Intimate Networks and Atlantic Ties in Seventeenth-Century America* (Chapel Hill: University of North Carolina Press, 2014), chap. 3. For an extensive study of Puritan New England's law and Indians with a concentration on Massachusetts, see Kawashima, *Puritan Justice*. Wendy Anne Warren's study of the rape of a slave in seventeenth-century New England offers a model for how to proceed with a fragmentary record of one moment in an individual's life ("'The Cause,'" 1032, 1049).

6. Kirsten Fischer, *Suspect Relations: Sex, Race, and Resistance in Colonial North Carolina* (Ithaca, NY: Cornell University Press, 2002), 9; Cornelia Hughes Dayton, *Women before the Bar: Gender, Law, and Society in Connecticut, 1639–1789* (Chapel Hill: University of North Carolina Press, 1995); Andrea Smith, *Conquest: Sexual Violence and American Indian Genocide* (Cambridge, MA: South End Press, 2005). Other historians have noted that intimate relations could build cross-cultural ties as well; see Romney, *New Netherland Connections*; Jennifer M. Spear, "Colonial Intimacies: Legislating Sex in French Louisiana," *William and Mary Quarterly* 60, no. 1 (2003): 75–98.

7. Sharon Block, *Rape and Sexual Power in Early America* (Chapel Hill: University of North Carolina Press, 2006); John Wood Sweet, *Bodies Politic: Negotiating Race in the American North, 1730–1830* (Philadelphia: University of Pennsylvania Press, 2007), 166; Dayton, *Women before the Bar*, chap. 5. For more on rape in colonial America, see Barbara S. Lindemann, "'To Ravish and Carnally Know': Rape in Eighteenth-Century Massachusetts," *Signs* 10, no. 1 (1984): 63–82; Harry B. Weiss, *An Introduction to Crime and Punishment in Colonial New Jersey* (Trenton, NJ: Past Times Press, 1960); Merril D. Smith, ed., *Sex without Consent: Rape and Sexual Coercion in America* (New York: New York University Press, 2001); Matthew Williams, "'To Lay Violent Hands': Prosecuting Sexual Violence in Colonial New York," *New York History* 95, no. 2 (2014): 172–92. Lindemann and Block depart in that they consider power more than the others, who tend to focus on legalities.

8. Kirsten Fischer and Jennifer Morgan, "Sex, Race, and the Colonial Project," *William and Mary Quarterly* 60, no. 1 (2003): 197–98.

9. Romney, *New Netherland Connections*, 16–18.

10. Strong, *Montaukett Indians*, 11–17; Strong, "Imposition of Colonial Jurisdiction," 561–64; Romney, *New Netherland Connections*, 270–73.

11. Strong, "Imposition of Colonial Jurisdiction," 564–66; Strong, *Montaukett Indians*, 19–31, 36–37, 43–55; Trigger, *Northeast*, 184–85.

12. Christoph, *Administrative Papers*, 66; Strong, "Imposition of Colonial Jurisdiction," 565; Strong, *Montaukett Indians,* 27, 32.

13. On colonization curtailing familiar avenues to male status, see Colin G. Calloway, *New Worlds for All: Indians, Europeans, and the Remaking of Early America* (Baltimore, MD: Johns Hopkins University Press, 1997), 168.

14. Daniel R. Mandell, "Shifting Boundaries of Race and Ethnicity: Indian-Black Intermarriage in Southern New England, 1760–1880," *Journal of American History* 85, no. 2 (1998): 479, 485; Romney, *New Netherland Connections*, chap. 3.

15. Christoph, *Administrative Papers,* 66; Strong, "Imposition of Colonial Jurisdiction," 567–69, 572; Peter C. Mancall, *Deadly Medicine: Indians and Alcohol in Early America* (Ithaca, NY: Cornell University Press, 1995), 74–83, 86–91. See also Christoph, *Administrative Papers,* 67, 69. For the Duke's Laws, see Historical Society of the New York Courts, "The Duke of York's Laws, 1655–1675," accessed January 30, 2016, http://www.nycourts.gov/history/legal-history-new-york/documents/charters-duke-transcript.pdf. On continued alcohol sales strengthening trust-based personal relationships in the Dutch era, see Romney, *New Netherland Connections,* 165.

16. Christoph, *Administrative Papers*, 63–64, 65. Local town historians and genealogists are uncertain of either woman's maiden name, and so to distinguish them I refer to the Mary Miller married to John and at the center of the rape trial as simply "Mary" and distinguish the other witness as "Mary (George)." It is possible the women were sisters-in-law, though again, town historians are uncertain, since George is not clearly identified as John's brother, and it appears there were two families of Millers with different European roots in early East Hampton. See Jeannette Edwards Rattray, *East Hampton History, Including Genealogies of Early Families* (East Hampton, Long Island, NY: Jeannette Edwards Rattray, 1953), 446–49.

17. Rattray, *East Hampton History,* 74, 96, 446.

18. Christoph, *Administrative Papers*, 62–63. Additional court documents, especially those recording testimony, referred to him as "Nangenutch alias Will," "Will the Indyan," or simply "Will."

19. On adopting and performing complex identities, see Robert S. Grumet, *The Munsee Indians: A History* (Norman: University of Oklahoma Press, 2009), 12–13; Michael Witgen, *An Infinity of Nations: How the Native New World Shaped Early North America* (Philadelphia: University of Pennsylvania Press, 2012), 89–90, 105–6; James H. Merrell, "'The Cast of His Countenance': Reading Andrew Montour," in *Through a Glass Darkly: Reflections on Personal Identity in Early America,* ed. Ronald Hoffman, Mechal Sobel, and Frederika J. Teute (Chapel Hill: University of North Carolina Press, 1997), 13–39. For examples of the extensive literature on the identities and roles of cultural brokers, see Timothy J. Shannon, "Dressing for Success on the Mohawk Frontier: Hendrick,

William Johnson and the Indian Fashion," *William and Mary Quarterly* 53, no. 1 (1996): 13—42, esp. 18—19; Nancy L. Hagedorn, "'A Friend to Go between Them': The Interpreter as Cultural Broker during Anglo-Iroquois Councils, 1740—70," *Ethnohistory* 35, no. 1 (1988): 60—80; Margaret Connell Szasz, *Between Indian and White Worlds: The Cultural Broker* (Norman: University of Oklahoma Press, 1994); Daniel K. Richter, "Brokers and Politics: Iroquois and New Yorkers," in *Trade, Land, Power: The Struggle for Eastern North America* (Philadelphia: University of Pennsylvania Press, 2013), 113—32; Alan Taylor, "Captain Hendrick Aupaumut: The Dilemmas of an Intercultural Broker," *Ethnohistory* 43, no. 3 (1996): 431—57.

20. Barbara J. Fields and Karen E. Fields, "How Race Is Conjured," *Jacobin*, June 29, 2015, https://www.jacobinmag.com/2015/06/karen-barbara -fields-racecraft-dolezal-racism/; Falzetti, "Archival Absence," 9. For a fuller discussion, see Barbara J. Fields and Karen E. Fields, *Racecraft: The Soul of Inequality in American Life* (New York: Verso, 2012).

21. Strong, "Imposition of Colonial Jurisdiction," 566; Falzetti, "Archival Absence," 9.

22. Christoph, *Administrative Papers,* 65, 68; Block, *Rape and Sexual Power,* 20—26, 40—42, 131—32. For a fuller discussion of jurist Sir Matthew Hale's rules for evaluating rape claims, see Block, *Rape and Sexual Power,* 129—36; Dayton, *Women before the Bar,* 246—47.

23. Christoph, *Administrative Papers,* 64; Terri L. Snyder, "Sexual Consent and Sexual Coercion in Seventeenth-Century Virginia," in Smith, *Sex without Consent,* 53—56; Block, *Rape and Sexual Power,* 90—121.

24. Christoph, *Administrative Papers,* 64, 65.

25. Ibid., 64.

26. Ibid., 65, 66.

27. Ibid., 65; Block, *Rape and Sexual Power,* 25—26, 61.

28. Christoph, *Administrative Papers,* 64, 68—69; Block, *Rape and Sexual Power,* 26—27. For another instance of lighting a pipe in the course of a sexual assault, see Godbeer, *Sexual Revolution,* 94.

29. Block, *Rape and Sexual Power,* 26, 61.

30. Christoph, *Administrative Papers,* 66; Mancall, *Deadly Medicine,* 79—82.

31. Christoph, *Administrative Papers,* 68, 72. On women in Eastern Algonquian and Montaukett societies, see Alice Nash, "'None of the Women Were Abused': Indigenous Contexts for the Treatment of Women Captives in the Northeast," in Smith, *Sex without Consent,* 17; James Homer Williams, "Coerced Sex and Gendered Violence in New Netherland," in Smith, *Sex without Consent,* 62; Strong, *Montaukett Indians,* 28; Strong, "Imposition of Colonial Jurisdiction," 565.

32. Nash, "'None of the Women,'" 13, 17; Romney, *New Netherland Connections,* chap. 3, esp. 172. See also Ann Little, *Abraham in Arms: War and Gender in Colonial New England* (Philadelphia: University of Pennsylvania Press, 2007), 2.

33. Christoph, *Administrative Papers,* 63—64; Block, *Rape and Sexual Power,* 79—80; Robert Blair St. George, "Witchcraft, Bodily Affliction, and Domestic Space in Seventeenth-Century New England," in *A Centre of Wonders: The Body*

in Early America, ed. Janet Moore Lindman and Michele Lise Tarter (Ithaca, NY: Cornell University Press, 2001), 22.

34. Christoph, *Administrative Papers*, 62, 71—72.

35. On nonsexual charges for crimes involving sexual coercion, see Block, *Rape and Sexual Power,* 158; on the stature of the Chatfield and Miller families, see Rattray, *East Hampton History,* 74, 96, 446.

36. Christoph, *Administrative Papers*, 71; Mandell, "Shifting Boundaries," 479; Stuart Banner, *How the Indians Lost Their Land: Law and Power on the Frontier* (Cambridge, MA: Harvard University Press, 2005), 57—59. On Indians and crime in early New York, see Douglas Greenberg, *Crime and Law Enforcement in the Colony of New York, 1691—1776* (Ithaca, NY: Cornell University Press, 1976), 58.

37. Christoph, *Administrative Papers,* 65; Fischer, *Suspect Relations,* 15. For the attack on Annah, see Strong, "Imposition of Colonial Jurisdiction," 571; Rattray, *East Hampton History,* 74, 96. For interpretations of attacks on houses, see St. George, "Witchcraft," 24—25; Robert Blair St. George, *Conversing by Signs: Poetics of Implication in Colonial New England Culture* (Chapel Hill: University of North Carolina Press, 1998), 121; Little, *Abraham in Arms,* 104—5.

38. On women's testimony, see Dayton, *Women before the Bar,* 31—32, 238—39; Williams, "Prosecuting Sexual Violence," 174. On courts considering patterns of behavior but sometimes discounting them, see Godbeer, *Sexual Revolution,* 87, 113; Dayton, *Women before the Bar,* 240.

39. Christoph, *Administrative Papers*, 66—69, 71. Executions in rape cases were fairly rare; see Baker, "American Indian Executions"; Else L. Hambleton, "'Playing the Rogue': Rape and Issues of Consent in Seventeenth-Century Massachusetts," in Miller, *Sex without Consent,* 37; Godbeer, *Sexual Revolution,* 87, 102; Strong, "Imposition of Colonial Jurisdiction," 574.

40. Christoph, *Administrative Papers*, 62, 70, 71—72.

41. On these juridical debates, see Block, *Rape and Sexual Power,* 135—39; Williams, "Prosecuting Sexual Violence," 15.

42. Fischer, *Suspect Relations,* 56—57; Louis Montrose, "The Work of Gender and Sexuality in the Elizabethan Discourse of Discovery," in *Discourses of Sexuality: From Aristotle to AIDS,* ed. Donna C. Stanton (Ann Arbor: University of Michigan Press, 1992), 138—84; Karen O. Kupperman, "Presentment of Civility: English Reading of American Self-Presentation in the Early Years of Colonization," *William and Mary Quarterly* 54, no. 1 (1997): 193—228; Williams, "Prosecuting Sexual Violence," 190; Godbeer, *Sexual Revolution,* 174.

43. Christoph, *Administrative Papers,* 70—71.

44. Ibid., 71; Block, *Rape and Sexual Power,* 61; Dayton, *Women before the Bar,* 238—39.

45. Strong, "Imposition of Colonial Jurisdiction"; Strong, *Montaukett Indians,* 32—34; Historical Society of the New York Courts, "The Duke of York's Laws, 1655—1675."

46. On English officials holding entire New England Algonquian communities responsible for individual crimes, see David J. Silverman, *Faith and Boundaries: Colonists, Christianity, and Community among the Wampanoag*

Indians of Martha's Vineyard, 1600—1871 (New York: Cambridge University Press, 2005), 87.

47. Christoph, *Administrative Papers*, 71; Historical Society of the New York Courts, "The Duke of York's Laws, 1655—1675." The Duke's Laws were consistent with prevailing legal attitudes in Europe, though they were unevenly applied in the Americas. Deborah Rosen has pointed out that between the thirteenth and eighteenth centuries, European commitments to a universalistic approach "assumed all humans had the same natural rights and all nations had an obligation to provide the protections of fundamental law universally" but that with regard to the Americas they constantly "found ways to justify the European practice of applying different rules to indigenous peoples," in particular pointing to "Indians' nonconformity with European notions of normal, moral behavior" (*Border Law: The First Seminole War and American Nationhood* [Cambridge, MA: Harvard University Press, 2015], 113—16, quotes from 113, 114, 116). For Nangenutch's escape, see Peter R. Christoph and Florence A. Christoph, eds., *Books of General Entries of the Colony of New York, 1664—1673: Orders, Warrants, Letters, Commissions, Passes and Licenses Issued by Governors Richard Nicolls and Francis Lovelace*, New York Historical Manuscripts: English (Baltimore, MD: Genealogical Publishing Co., 1982), 191—92, 200—201; Strong, "Imposition of Colonial Jurisdiction," 574. Interestingly, a second Indian convicted of rape in New York in 1669 also escaped from prison; see Victor Hugo Paltsits, ed., *Minutes of the Executive Council of the Province of New York: Administration of Francis Lovelace, 1668—1673* (Albany: State of New York, 1910), 1:323. On Native notions of justice, which frequently emphasized retribution rather than revenge, see Witgen, *Infinity of Nations*, 200—11; on coexisting systems of law in early America, see Sidney L. Harring, "Indian Law, Sovereignty, and State Law: Native People and the Law," in *A Companion to American Indian History*, ed. Philip J. Deloria and Neal Salisbury (Malden, MA: Blackwell Publishers, 2002), 447.

48. Christoph and Christoph, *Books of General Entries*, 191—92, 243, 271; Strong, "Imposition of Colonial Jurisdiction," 575—80; Strong, *Montaukett Indians*, 37—39.

49. Strong, "Imposition of Colonial Jurisdiction," 576—82. For a more complete account of Montaukett land loss, see Strong, *Montaukett Indians*.

50. Paltsits, *Minutes of the Executive Council*, 33, 240; Christoph and Christoph, *Books of General Entries*, 277.

RANDALL AKEE, VALENTINA DIMITROVA-GRAJZL, PETER GRAJZL, AND RICHARD M. TODD

From Gaming to Justice?
A Note on the Effect of American Indian
Casinos on Tribal Judicial Systems

AN EFFICIENT AND IMPARTIAL JUDICIAL SYSTEM is essential to economic development. The judiciary plays a central role in upholding property rights and promoting commerce in large-scale anonymous markets where reputation-based relational contracting loses its efficacy (see, e.g., Dixit 2003; Stephenson 2007). An effective judiciary has been shown to foster investment, entrepreneurship, industrial activity, and credit (see, e.g., Chemin 2009a, 2009b, 2012; Jappelli, Pagano, and Bianco 2005; Visaria 2009). In the context of Indian Country in particular, recent empirical evidence suggests that differences in legislative frameworks that structure the functioning of judicial institutions are an important driver of disparities in socioeconomic outcomes (see, e.g., Goldberg and Champagne 2007; Anderson and Parker 2008; Dimitrova-Grajzl, Grajzl, and Guse 2014; Dimitrova-Grajzl, Guse, and Todd 2015; Wellhausen 2017). This raises the question of what factors impact and facilitate the development of an effective judiciary in Native communities.

In Indian Country, access to an effective judiciary has been limited as a consequence of a long history of federal encroachment on tribal sovereignty, inadequate government funding, and a maze of jurisdictional overlaps and limits. To fill the resulting institutional vacuum, tribal communities have striven to expand and enhance their own tribal judicial systems. Given that "tribal justice systems have been underfunded for decades" (US Commission on Civil Rights 2003, 77), financial constraints have been the main obstacle in this regard.

In such an environment, characterized by severe resource scarcity, the American Indian gaming industry has emerged as a mechanism capable of relaxing tribal financial constraints (Akee, Spilde, and Taylor 2015). Indeed, a key goal of the 1988 Indian Gaming Regulatory Act (IGRA) was to promote "tribal economic development, self-sufficiency, and strong tribal governments" (Indian Gaming Regulatory Act 1988). The implementing regulations explicitly recognized tribal government spending to enhance the judicial system as "allowable expenditures of gaming revenues" (National Indian

Gaming Commission 2005). In addition, gaming conceivably creates additional demand for tribal judicial services.

The socioeconomic impact of gaming in Indian Country has been explored by a handful of previous studies (see, e.g., Evans and Topoleski 2002; Reagan and Gitter 2007; Anderson 2013). However, to date, no contribution has empirically examined the link between gaming and tribal institution building, in particular, the development of tribal judicial systems. We evaluate how the presence of the American Indian gaming industry has impacted one basic yet salient dimension of tribal judicial systems: their extensiveness. Our analysis thereby fills an important gap in the emerging empirical literature that examines the causes and consequences of institutional development in Indigenous communities (see, e.g., Cornell and Kalt 2000; Dippel 2014; Akee and Jorgensen 2014; Akee, Jorgensen, and Sunde 2015; Aragón 2015).

Data

The source of our data on tribal justice systems is the 2002 Census of Tribal Justice Agencies in American Indian and Alaska Native Jurisdiction. We measure the size of a tribal justice system with the sum of all part-time and full-time personnel working within the tribal justice system (*Tribal Justice System Staff*). Personnel is the key input in the administration of justice (see, e.g., Beenstock and Haitovsky 2004; Dimitrova-Grajzl et al. 2012; Dimitrova-Grajzl, Grajzl, and Zajc 2014; Dimitrova-Grajzl et al. 2016; Grajzl and Silwal 2017) and, therefore, an appropriate measure of the extensiveness of a tribal justice system. We concentrate our analysis on reservations with a population of at least five hundred in year 2000. Our dataset covers 106 reservations from twenty-three states; 97 of these 106 reservations have a tribal justice system.

Our focal explanatory variable, *Gaming*, is Conner and Taggart's (2013) and Taylor and Kalt's (2005) dummy equal to 1 if the tribe associated with a specific reservation in year 2000 operates a class II (e.g., bingo facility) or class III (Las Vegas—style casino) gaming facility. Our 1990 reservation-level controls come from Akee and Taylor (2014) and include total population, percent of adults with a college degree, percent unemployed, median household income, and percent of population that is American Indian.

Empirical Strategy

The distribution of *Tribal Justice System Staff* with a mean of 15.5 and a standard deviation of 12.8 is positively skewed. In regression analysis, we therefore use the logged value of (*Tribal Justice System Staff* + 1). We estimate the following model:

$$\log(Tribal\ Justice\ System\ Staff + 1)_i = \beta_0 + \beta_1 \times Gaming_i + X_i'\gamma + \varepsilon_i,\ (1)$$

where X_i is the vector of controls for reservation i, ε_i is the error term, and β_1 is the coefficient of interest. The focal explanatory variable, *Gaming*, is likely endogenous: tribal choice to develop a gaming industry may be driven by unobservables that also affect the extensiveness of the tribal justice system, rendering OLS estimates of (1) biased. To address this concern, we adopt an instrumental variable (IV/2SLS) approach. We instrument for *Gaming* with Cookson's (2010) *Racetrack Betting,* which equals 1 if the reservation's state allows non-Indians to operate off-reservation racetrack betting operations. Cookson (2010) shows that *Racetrack Betting* and the presence of American Indian casinos are negatively correlated: reservations that face competition in the state-level gambling market are, all else equal, less likely to operate a casino. *Racetrack Betting*, however, should not exhibit an effect on the extensiveness of the tribal justice system through any other channel but *Gaming*.

Because we observe *Tribal Justice System Staff* only when the tribal justice system actually exists, a further concern for our analysis is that the unobservables that help explain the extensiveness of a tribal justice system may be correlated with the unobservables that help predict the existence of the tribal justice system. To address this potential sample selection problem, we also combine our IV/2SLS approach with Heckman's (1979) two-step (Heckit) method (Wooldridge 2002, 568). Specifically, in the first step (sample selection equation), we estimate a probit with *Tribal Justice System* dummy (equal to 1 if a tribal justice system exists) as the outcome variable. The explanatory variables include the full set of socioeconomic controls, as well as two additional variables, *Racetrack Betting* and *State Jurisdiction,* which equals 1 if criminal or civil matters, or both, on a reservation are under predominant state rather than tribal jurisdiction (see Goldberg 2010). We expect reservations under state jurisdiction to be less likely to develop an Indigenous (tribal) justice system. The presence or absence of state jurisdiction, however, should not exhibit a direct effect on the extensiveness of the tribal justice system if one exists. In the second step, we estimate the IV/2SLS model, with the inverse Mills ratio, computed from the corresponding step one (probit) estimates and all exogenous variables included among the explanatory variables. We base statistical inference on heteroscedasticity-robust standard errors clustered at the state level to correct for plausible correlation of error terms within a state.

TABLE 1.

Main Results

EXPLANATORY VARIABLES	(1) OLS WITHOUT SOCIOECONOMIC CONTROLS	(2) OLS WITH SOCIOECONOMIC CONTROLS	(3) IV/2SLS	(4) HECKIT + IV/2SLS
Gaming	0.2151**	0.3719***	1.3759***	1.3682***
	(0.0995)	(0.1213)	(0.4365)	(0.4201)
Population (in thousands)		0.0391*	0.0452***	0.0303**
		(0.0208)	(0.0128)	(0.0125)
Percent college degree		0.0066	0.0091	-0.0037
		(0.0158)	(0.0123)	(0.0121)
Percent unemployed		-0.0287*	-0.0534***	-0.0527***
		(0.0155)	(0.0181)	(0.0189)
Median household income (in US$1,000)		-0.0177	-0.0241	-0.0047
		(0.0145)	(0.0162)	(0.0134)
Percent American Indian		0.0101***	0.0170***	0.0174***
		(0.0025)	(0.0035)	(0.0036)
Inverse Mills ratio				-1.1373***
				(0.3184)
R-squared	0.0178	0.1441		
Number of observations	97	97	97	97

NOTES: The outcome variable is log(*Tribal Justice System Staff* + 1). In all tables, the standard errors reported in parentheses are heteroscedasticity-robust and clustered at the state level.

*, **, and *** denote statistical significance at the 10, 5, and 1 percent level, respectively. Variable definitions and descriptive statistics are provided in the supplementary appendix.

Results

Our main results are presented in table 1. Columns 1 and 2 show the OLS results without and with socioeconomic controls, respectively. Based on the estimates in column 2, the presence of gaming on a reservation is, ceteris paribus, associated with, on average, a 45 percent increase in the number of tribal justice system personnel. OLS estimates are likely biased, as argued above. The IV/2SLS estimates are shown in column 3 and indicate that the presence of gaming on a reservation, ceteris paribus, increases the number of tribal justice system personnel by nearly threefold. The corresponding first-stage results are shown in column 1 of table 2. As expected, *Gaming* is statistically significantly negatively associated with *Racetrack Betting*. The

F-statistic for the test of excluded instruments equals 10.17. Our instrument is thus adequately strong in a statistical sense.

The estimates when combining IV/2SLS and Heckit approaches are presented in column 4 of table 1. The implied magnitude of the effect of gaming is very similar to that based on the IV/2SLS estimates. The corresponding estimates for the sample selection equation and the first stage of the IV/2SLS model are presented in columns 2 and 3 of table 2. As conjectured, *State Jurisdiction* is statistically significantly negatively associated with *Tribal Justice System*. *Racetrack Betting* continues to be a strong instrument for *Gaming*.

TABLE 2.

First Stage and Sample Selection Equation Estimates

	FIRST STAGE (OLS) FOR IV/2SLS ESTIMATES IN COLUMN 3 OF TABLE 1	SAMPLE SELECTION (PROBIT) AND FIRST STAGE (OLS) FOR HECKIT + IV/2SLS ESTIMATES IN COLUMN 4 OF TABLE 1	
EXPLANATORY VARIABLES	(1) OUTCOME VARIABLE: GAMING	(2) OUTCOME VARIABLE: TRIBAL JUSTICE SYSTEM	(3) OUTCOME VARIABLE: GAMING
Population (in thousands)	-0.0055	0.6865*	-0.0034
	(0.0072)	(0.4097)	(0.0088)
Percent college degree	-0.0020	0.0584	-0.0002
	(0.0089)	(0.0613)	(0.0096)
Percent unemployed	0.0150	-0.0087	0.0152
	(0.0120)	(0.0498)	(0.0119)
Median household income (in US$1,000)	0.0061	-0.1102*	0.0039
	(0.0091)	(0.0589)	(0.0091)
Percent American Indian	-0.0044	-0.0057	-0.0047*
	(0.0027)	(0.0140)	(0.0026)
Racetrack betting	-0.3707***	-0.6893	-0.3873***
	(0.1162)	(0.8662)	(0.1278)
State jurisdiction		-1.5277*	-0.0601
		(0.7841)	(0.1034)
Inverse Mills ratio			0.1932
			(0.1987)
F-test of excluded instruments	10.17		9.18
Number of observations	97	106	97

Notes: The table reports estimated coefficients. See notes under table 1.

Table 3 summarizes the results of a series of robustness checks. Columns 1—7, where we drop the states with the most observations, demonstrate that our results are not driven by any particular geographic region. Column 8 shows that our results continue to hold if we use the sample of only the largest reservations. Column (9) confirms that our results are further robust to restricting the sample to the subset of reservations which had a functioning tribal justice system already prior to emergence of the gambling industry in Indian Country in the late 1980s. The first stage (not shown) of the IV/2SLS regression in column (9) continues to be strong (the F-statistic for the test of excluded instruments equals 10.67).

TABLE 3.

Robustness Check

	SAMPLE				
ESTIMATION METHOD	**(1) WITHOUT WASHINGTON**	**(2) WITHOUT NEW MEXICO**	**(3) WITHOUT ARIZONA**	**(4) WITHOUT SOUTH DAKOTA**	**(5) WITHOUT WISCONSIN**
OLS	0.4085***	0.3177*	0.4027***	0.3775***	0.3953***
IV/2SLS	1.5013***	1.6160^{+}	1.3206***	1.5905***	1.4051***
Heckit + IV/2SLS	1.4412***	n.e.	1.3850**	1.6673***	1.2968***
Number of observations	81	83	87	89	90

	SAMPLE			
ESTIMATION METHOD	**(6) WITHOUT MINNESOTA**	**(7) WITHOUT MONTANA**	**(8) POPULATION IN 2000 > 1,000**	**(9) TRIBAL JUSTICE SYSTEM EXISTS SINCE BEFORE 1985**
OLS	0.3492***	0.3262***	0.4082***	0.3470***
IV/2SLS	1.3484***	1.3231***	1.5920***	0.9979***
Heckit + IV/2SLS	1.3472***	1.3578***	1.8298***	
Number of observations	90	91	83	77

NOTES: The table reports estimates of the *Gaming* coefficient. All regressions include the full set of controls as featured in columns 2—4 of table 1. See notes under table 1.

+ denotes a statistical significance at the 10 percent level for a one-sided test.

n.e. stands for "not estimable" (*State Jurisdiction* = 0 predicts the value of *Tribal Justice System* perfectly in the corresponding probit regression).

Conclusion

We demonstrate empirically that American Indian gaming on reservations increases the extensiveness of tribal justice systems as measured by the size of total tribal justice system personnel. Addressing endogeneity and sample selection concerns, we show that this effect of reservation gaming is robust and noteworthy in magnitude. Our results therefore imply that the tribal gaming industry as implemented through the IGRA, primarily by relaxing tribal budget constraints, as well as potentially by contributing to a demand for judicial services, enhanced the judicial branch of tribal governments. More generally, our analysis shows that commercial projects that significantly boost tribal government revenue, as many casinos do, may exert a positive effect on the institutional capacity of a Native community.

RANDALL AKEE is an associate professor in the Department of Public Policy and American Indian Studies at UCLA. He is currently a David Rubenstein Fellow at the Brookings Institution in Washington, DC, in the Economic Studies Division.

VALENTINA DIMITROVA-GRAJZL is an associate professor of economics at the Virginia Military Institute. Her teaching and research focus on economics of institutions, Indigenous economics, postsocialist economies and polities, economic history, and law and economics.

PETER GRAJZL is Ehrick Kilner Haight Sr. Term Associate Professor of Economics at Washington and Lee University. His research spans the fields of comparative institutional economics, law and economics, and political economics with applications to American Indian studies.

RICHARD M. TODD is a vice president at the Federal Reserve Bank of Minneapolis and advisor to the bank's Center for Indian Country Development and Community Development Department. His current work focuses on Indian Country land, housing, education, and business development issues.

Appendix

TABLE A1. Variable Definitions

VARIABLE NAME	DESCRIPTION	SOURCE
Tribal justice system staff	Sum of all part-time and full-time personnel (tribal court judges, appellate court judges, court administrators, court interpreters, prosecutors, public defenders, probation officers, parole officers, peacemakers, bailiffs, staff attorneys, and support staff) working within the tribal justice system. Data from year 2002.	2002 Census of Tribal Justice Agencies in American Indian and Alaska Native Tribal Jurisdictions, question B12
Gaming	Dummy equal to 1 if the reservation or American Indian tribal statistical area is associated with a tribe operating a class II or class III gaming facility as of January 1, 2000; and 0 otherwise.	Conner and Taggart (2013), Taylor and Kalt (2005)
Population	Total population 16+ years old, all races. Data from year 1990.	1990 census
Percent college degree	Percent of population with a college degree, all races. Data from year 1990.	1990 census
Percent unemployed	Percent of unemployed in total labor force, all races. Data from year 1990.	1990 census
Median household income	Median household income, all races. Data from year 1990.	1990 census
Percent American Indian	Percent of population 16+ years old that is American Indian. Data from year 1990.	1990 census
Tribal justice system	Dummy equal to 1 if the tribe living on the reservation operates a tribal justice system, defined as the entire judicial branch, and employees thereof, of an Indian tribe, including (but not limited to) traditional methods and forums for dispute resolution, lower courts, appellate courts (including intertribal appellate courts), alternative dispute resolution systems, and circuit rider systems, established by inherent authority whether or not they constitute a court of record; and 0 otherwise. Data from year 2002.	2002 Census of Tribal Justice Agencies in American Indian and Alaska Native Tribal Jurisdictions, question B1
Racetrack betting	Dummy equal to 1 if the reservation's state allows non-Indians to operate racetrack betting operations and 0 otherwise. Data from prior to year 2000.	Cookson (2010)
State jurisdiction	Dummy equal to 1 if the criminal or civil matters, or both, on a reservation are under predominant state jurisdiction either due to Public Law 280 or other federal acts; and 0 otherwise. Data from year 2000 or prior.	Goldberg (2010)

TABLE A2. Descriptive Statistics

VARIABLE NAME	NUMBER OF OBSERVATIONS	MEAN	STANDARD DEVIATION	MINIMUM	MAXIMUM
Tribal justice system staff	97	15.48	12.83	0	75
Gaming	97	0.7732	0.4209	0	1
Population	97	3742.1	4958.3	202	31,306
Percent college degree	97	9.78	5.33	1.22	28.50
Percent unemployed	97	15.50	7.83	3.85	35.98
Median household income	97	19,282.1	5,670.0	9,871	40,948
Percent American Indian	97	50.70	31.27	2.63	100
Tribal justice system	106	0.9151	0.2801	0	1
Racetrack betting	97	0.2165	0.4140	0	1
State jurisdiction	106	0.3679	0.4845	0	1

Note

We are grateful to Thaddieus Conner, Anthony Cookson, and Miriam Jorgensen for sharing their data. For helpful comments and suggestions on the manuscript, we thank Miriam Jorgensen; Laurel Wheeler; participants at the annual meeting of the Midwest Economic Association and at a faculty seminar at Virginia Military Institute; two anonymous reviewers; and the editors, Jean O'Brien and Robert Warrior.

Works Cited

Akee, R. K. Q., and M. Jorgensen. 2014. "Property Institutions and Business Investments on American Indian Reservations." *Regional Science and Urban Economics* 46: 116—25.

Akee, R. K. Q., M. Jorgensen, and U. Sunde. 2015. "Critical Junctures and Economic Development: Evidence from the Adoption of Constitutions among American Indian Nations." *Journal of Comparative Economics* 43, no. 4: 844—61.

Akee, R. K. Q., K. A. Spilde, and J. B. Taylor. 2015. "The Indian Gaming Regulatory Act and Its Effects on American Indian Economic Development." *Journal of Economic Perspectives* 29, no. 3: 185—208.

Akee, R. K. Q., and J. B. Taylor. 2014. *Social and Economic Change on American Indian Reservations: A Databook of the US Censuses and American Community Survey, 1990—2010.* Sarasota, FL: Taylor Policy Group, Inc.

Anderson, R. J. 2013. "Tribal Casino Impacts on American Indians' Well-Being: Evidence from Reservation-Level Census Data." *Contemporary Economic Policy* 31, no. 2: 291–300.

Anderson, T. L., and D. P. Parker. 2008. "Sovereignty, Credible Commitments and Economic Prosperity on American Indian Reservations." *Journal of Law and Economics* 51, no. 4: 641–66.

Aragón, Fernando M. 2015. "Do Better Property Rights Improve Local Income? Evidence from First Nations' Treaties." *Journal of Development Economics* 116: 43–56.

Beenstock, M., and Y. Haitovsky. 2004. "Does the Appointment of Judges Increase the Output of the Judiciary?" *International Review of Law and Economics* 24, no. 3: 351–69.

Chemin, M. 2009a. "Do Judiciaries Matter for Development? Evidence from India." *Journal of Comparative Economics* 37, no. 2: 230–50.

———. 2009b. "The Impact of the Judiciary on Entrepreneurship: Evaluation of Pakistan's Access to Justice Programme." *Journal of Public Economics* 93, no. 1–2: 114–25.

———. 2012. "Does Court Speed Shape Economic Activity? Evidence from a Court Reform in India." *Journal of Law Economics and Organization* 28, no. 3: 460–85.

Conner, T., and W. A. Taggart. 2013. "Assessing the Impact of Indian Gaming on American Indian Nations: Is the House Winning?" *Social Science Quarterly* 94, no. 4: 1016–44.

Cookson, J. A. 2010. "Institutions and Casinos on American Indian Reservations: An Empirical Analysis of the Location of Indian Casinos." *Journal of Law and Economics* 53, no. 4: 651–87.

Cornell, S., and J. P. Kalt. 2000. "Where's the Glue? Institutional and Cultural Foundations of American Indian Economic Development." *Journal of Socio-economics* 29, no. 5: 443–70.

Dimitrova-Grajzl, V., P. Grajzl, and A. J. Guse. 2014. "Jurisdiction, Crime, and Development: The Impact of Public Law 280 in Indian Country." *Law and Society Review* 48, no. 1: 127–60.

Dimitrova-Grajzl, V., P. Grajzl, A. Slavov, and K. Zajc. 2016. "Courts in a Transition Economy: Case Disposition and the Quantity-Quality Tradeoff in Bulgaria." *Economic Systems* 40, no. 1: 18–38.

Dimitrova-Grajzl, V., P. Grajzl, J. Sustersic, and K. Zajc. 2012. "Court Output, Judicial Staffing, and the Demand for Court Services: Evidence from Slovenian Courts of First Instance." *International Review of Law and Economics* 32, no. 1: 19–29.

Dimitrova-Grajzl, V., P. Grajzl, and K. Zajc. 2014. "Understanding Modes of Civil Case Disposition: Evidence from Slovenian Courts." *Journal of Comparative Economics* 42, no. 2: 924–39.

Dimitrova-Grajzl, V., A. J. Guse, and R. M. Todd. 2015. "Consumer Credit on American Indian Reservations." *Economic Systems* 39, no. 3: 518–40.

Dippel, Christian. 2014. "Forced Coexistence and Economic Development: Evidence from Native American Reservations." *Econometrica* 82, no. 6: 2131–65.

Dixit, A. 2003. "Trade Expansion and Contract Enforcement." *Journal of Political Economy* 111, no. 6: 1293–317.

Evans, W. N., and J. Topoleski. 2002. "The Social and Economic Impact of Native American Casinos." NBER Working Paper 9198.

Goldberg, C. 2010. "Tribal Jurisdictional Status Analysis." http://www.tribal-institute.org/lists/tjsa.htm.

Goldberg, C., and D. Champagne. 2007. "Is Public Law 280 Fit for the 21st Century? Some Data at Last." *Connecticut Law Review* 38, no. 4: 697–729.

Grajzl, P., and S. Silwal. 2017. "The Functioning of Courts in a Developing Economy: Evidence from Nepal." *European Journal of Law and Economics*, forthcoming. DOI: https://doi.org/10.1007/s10657–017–9570–7.

Heckman, J. J. 1979. "Sample Selection Bias as a Specification Error." *Econometrica* 47: 153–61.

Indian Gaming Regulatory Act. 1988. Public Law 100-497. 100th Congress.

Jappelli, T., M. Pagano, and M. Bianco. 2005. "Courts and Banks: Effects of Judicial Enforcement on Credit Markets." *Journal of Money, Credit and Banking* 37, no. 2: 223–44.

National Indian Gaming Commission. 2005. "Use of Gaming Revenues Bulletin." https://www.nigc.gov/compliance/detail/use-of-net-gaming-revenues-bulletin.

Reagan, P. B., and R. J. Gitter. 2007. "Is Gaming the Optimal Strategy? The Impact of Gaming Facilities on the Income and Employment of American Indians." *Economics Letters* 95, no. 3: 428–32.

Stephenson, M. 2007. "Judicial Reform in Developing Countries: Constraints and Opportunities." In *Beyond Transition*, edited by F. Bourguignon, and B. Pleskovic, 311–28. Washington, DC: World Bank.

Taylor, J. B., and J. P. Kalt. 2005. *American Indians on Reservations: A Databook of Socioeconomic Change between the 1990 and 2000 Censuses*. Harvard Project on American Indian Economic Development.

US Commission on Civil Rights. 2003. *A Quiet Crisis: Federal Funding and Unmet Needs in Indian Country*. Washington, DC.

Visaria, S. 2009. "Legal Reform and Loan Repayment: The Microeconomic Impact of Debt Recovery Tribunals in India." *American Economic Journal: Applied Economics* 1, no. 3: 59–81.

Wellhausen, R. L. 2017. "Sovereignty, Law, and Finance: Evidence from American Indian Reservations." *Quarterly Journal of Political Science* 12, no. 4: 405–36.

Wooldridge, J. M. 2002. *Econometric Analysis of Cross Section and Panel Data*. Cambridge, MA: MIT Press.

KRISTINA JACOBSEN AND SHIRLEY ANN BOWMAN

"Don't Even Talk to Me if You're Kinya'áanii [Towering House]": Adopted Clans, Kinship, and "Blood" in Navajo Country

For citizens of the Navajo diaspora

Diné comedy duo James and Ernie perform in the Navajo reservation border-town of Farmington, New Mexico.[1] In the routine, we are in a smoky bar: a Diné country western band, Aces Wild, is playing a popular song ("The Aces Wild Song"), Navajo couples are two-stepping to the music, and various Diné men are trying unsuccessfully to pick up women in the bar. "Hey baby, what's your CLAN?" one man asks with exaggerated intonation of the woman sitting next to him. With an air of impatience, the woman rolls her eyes and tells off the inquiring man: "Don't even TALK to me if you're Kinya'áanii!"[2]

HOW DO CLANS FIGURE INTO contemporary Navajo life, and what personality traits might be attached to, say, Kinya'áaniis, or members of the Towering House clan, that would make individuals from this clan more or less attractive as potential mates? What can we learn about Navajo or Diné histories of cultural mixture, belonging, and inclusion through the many "adopted" Navajo clan names?[3] Given that close to half of all Diné citizens now live off the Navajo Nation, what might a contemporary ethnography of Navajo kinship, a topic so tirelessly explored by early anthropologists to Navajo country (see Reichard 1928; Franciscan Fathers 1910, 424; Matthews 1894, 1897), look like?[4]

This article examines ideologies surrounding the Diné kinship system, or *k'é*, in which Diné people are connected to one another through an elabo-rate matrilineal descent network of systems of obligation and reciprocity, otherwise known as the clan system (*dóone'é*).[5] As elsewhere, kinship in Diné contexts is culturally specific, cultivated through daily use, and not a given, natural fact. As Gary Witherspoon noted over forty years ago, "The point here is that there is no set of biological or sexual ties unless they are said by the culture to exist. The nature of these ties, if they exist, is cultur-ally explained, and the meaning attributed to such ties is culturally derived and assigned. Each culture independently explains the nature and meaning of kinship" (1975, 12). Using oral histories, interviews, archival materials, humorous memes, comedy routines, data from Bureau of Indian Affairs and Indian census rolls, and contemporary scholarship from Diné scholars, we foreground the story of so-called adopted clans, or clans that reveal the Diné practice of adopting and incorporating non-Diné peoples into Navajo society as a way to solidify kin relationships. For example, out of some fifty-three clans identified by anthropologist Gladys Reichard in 1928, twenty-one, or over one-third, are listed as adopted clans or as clan names created for individuals or other Pueblo or Mexican groups that originally came from outside the Navajo Nation (1928, 16). Putting these various sources in conversation with one another, we attend to the "floating gap" (Vansina 1985, 23; cf. Gardner 2015) that exists between the "mythic time" of clan histories and the "calendrical time" of Diné settler-colonial histories from Spanish contact (ca. 1539) onward, dwelling in the space of possibility between the two histories. Using clans as a window into the ways Diné society historically included and incorporated non-Navajos into the fabric of the Navajo Nation, we probe what implications these stories might have for a Diné politics of citizenship and belonging today.

Our goal is not to focus on clan histories and clan-internal stories per se—this is neither the appropriate medium nor the forum to share such typically private and culturally intimate stories—but rather to foreground Diné adoptive practices in order to broaden what we currently perceive as a discourse of "purism" around blood quantum and "being Navajo" experienced by many, including coauthor Bowman, in Navajo communities both on the reservation and off today (Barker 2011; Cody 2016; Denetdale 2006; Kauanui 2008; L. Lee 2007; Jacobsen-Bia 2014; Spruhan 2007, 2018; Webster 2015). Moreover, by suggesting that Navajos were remarkably open to a variety of categories of citizenship, we do not mean to indicate that being Navajo, then or now, is up for grabs or that one can simply wake up and proclaim oneself to be Native or Navajo.[6] Nor do we mean to imply, as many anthropologists have before us, that this in any way makes Navajo citizens less "authentically" Indigenous or that fluid identities are unique to the Navajo Nation among other North American Indigenous communities. To the contrary, clans and kinship are deeply embedded, intricate, and continue to be guidelines for many as to how the world should be ordered; methods of incorporation were (and often still are) strategic and premised on extant relationships, senses of connection, and shared history, and those who became "Navajo" had to visibly demonstrate their investment in a Navajo polity through their actions and ability to act, socialize, and speak in Diné ways. We also understand Native identity primarily as a political rather than a racial assignation, and being enrolled in a federally or state-recognized tribe is an important part of this process. Finally, our framing of Navajo Nation here crucially includes Diné citizens living both on and off the formal Navajo Nation; this includes the many Diné citizens living in southwestern "bordertowns" such as Albuquerque, New Mexico, and Phoenix and Flagstaff, Arizona, but also Denver, Los Angeles, and Chicago (Navajo Division of Health and Navajo Epidemiology Center 2013). It also includes the many Diné citizens across the United States—over 10 percent of Diné citizenry—who currently serve in the military (Jacobsen 2017; Denetdale 2006; Schilling 2014).

We conclude by reflecting on settler colonialism's impact on relationships between and among Navajos with the advent of the first Indian census in 1885 and the creation of the Navajo Nation Adoption Law in 1934, when the Navajo Tribal Council stipulated that a person cannot become a member of the Navajo Nation by adoption (Austin 2007, 193). While the Spanish colonial period (1539–1821) is acknowledged as the driving force behind increased tensions and divisions between Diné, Pueblo, and Ute peoples (Zolbrod 1984; Forbes 1960), the advent of the American occupation of the Southwest (1848 to the present) and the practice of taking a "census" not only exacerbated these same tensions but also created new Navajo-internal divisions, many of them based on enrollment, land allotment, and, in more recent decades, the measuring of someone's percentage or degree of "Indian blood," also known as blood quantum.[7] Crucially, the creation of a census seems to be linked to the cessation of adoption practices and the creation of new clans. Although Reichard recorded two new clans (both Pueblo or pre-Puebloan in origin) that appear to have been created postcensus, between 1890 (when Washington Matthews recorded his list of forty-four clans) and 1910, these seem to be some of the last formally designated new clans added to the current clan structure within Diné society; today, they are formally included and colloquially referred to on the reservation as "adopted" clans, despite what Reichard notes as the very common "principle of adoption of a foreign people" within Diné society (1928, 27–28). Thus, the creation of a census signaled the beginning of the end of the existing elasticity within Diné kinship structures to create new clans for outside groups with whom Diné peoples came into contact.

Diné Clan Characteristics

Today there are over seventy active clans on the Navajo Nation, and clans are further divided into nine major clan groupings (Lapahie 2001; Littleben 2010), creating numerous taboos as to whom one can and cannot marry or date (dating someone with whom you share a first or second clan is considered akin to incest, since that means you are brother/sister).[8] The role of clans is threefold, including exogamy, or marrying outside one's primary clan groups, hospitality, and ceremonial practices. As Witherspoon articulated this, "Two persons who have the same matrilineal descent identity *should not marry or experience sexual intercourse, should provide food and lodging for each other while one or the other is traveling away from home, and should help each other during a ceremony for one or the other.* These acts of solidarity realize the affective and functional meanings of the concept of matrilineal descent" (1975, 42, italics added).

However, not all Diné people go by or believe in the clan system, for example, Diné citizens who belong to one of the many Navajo-led neo-Pentecostal churches on the reservation (Marshall 2016a, 2016b). Some urban-identified Diné, including some of our students at the University of New Mexico and at Diné College, Crownpoint, also do not follow the clan system or "know" their clans. For those who do adhere to the clan system, being related to someone by clan is a strong bond, and certain clans are associated—historically and contemporarily—with specific areas of the Navajo reservation and are territorially restricted (Reichard 1928, 20). For example, the New Mexico reservation town of Tohatchi is known for clans such as Bit'ahnii (Folded Arms People) and Tódich'íi'nii (Bitterwater People), while many members of the Towering House clan, the clan mentioned by James and Ernie in their routine at the beginning of this piece, reside in the town of Crownpoint (T'iis Ts'óóz Ndeeshgiizh), the location where one iteration of this clan is said to originate.[9] Similarly, the Deeshch'íi'nii clan, understood to be Apache in origin, is named after a canyon in the Cibecue area of Western Apache country (Lapahie 2001).

Clans also carry certain professional, phenotypic, and psychological traits and taboos, and some clans are assigned more prestige than others. For example, in coauthor Bowman's experience, Kinya'áaniis are a high-status clan known for their leadership and rhetorical skills and for often holding powerful positions within Navajo society. Numerous Navajo Nation Council delegates are Kinya'áaniis. Folded Arms People (Bit'ahnii) are known for being harsh, scolding, and sometimes self-centered; they are also known for sometimes having a lighter skin tone compared to other Diné clan groups. Bit'ahniis also have high expectations for those around them, emphasizing the Diné belief that "t'áá áko ajit'éego" (if it is to be, then it's up to me), and this raises the bar for anyone related to a Bit'ahnii. Members of the Bitterwater clan (Tódich'íi'nii) also hold significant Diné cultural capital and are known primarily as educators, philosophers, counselors, and Medicine People, or traditional healers. Sleep Rock people (Tsénahabiłnii) are known for being very caring and for "making you feel like you belong" (Bowman 2016). They are also linguistically demonstrative, using lots of kinship terms for those they care about, such as *shiyázhí* (my little one) and *she'awéé'* (my baby/sweetheart). Water Comes Together (Tó Aheedlíinii) clan members can be flirtatious, "jollied out" (Bowman 2016), and sometimes fickle in nature. Salt clan (Áshįįhí) members originate from Salt Woman, who is known for her generosity and for having made the first baby laugh. Therefore, they are often happy-go-lucky and always smiling, and they also love to laugh, known in Navajo as *ayóo badahozhǫ́*.

There are four clans created by the Diné deity known as Asdzą́ą́ Nádleehí, or Changing Woman (Zolbrod 1984; Lapahie 2001): Towering House (Kinya'áanii), Bitterwater (Tódich'íí'nii), Mud (Hashtl'ishnii), and One Who Walks Around (Honaghaahnii) (see Lapahie 2001). These clans form the basis for the Western Water clans, and although they are colloquially referred to as the four "original" clans, these clans likely came into formation around the same time that clans in the eastern part of Diné Bikéyah were also first forming (Thompson 2017). Crucially, in a Diné cosmology, one is an equal balance of all four clans (Bowman 2011), and one should never let one clan—or that one clan's characteristics—dominate the others.

If a Diné person has four Navajo grandparents, then they will have four Diné clans—maternal, paternal, mother's father, and father's father, and typically presented in this order.[10] The first or maternal clan is considered to be the most important in being identified (and identifying oneself) as Diné.[11] Having a Navajo clan connects one to a much larger group of people and is a central way not only of signifying Diné identity but of immediately establishing a relationship to others in one's clan group. Indeed, some Diné introduce their clans before introducing themselves by name or even identifying themselves as Native or Navajo: the clan identification takes precedence.[12] Sharing kinship means that everywhere one travels where there are other Navajos, one gains not only a relative but also a sense of belonging.[13] For example, contrasting current rhetoric where "full Navajo" means a "full-blooded," "4/4," or someone who has four Navajo grandparents, acknowledging kinship and "knowing" one's clans is what makes someone, according to a traditional Diné perspective, a "full Navajo" (Bowman 2016).

Contrasting a Navajo discourse where Diné clans are portrayed as "always" having come exclusively from within Diné society (Tribal Employee Blogspot 2015; Tom 1997), we know from both clan histories and historical records that as many as one-third of Navajo clans are in fact "adopted" clans (Lapahie 2001; Bowman 2009; Reichard 1928; Lapahie 2001). In many cases, adopted clans were created after non-Diné women and children were brought back to the Navajo Nation through various encounters during the Journey Narrative and, later, after raids and hostage taking.[14] Crucially, whatever the method of contact, these groups were typically and then actively incorporated into Diné society through the creation of a Navajo clan (Thompson 2009).

Clan names themselves originate typically from place-names, as referenced earlier, but also from characteristics of certain individuals belonging to a clan group whose prominence is marked by a renaming of that clan to honor them and from names of outside groups—typically Pueblo, Apache, Ute, or Mexican—or specific clans of members from outside groups (Reichard 1928). Speaking to this diversity of clan origins, Reichard further demarcated four groupings for the origins of clan names, including (1) local or place-names, (2) Pueblo names or Pueblo clan names, (3) nicknames belonging to individuals that become clan names, and (4) names of "alien" tribes (1928, 16). Importantly, clan stories vary significantly from clan to clan and family to family; thus, there is not always common agreement on the elements, for example, of the Diné Bahane', nor is there one set agreed-upon narrative (L. Lee 2012; Bauman 2009). Thus, clan origin stories themselves are yet another example of the internal diversity—and the space that is made and allowed for multiple versions of a single narrative to coexist—with Diné social spaces both historically and in the present moment.

"Adopted" and "Related" Navajo Clans: Methods of Incorporation and Social Elasticity

Diné society has adopted groups from outside Navajo society from the beginning; this is documented in part 4, the final section of the Diné Journey Narrative and Creation Scriptures, also known as the Gathering of the Clans (Zolbrod 1984; L. Lee 2012; Denetdale 2006).[15] Because of the diversity represented in this final section, Diné society has also been referred to as the "first melting pot culture" (Zolbrod 2016).[16] For example, clans were often created when descendants of Ute, Apache, Pueblo, Spanish, and Mexican war captives were incorporated into Diné society (Thompson 2009, 134). Alternately, clans of Athabaskan-speaking peoples from as far west as the Pacific Ocean also migrated into Navajo country seeking their kin and eventually became Navajos (Matthews 1897; Thompson 2017). According to Harrison Lapahie (2001), many of these clans either were imprisoned with Diné people at Hwéeldi (Fort Sumner) and traveled back with them to Dinétah, such as the Chiricahua and Mescalero Apaches, or were groups with whom Diné met up on the way back from the long walk en route to Dinétah.[17] This includes present-day clans such as the Mexican People Clan (Naakaii Dine'é), Ute clan (Nóóda'í Dine'é), and Apache clans such as the White Mountain Apache Clan (Dziłgha'í Dine'é), Mescalero Apache Clan (Naashgalí Dine'é), and Chiricahua Apache Clan (Chishí Dine'é). Adopted Pueblo clans include the Hopi clan

(Kiis'áanii), Tewa clan (Naashashí, i.e., the Tewa-speaking peoples of New Mexico), the Zuni clan (Naasht'ézhí) and the Zia (Weaver) clan (Tł'ógí).[18]

Interestingly, there is also documentation of some groups wishing to become a part of the fabric of Diné society but not being accorded this status. Typically, this seems to have been based on geographic proximity and that group's willingness to culturally become Diné rather than premised on them being outsiders. For example, in Diné historian Lapahie's (2001) version of the years following the return from Fort Sumner and migration patterns of Dine'é, he notes:

> As the years passed, most of the people of Dinétah started moving around from place to place, and other American Indian tribal bands were adopted into the Navajo tribe. When the Diné moved back from Hwéeldi (Ft. Sumner), New Mexico, in the 1860s, some newcomers joined them on their walk back home. These people had also been imprisoned and now formed their own clans, the Chíshí Dine'é (Chiricahua Apache Clan) and Naashgalí Dine'é (Mescalero Apache Clan). *It is said that these people tried, but were not accepted by many Diné.* The Beiyóodzíne' [text missing here] (Paiutes) from Naatsis'áán (Navajo Mountain) were adopted but were left there because of differences over religious matters. The people (Diné) then moved down toward the south, where they left the Chíshí (Chiricahua Apaches), and adopted the Mexicans (Naakaii). Then they went to the east, where the Naashgalí (Mescalero Apaches) decided to stay. The Mescaleros now live from Albuquerque (Be'eldííldahsinil) all the way down to the home of the Naakaii (Mexicans). From there, the Diné again moved to the vicinity of Dibé Nitsaa (La Plata Mountains), where the Beehai (Jicarilla Apaches) eventually settled. (Lapahie 2001, italics added)

In the Gathering of the Clans, stories also chronicle the multitude of ways that these outsiders became a part of the fabric of contemporary Diné society. What is striking about each narrative in the Gathering of the Clans is the variety of methods for incorporation and inherent flexibility within Diné society to allow new social groups the level of autonomy—or integration—that they desired once they came into contact with Diné society. Also of note is the extensive contact between Navajos and Puebloan and Apachean groups and how relatively recently many of these outside groups joined the Navajo Nation and were given adopted or related clan status. In other words, while clan adoption is a practice going back to the Diné Creation Stories, it also was used as a standard method of incorporation until quite recently.[19]

In these stories, identities are fluid, based less on "ethnicity" and more on the ability to behave in a cooperative manner and successfully integrate oneself socially. Clans, regardless of origin, are egalitarian. Clan names are given based on place of origin, method of encounter, behaviors associated with that group, and even the perceived physical appearance of said group. Thus, kinship is created based on a sense of *k'é,* or relatedness between groups, rather than by shared ethnicity or "blood" per se.

The specific origins or nature of encounter with the adopted "outside" group also seems to play a role in the designation of "real" versus "slave" adopted clans. However, those who descend from so-called slave clans do not identify with this designation. As Reichard poignantly states: "Some also claim that some branches of adopted clans are 'real' while others are 'slave' clans. We found numerous members of the 'real' clan but no one among 3500 souls who confessedly belonged to a 'slave' branch—consequently in practice all are 'real'! There is little doubt that captives were often slaves, but since Navajo social organization did not tend to encourage the institution of slavery as it is commonly understood those individuals became acknowledged members of the Navajo tribe with a few generations" (1928, 15–16).

Environmental determinism also plays a role in clan characteristics. For example, an offshoot of the Kinya'áaniis, Kinya'áanii Dził'ahnii (Towering House Mountain Cove People), originated in the Chuska Mountains, two hours west of the Kinya'áaniis from Crownpoint. As rugged mountain people, they are known for their independence, their can-do spirit, and their ability to make do with whatever comes their way.

While clans have equal status in relation to one another, they vary in their degree of "firstness," or proximity to the four original clans created by Changing Woman. This, in turn, determines how they are grouped in a contemporary Navajo clan chart showing relationality between the various clans. Thus, different groups were adopted and incorporated to varying degrees and with differing levels of cultural independence, something we can see by looking at a clan chart showing contemporary relations between clans. In many of these charts (e.g., Lapahie 2001), we see a fourfold hierarchy of clans based on degree of firstness or connections to firstness, where the four "original" clans come first, followed by clans "related" to the original clan and included in that clan grouping. Next we see clans "adopted" into one of the nine primary clan groups, followed by "other" clan groups that are acknowledged but have not been adopted into a clan relationship (clan groups 10–21) but are listed as clan groups in their own right (Lapahie 2001). These include the Tewa (Naashashí), Ute (Nóóda'í Dine'é), and Mescalero Apache (Naashgalí) clans. Finally, we have groups, including other nationalities, not included in the clan charts at all.

What clan charts fail to show us, however, is the actual fluidity in terms of adoption practices, practices that were in fact anything but linear, finite, and fixed. Outside groups merged with Diné society, retained their own clans, merged clans, left for long periods of time, and returned, and adoption was not an overnight process. So the boundaries of Diné society, while cohesive and coherent, were also porous.

Another factor in determining which clans are "related" and which clans are "adopted," for example, is geographic proximity and intermarriage. Tribes and communities that lived or live in close proximity to Diné Bikéyah—an area spanning the Four Corners region and enclosed by the four Sacred Mountains—were more likely to acquire their own Navajo clan. Additionally, individuals or communities that intermarried with Navajos, for example, Mą'ii Deeshgiiznii (Jemez / Coyote Pass clan), Naakai Dine'é (Mexican People Clan), or Nasht'ézhí Dine'é (Zuni Clan), were also more likely to be given a "Navajo" clan. For example, Gladys Reichard noted that citizens of Zuni Pueblo at that time noted that Navajos of Zuni origin "still retain the language of the mother tribe (i.e., the Zuni language)" and are "counted among the best blanket-makers and artisans of the Navajo" (1928, 15).

Looking from yet another perspective, however, it is also possible to say that all Diné clans are "adopted" clans and that a demarcation between "us"—Navajos—and "them"—non-Navajos—really only began with the incorporation of the Ute clan. As Diné archaeologist Kerry Thompson notes, according to the stories collected by anthropologist Washington Matthews in the nineteenth century, "one could argue that all clans are 'adopted'—the narratives he's collected describe a gathering of people and it isn't until the Ute clan comes into being that there is a distinction between the way 'we' act and the way 'they' act" (2017). Thus, terms such as "incorporation" and "social elasticity" might be more productive than a term such as "adoption" to describe processes where newer social groups—Athabaskan clans, other Native tribes, and non-Native groups—are incorporated into Diné society.

Clans also help us to understand contemporary indigeneity in North America, including the location of other present-day Athabaskan or Dené communities as a part of the Navajo diaspora in the Fourth World. For example, Changing Woman, the deity who created the first four clans descending from the Western Water clans, spent many years living on the West Coast, allegedly near present-day Santa Barbara, California, which would explain why speakers of related Athabaskan (Dené) languages are also found in California today (Zolbrod 1984).[20] Similarly, in the Journey Narratives we see stories of an Apache scout who got lost and eventually took his people far northward, becoming the Diné Nááhódlóonii (Other Navajo People), explaining an Athabaskan presence in western Canada and Alaska from a Diné perspective (Ives 2003; Ruhlen 1998; Wilson 1970; Zolbrod 1984). Using the Journey Narratives as the means for understanding the extent to which Navajo and non-Navajo groups became interconnected—the gradation—we gain deeper insight into contemporary forms of Diné identity and belonging.

"What's Your Chart Number?": The Navajo Census, Tribal Enrollment, and Blood Quantum

> James and Ernie are now on a different stage, this time depicting a scene in an Indian Health Service (IHS) clinic on the reservation. As James enters the clinic and signs in for his appointment, a matronly BIA employee (Ernie) at the service window asks him in an irritated voice, as if he has already done something to offend her: "What's your CHART number?" Laughter erupts from the mostly Navajo crowd attending the show.[21]

"Chart numbers" are often used in addition to names and birth dates at publicly funded health care facilities in Indian Country for purposes of identification. IHS (and BIA) desk clerks are notoriously grumpy and, in this comedy routine, relish reinforcing the red tape associated with unwieldy federal agencies ostensibly designed to serve Indian people. In this case, chart numbers are also linked to census numbers, or the number a Native American or Navajo is assigned verifying his or her political identity as an "Indian" at the federal level.[22] In places like IHS facilities, census numbers are also sometimes bureaucratically linked to an individual's CDIB, or Certificate Degree of Indian Blood, and in some cases a person's CDIB is required before an individual can apply for tribal citizenship (Spruhan 2018, 175). Thus, "chart number" in this comedy routine acts as a generic stand-in phrase for a variety of identification numbers and gatekeeping mechanisms used to designate, quantify, and verify an individual's identity as an "Indian" in ways that are, depending on whom you ask, seen as either tedious yet necessary or ridiculous, pointless, and diminishing. So while having a census number is separate and distinct from being enrolled in one's tribal nation—one can have a census number, for example, but not be enrolled in a tribal nation and vice versa—what we argue here is that both the taking of the census and tribal enrollment practices have equally affected the ability to continue to incorporate outside groups into Navajo communities.

Referred in local parlance on the Navajo Nation as simply a CIB, the Diné-specific version of the CDIB—the Certificate of Navajo Indian Blood, or CNIB—is a legal document issued by the Navajo Nation Office of Vital Records and Information (NNOVRI) to quantify the percentage of Navajo "blood" an individual possesses (Begay in L. Lee 2014; Thompson, forthcoming). In the case of the Navajo Nation, which, like all federally recognized tribes, determines its own enrollment criteria, one must possess one-quarter or more "Navajo" blood, and ancestry must be traced to one of two BIA rolls, one from 1928 and one from 1940, in order for someone to be enrolled as a Navajo citizen. In the case of the Navajo Nation, the CNIB is a nonlaminated 8½-by-11 green piece of paper (Spruhan 2018, 170).

CNIBs create a dividing line between those who have one and those who do not. As Paul Spruhan notes, a CNIB is "the key that unlocks educational loans, medical services, employment preference, or other federal benefits unique to Native Americans" (2018, 171); a CNIB is required, for example, to vote in Navajo Nation elections and apply for Navajo Nation scholarships, and it acts as the bureaucratic standard of documentation for many other services available only to individuals enrolled in the Navajo Nation.[23] Moreover, while some tribes issue two different documents, or a CDIB for federal purposes and a tribal membership document for tribal purposes, the Navajo Nation uses the CNIB for both, thus blurring the boundaries between blood quantum, tribal citizenship, and the relationship between the two (Spruhan 2018, 176).

The BIA rolls to which an enrolled Navajo must trace their ancestry were instituted by the Bureau of Indian Affairs beginning with the first Navajo BIA roll in 1928. The second roll, created in 1940, is the roll to which new enrollees are added by the NNOVRI, even today. In this case, blood quantum for today's enrollees is calculated based on the blood quantum of the original enrollees on the 1928 or 1940 roll to which one's ancestry is traced. As Indigenous studies scholar J. Kehaulani Kauanui (Kanaka Maoli) describes the process of quantifying "Indian" blood percentages, "Blood quantum is a fractionalizing measurement—a calculation of 'distance' in relation to some supposed purity to mark one's proximity to a 'full-blood' forebear" (2008, 2).

Further complicating our understanding of clans and kinship, when the NNOVRI assesses Navajo "blood quantum" or percentage of "Navajo" blood and issues a CNIB to a Navajo citizen (Begay 2011; Spruhan 2017), adopted clans such as Mexican People Clan (Naakai Dine'é) and Jemez / Coyote Pass clan (Ma̜'ii Deeshgiizhnii) are counted as "Navajo" blood, despite origin narratives and historical references offered explicitly to the contrary. Groups incorporated after the 1880s, by contrast, are by and large not given Diné clan names and thus are treated as "non-Navajo" and not counted on a CNIB as "Navajo" blood. Thus, a contemporary CNIB represents in microcosm many of the internal contradictions and historical demarcations in the shifting landscape of Diné kinship, adoption, and blood quantum.

Enumeration and quantification of Navajo bodies and Navajo "blood" by both the tribe and the federal government in the form of the census number and the CDIB—and the sheer ridiculousness of the bureaucracy that accompanies this world and the futility of actually measuring Navajo blood in the biological sense—are part of what James and Ernie are making fun of in this skit.

The Navajo Census

Following the removal period to Hwéeldi (Bosque Redondo in Fort Sumner, New Mexico), known as the Long Walk (1864–68), Navajo people returned to a portion of their original homeland in the American Southwest, Diné Bikéyah. Less than twenty years after their return, in 1885, the first Navajo census was conducted, a practice designed to enumerate Navajo bodies.[24] It planted the seeds for the concept of "enrollment" in a federally recognized tribe as part of what it meant to be counted as "Indian."[25]

With the creation of the census, the more organic practice of adopting clans seems to have largely stopped, and from this point forward outside groups that interacted with Diné society were given Navajo names indicating separate and demarcated tribal and ethnic groups existing outside of the kinship system, or what Reichard referred to as "alien" clans (Thompson 2016; Lapahie 2001; Reichard 1928, 29). Even so, in a Navajo census conducted as late as 1915 by BIA Superintendent Peter Paquette (Diné) for the Navajo Agency, maternal clans, although not required by the US Census Bureau, are listed for each of the 11,915 Navajos documented in the census (Paquette 1915, A-1, 56), showing the continued importance of kinship not only for Diné people but also for BIA administrators and enumerators. A Navajo clerk working for the agency, John Walker, was hired exclusively to attend to the documentation of names and clans for everyone listed in the census (Paquette 1915, B-11). Moreover, attesting to continued forms of adoption in some form, in the enumeration of Diné families in this census, adopted children were matter-of-factly given the mother's Navajo clan (Paquette 1915, 56).

Blood quantum as part of the Indian census came much later, between 1928 and 1930, and a minimum blood quantum of one-quarter "Navajo" blood—the criterion used today to determine Diné citizenship—wasn't adopted by the Navajo Nation until 1953 (Spruhan 2007; Thompson, forthcoming). Indian agents were first required to include degree of Indian "blood" in Indian census documentation in 1928, but the criteria changed frequently thereafter: initial requirements were general and vague, and subsequent criteria became more and more concerned with minutiae and "precision" (Indian Census Rolls). For example, in 1930 agents had to compress a person's blood quantum into one of three categories, even if that person didn't technically fit into these categories: "F" for "full blood"; "¼+" for one-quarter or more Indian blood; and "¼-" for less than one-quarter. By 1933 these categories were expanded to include "F," "¾," "½," "¼," and "⅛," and later still, all agents were encouraged to be "exact if possible" (Indian Census Rolls). However, as the US Census Bureau acknowledges, "If someone used the 1930 blood quantum information in retrospect it could lead to mistakes, since it is *not* possible to start from an artificially compressed category and then *accurately* return with greater detail" (Indian Census Rolls). Blood quantum in the case of the census is not—and never was—grounded in scientific fact, and it is historically discordant with systems used prior to its invention to assess Indigenous belonging (Bond, Brough, and Cox 2014; Perdue 2010; TallBear 2013; Villazor 2008).

After the institution of the census and census blood quantum requirements, the method of naming outside groups also changed, shifting to names that became based more on physical descriptions and less on the nature of the kinship relationship between Navajo and non-Navajo groups. In stark contrast to the flexible nature of prior methods of incorporation, these names chronicle the initial nature of encounter—often military in nature—and reflect broader American xenophobic discourse about said groups. For example, in examining a list of Navajo names for contemporary nationalities, many of them created during World War II, the current word for Russian is Bi'éé' Daalchíi'ii, or the Ones with the Red Shirts, a reference to Communist era, Cold War relations between the United States and Russia.[26] Similarly, Germans are called Béésh Bich'ahii, or "Metal Helmets," a reference to World War II and Diné encounters with German soldiers. Chinese people are Bináá'ádaalts'ózí, or "Narrow Slit-Eyed People" (Young and Morgan 1987). It is significant to note that although there is significant intermarriage, there is no existing adopted clan for Anglo people, or Bilagáanas.

Today, blood quantum and enrollment have permeated Diné modes of thinking and being, including the ideas held by some citizens that all "real" Navajos have a census number and a CNIB and are enrolled in the Navajo Nation. Some believe that the more Navajo "blood" one has, the more "Navajo" one is. Like many other tribes, the Navajo Nation has adopted BIA rolls as the base rolls for determining citizenship, where ancestry is traced back using lineal descent to a specific roll, in this case from 1928 or 1940 (Spruhan 2008).[27] Thus, anyone not on these rolls or who happened to be living off the reservation for employment at the time a particular roll count was taken was not included on the rolls and therefore may not "count" as Navajo. Like most identity formations (Hall 2000; Hall and Bucholtz 2012), blood quantum is socially constructed, yet it continues to hold much social power in Diné social spaces today. Lenape scholar Joanne Barker has expanded upon the social construction of blood quantum and the power it holds, particularly for the ways in which a higher blood degree is linked to perceptions of social isolation, lack of Euro-American cultural assimilation, and biological "purity": "Language fluency and blood quantum were used as special tools for measuring isolation and, hence, authenticity against the presumed historical forces of assimilation that resulted in language loss and compromised blood degrees" (2011, 4). Linking this argument to settler colonialism's reach, Kauanui extends this analysis to the ways "blood dilation" can be used to delegitimize and ultimately dispossess Indigenous peoples, where "the 'inauthentic' status of Natives is a condition for sovereign dispossession in the service of settler colonialism" (2008, 25).

Contemporary Diné citizenship based on blood quantum is based on a calcified idea of "Indianness" that runs counter to historical and clan-based ideologies of Diné community building and social incorporation. As Thompson has noted, "Blood quantum bears no cultural relationship to the Navajo clan system. . . . The practices of census taking and 'measuring' blood quantum has 'fixed' the Navajo clan system at a moment in time. Adoption of new clans is no longer practiced, therefore, anyone who appears on the Navajo census roll has inherited a minimum of one clan that existed at the time the census became the rigid enumeration of membership we recognize today" (Thompson, forthcoming).

Becoming Diné: Methods of Incorporation and Adoption in Diné Bahane'

Looking at the history of Diné methods of incorporation and adoption, we see a very different story. The most common method of adoption in the Navajo Creation Scriptures and Journey Narratives—the Diné Bahane'—is for a new, exogamous group to be adopted by an already existing Diné clan. This clan, in turn, creates a new "adopted" clan for that group, where the new and old clan groups are henceforth considered "related" and can no longer marry one another; instead, they see one another henceforward as *k'éí*, or extended family. Thus, within the clan groups provided by Lapahie (2001) and Reichard (1928), we see clan groupings and then various related clans grouped within those clans. Significantly, once a woman had children with someone within a Diné clan group, she herself was given a new clan and considered to be Diné. This is seen, for example, in one version of the creation of the Kinłichʼííʼnii clan, a Puebloan group living along the Rio Grande that was attacked by members of the Diné clan group known as Tsiʼnaajinii, or Black Horizontal Forest People. One of the Tsiʼnaajinii warriors who conducted the raid took a Kinłichʼííʼnii woman for his wife during the raid, presumably by force. However, once the couple had children, she and the children were given a new clan, Kin Kinłichʼííʼnii, and at the end of her life she died as a Diné woman. As Zolbrod chronicles this event, "She became his wife and in time gave birth often. So it was that she also became the mother of many children and finally died at a ripe old age as a respected Navajo woman. From her descends the clan known as Kin Kinłich'íi'nii, which means Red House Clan in the language spoken by Bilagáana today" (1984, 308).[28] Thus, in this telling of this story, bearing children and being given a clan are what gives someone a Diné clan.

An alternate method of incorporation was for the children of a Pueblo woman and a Diné father to be assigned the mother's Pueblo clan name rather than her tribal origin name, which was sometimes then combined with the father's clan, creating a new synthetic clan combining the two names (Reichard 1928, 17–18). For example, if the Diné father was Tachíi'nii and the Pueblo mother's clan was Tobacco clan, then the child might then be Tobacco-Tachíi'nii (18). Thus, "a few concrete examples show the change from pueblo to Navajo type of clan names depending upon which group the female participant in the marriage belongs to" (19). The tendency for relating clans and creating alliances, even where none existed before, is seen as a prevalent feature of Diné society: "Pueblo women who married into the tribe gave their pueblo names to their children and thus clans with pueblo names originated. Or, it may be that in a tribe like the Navajo *where the tendency for relating clans was extremely strong* the woman was adopted into a Navajo clan and she and her children thereafter had a Navajo clan name" (17, italics added).

In other cases, moving to Navajo land from elsewhere on a voluntary basis and wanting to become Diné is enough to make a new group Navajo. As Zolbrod notes about one version of the arrival of a group of Apaches from south of the San Juan Valley to Diné Bikéyah, a group later adopted by the Tábąąhá, or Water's Edge clan: "They had left the land of the Apaches forever, and they now wanted to become Navajos" (1984, 306).[29] As with Kin Kinłich'íi'nii and Tsi'naajiniis, these two groups became so close that marrying someone from the other clan group is now considered taboo.

Linguistic histories are also foregrounded in the Gathering of the Clans and in the Diné Journey Narratives. In one story, the origin of the Navajo language, or Diné Bizaad, is actually brought by one of the most central clans in this section, the Water's Edge clan, or Tábąąhá, a clan that is considered to be Pueblo rather than Diné in origin: "The language that the people of Tábąąhá the Water's Edge Clan spoke was more like the modern Navajo language spoken today than that which members of the other clans spoke. For at this time their respective languages were not alike. Nor were they like languages spoken today. So less could be understood among them than is understood now" (Zolbrod 1984, 301). Tábąąhá introduced their language as a lingua franca that all gravitate toward, and Navajos as a group eventually agreed to allow this version of the language to become the one they regarded as "the" Navajo language.

Behavior and willingness to become a part of a larger entity within Diné society are also factors in determining how integrated an outside group becomes. Navajos and Utes have a long history of raiding one another, and even today there is sometimes tension between these two groups because of this history (Whyte 2010). In the following passage, we see perhaps some of the residual perceptions Diné people had of Ute people based on raids already conducted: "At first they (Utes) lived apart from the Navajos, for they were unruly and rude. But by and by *they learned to conduct them-selves acceptably and they gradually merged into the Navajo nation*. They formed the Nóóda'í Dine'é Clan, which means Ute People in the language that Bilagáana the White Man speaks" (Zolbrod 1984, 309, italics added). Once Utes adopted the common cultural practices of Diné people, they were permitted to join the Navajo Nation, and that subgroup (phratry) of Utes was then considered Diné.

Clans are also given as a status marker, and in some cases phenotype and the desire on the part of a Diné clan member to bestow a new clan upon another also determines the clan creation. In the story of the Yel-low People clan, a young Tábaahá woman becomes close with an Apache man whose band is visiting for the large winter ceremony, the Naachid. Together they leave to go back to Apache country, until her Navajo kin-folk, many years later, find her and convince her and her family to return to Diné Bikéyah. By this time, she has three grown daughters, who were "beautiful maidens by then with light skin and fair hair" (Zolbrod 1984, 310). In this case, their Apache father, now in Navajo country and with three Diné daughters, is bestowed proximate kinship and also dies as a Diné man. Zolbrod notes about the Tábaahá grandmother of the three girls: "Their grandmother, who admired them when she saw them for the first time, desired that they should become the founders of a new clan. Soon they were married, and as they raised families of their own their offspring became known as łitso dine'é. That name means Yellow People in the lan-guage of *Bilagáana* the White Man. *The father of those three women lived to a ripe old age and finally died as a respected Navajo*" (1984, 310-11, italics added).

Non-Navajos can also bestow clans on other Navajos as an indication of shared history and where naming of a clan is also a display of respect and an explicit demonstration of relationality between the namer and the named. For example, members of a then nameless clan from the west lived in Apache country, south of Diné Bikéyah, for a total of seven years. After finally deciding to return north to join other Navajos, they were named by an older Apache woman, who begins walking around them to demonstrate and embody the name she will soon give them:

"You came to live with us without a name," she said to them.

"And for seven years you have dwelt among us without a name.

"Without a name you have been our good friends. Without a name you have exchanged stories with our own people.

"Well, you should not leave us unnamed.

"That is why I have walked around you.

"From now on you shall be known as Honágháahnii the He Walks Around One Clan. Henceforth you shall no longer be nameless." (Zolbrod 1984, 334–35)

Also striking in the process of out-group incorporation is the degree of flexibility in how belonging and affiliation are determined. For example, in the case of Tábąąhá incorporation of members of the Paiute tribe, Paiutes desired both inclusion and the ability to retain some of their cultural practices, which are recognized and granted.[30] "At about the same time a band of Paiutes came and were likewise adopted. They too are members of that clan Tábąąhá to this very day, although *it is still understood that they are of a different origin and they retain some of their own traditions*" (Zolbrod 1984, 337, italics added). In this case, clan incorporation includes the ability to still assert difference and retain expressive practices considered central to that group's cultural identity.

Perhaps most essential to our analysis, the Gathering of the Clans provides clear evidence that adding outside groups to the polity known as the Navajo Nation was seen as an almost uniformly positive event, a strength-in-numbers approach in which equilibrium between and among groups was easily achievable: "Earlier the Navajos had been a small and a weak people. But now they found themselves numerous and strong" (Zolbrod 1984, 307). As the Franciscan Fathers, some of the earliest visitors to Navajo land to write about Diné language, clans, and history, noted in 1910, "The numerical increase of the clans is not due to the process of segmentation of existing clans, but to one of adoption of new peoples which were met in the course of the journey to the present habitat of the tribe. Accordingly, the phratry is eliminated, in fact, it is unknown to the Navajo, who makes no such distinction. *Each clan, therefore, forms a separate whole, which is socially the equal of others with whom it is perchance affiliated by consanguinity or adoption*" (quoted in Zolbrod 1984, 416n26, italics added).[31]

Another way to understand the elasticity of kinship and Diné willingness to create new clans is through the lens of how ceremonial and culturally specific knowledge is passed down in Diné society. This contrasts greatly to how ceremonial knowledge is passed down, for example, in neighboring Pueblo communities. Whereas in many Pueblo societies ceremonial stories, songs, and dances are exclusively passed down through one's clan, and thus extinction of a clan indicates the death of the stories themselves, in Diné society this knowledge is passed down through clans and one's relationship to clans. Songs can also be transmitted to those who express sustained interest, whether they are affiliated by clan or not. For Diné people, more flexibility is built into the transmission of this knowledge. Thus, "although Navajo clans have powerful social and economic functions, such as regulating marriage and consequent friendly affiliation and serving to keep individual property within the clan" (Reichard 1928, 32), ceremonial stories can remain vital and alive even if a clan that bore that knowledge is no longer an active clan.

One final framework for understanding the willingness to create new clans where none existed before is the fundamentally Diné desire to shift from more general kinship-based forms of solidarity and cooperation, known as *k'é*, to the more specific kind of solidarity that is experienced between and among kinspeople of the same descent group, known as *k'éí*. Creating clans that are considered "related" to Diné clans creates *k'éí* expeditiously and often within one generation. As Witherspoon notes on the distinction between *k'é* and *k'éí*,

> "K'ei" [now more commonly spelled with a high tone as *k'éí*] refers to a special kind of solidarity which exists among those related according to Navajo concepts and categories of descent. The suffixing of an "i" on "k'e" [now more commonly spelled with a high tone as *k'é*] is the same kind of linguistic phenomenon as the suffixing of an "e" on "dine." It means in this case a particular or special kind of k'e. Thus when a Navajo says "shik'ei" ("my relatives by descent") he is identifying an exclusive group of people with whom he especially relates according to the concepts of ideals of k'e. (1975, 120)

In applying the histories of new clan creation to contemporary Navajo Nation law, we see numerous discrepancies between these histories and what exists in the Navajo Tribal Code. Significantly, the creation of such clans from the Creation Scriptures and Journey Narratives up through the early twentieth century directly contradicts the language of a resolution passed in 1934 by the newly formed Navajo Tribal Council explicitly stating that non-Diné persons could not be adopted into the Navajo Nation.[32] More formally codified into law in 2005 as 1 N.N.C. § 702, the law states that "no Navajo law or custom has ever existed or exists now, by which anyone can ever become a Navajo, either by adoption, or otherwise, except by birth" (quoted in Austin 2007, 194). It then goes on to state that "all those individuals who claim to be a member of the Navajo Nation by adoption are declared to be in no possible way an adopted or honorary member of the Navajo People" (195). Interestingly, this law, adopted to prevent non-Indian claims of Navajo adoption, particularly from movie stars working on Navajo land at that time, was not concerned with the prevention of adopted clans per se

(Spruhan 2007, 2017). Regardless, this resolution seems to solidify and provide yet another endpoint to the cessation of new clan adoption begun by the creation of the census.

However, as legal scholar Raymond Austin (Diné) crucially notes, "This law obviously ignores the heterogeneity of the Navajo people. Several Navajo clans trace their roots to members of surrounding Indian tribes (e.g., Pueblos, Zuni, Jemez, Hopi, Ute, and Apache and even Mexican) who were adopted by Navajos. *The statement that no Navajo custom has ever existed that permitted non-Navajos to be adopted into the Navajo Nation is patently false*" (2007, 194, italics added).

Contemporary Diné Kinship: "FUNNY Navajo MEMES"

Today, kinship and ideas of *k'é* continue to hold weight and significance in Diné social spaces, albeit differentially and often determined by age, place of residence, and to what extent one may be either Christian or urban identified, among various other criteria. However, one way in which clans continue to hold social power and to circulate among younger Dine'é is through humor shared on social media. Questions of kinship, blood quantum, and belonging surface through humorous Diné memes, where humor can be a powerful way to foreground sensitive thematics in ways that provoke conversation. Nowhere, perhaps, are these thematics of kinship addressed more directly than in the anonymous Diné humorists for the Facebook page "FUNNY Navajo MEMES."[33] Written using intentionally colloquial, everyday language and sometimes employing what is referred to as a "rez" accent to represent specific Diné speaker types and class affiliations, these memes represent a microcosm of contemporary Navajo political and cultural issues that are top of mind to Diné citizens. Delivered through the lens of humor through social media, memes not only allow multiple frames of interpretation and analysis but also, significantly, create space for dialogue and critical reflection around often raw and sensitive topics (see Jacobsen and Thompson, forthcoming). Indeed, because these memes can be controversial, the authors of "FUNNY Navajo MEMES" choose to remain anonymous in order to give themselves the artistic freedom to post memes about what they really feel without fear of repercussion ("FUNNY Navajo MEMES" 2017a).

In one meme, we see a dating scenario in which a man is asked for his clans by a potential partner to determine his dating eligibility (Figure 1). In the meme we are brought into the intellectual headspace of this man assessing whether he wants to date the person asking the question and then deciding whether he should give his "real clans," which presumably aren't related to the person asking and make him dating-eligible, or his "fake clans," selected

FIGURE 1. "'Real' Clans and 'Fake' Clans." Courtesy of "FUNNY Navajo MEMES," copyright 2017.

in order to ward off further interest. (The assumption is that his "fake clans" would be the same as those of the person asking the question, thus making these two people ineligible to date.) As he wipes his sweating brow, emphasis is placed on the anxiety created through having to make these decisions as part of early dating protocol and the parallels this might have with contemporary Diné citizens having to make similar assessments in the very early stages of dating another Diné individual. Thus, although the image shows the man selecting his "fake" clans, as the viewers we don't know the final outcome of this scenario, and thus the palpable sense of anxiety and prevarication is foregrounded.

In a second meme, we see a photo of George W. Bush with his "bluff" face on, and above the image we read: "When someone asks for your clans but you don't know it" (Figure 2). Here again the implication is that even for perhaps more urban-identified and younger Diné who may not "know" their clans or may not use clans to navigate their own senses of connection to other Diné people or for dating parameters, clans are part of one's cultural patrimony as a Diné person, and one should still "know" them, regardless. A more sinister interpretation offered to us by some of our students who read this meme is that the person asking the question—perhaps an older Navajo-language speaker—may know that the younger person doesn't know her or his clans but is asking the question anyway, thus using the question as a form of culture shaming. Therefore, the chagrined face of "W" stands in for a Diné individual's own potential sense of embarrassment or the sense of a need to "fake it" when this question—"What are your clans?" or "há'áát'íí ádóone'é nilį?"—about kinship and belonging inevitably arises or is posed to them by other Diné-identified individuals.

A third meme that powerfully and controversially drives home perceptions

When someone asks for your clans but you don't know it

FIGURE 2. "Knowing Your Clans." Courtesy of "FUNNY Navajo MEMES," copyright 2017.

between phenotype, blood quantum, enrollment, and the inchoate but powerful desire to belong to a human community, whether politically or symbolically, is exemplified in the following image, which reads: "How that 1/16th Navajo looks when they qualify for that C.I.B." (Figure 3). The image, referencing a well-known moment from the film *Charlie and the Chocolate Factory* (2005), shows the facial expression of the protagonist when he learns that he has been given the coveted and elusive "golden ticket" to enter the chocolate factory, his life's dream. This meme, open to multiple interpretations, shows a phenotypically Anglo protagonist ostensibly looking not at his golden ticket but at his CNIB, the piece of paper that grants him enrollment status in the Navajo Nation. Thus, the CNIB is made analogous to a sort of entry prize or secret membership, something that is perhaps based more on chance than on circumstances, akin to winning the lottery. One of the implications here, therefore, is that the less Navajo "blood" one has, the less phenotypically Navajo one appears to be, or that the "1/16th Navajo," by definition, looks less "Navajo" than a Navajo with a higher blood quantum. A second implication, however—and one that is seemingly framed very much from the perspective of someone who has "more" Navajo blood and who identifies as Diné—is that those who supposedly want "in" on this exclusive club—of citizenship and belonging to the Navajo Nation—are overjoyed when they finally feel like they belong, marked here by the possession of a singular piece of paper, the CNIB, expressed through the joyful countenance of the blonde-haired young protagonist.

How that 1/16 Navajo looks when they qualify for that C.I.B. . .

FIGURE 3. "How That 1/16 Navajo Looks When They Qualify for That C.I.B." Courtesy of "FUNNY Navajo MEMES," copyright 2017.

Alternately, and less charitably, the joyful expression could be interpreted as that of a noncitizen, a "1/16th Navajo" who is delighted because he has "fooled" the system by claiming to be one-quarter Navajo, the minimum blood quantum required for enrollment in the Navajo Nation. This meme is also a powerful commentary on the ways that ideas of blood and blood quantum have overtaken kinship in determining belonging and social citizenship, where having a primary Navajo clan is no longer necessarily the primary marker of what makes one Diné; instead, the primary marker is the possession of a CIB.

A final meme circulating as of December 2017 on social media and accessed through the Facebook page "Diné Rights and Politics" (2018) beautifully encapsulates the shifting landscapes of blood quantum, tribal identification, and aesthetics, in this case through hairstyle and how this signifies differing Native identities in the contemporary moment (Figure 4). It also emphasizes how early socialization into differing Native identities begins and how ideas of social difference play out between peers in institutional spaces such as schools. In this meme, a note is being passed by two young grade school girls in a classroom. The note receiver, who is presumably Navajo, at first looks excited to be receiving a clandestine note in the space of the classroom and wears a big smile on her face. In the second image, her facial expression has shifted to one of irritation and perhaps dismay as she reads the contents of the note: "Guuurl you're full Navajo why you got Hopi bangs."

Here, a traditional "Hopi" hairstyle, where bangs that are cut straight across the front of one's forehead are sometimes a prominent feature for more traditionally oriented Hopi citizens, is being juxtaposed against the blood quantum of the Navajo girl, referenced in the note as being "full Navajo." More specifically, bangs play a key role in Hopi ceremonial life, where a young woman participating in the Hopi Butterfly dance, for example, grows out her bangs (or has artificial ones affixed) in order to affix her ceremonial headdress, known as a *kopatsoki*, to them (Lomahaftewa 2018).[34] Thus, the note writer is conflating cultural identity with blood quantum, where having four Navajo grandparents, or being "full Navajo," indicates the note writer's belief that her classmate is more Navajo than someone with a lower blood quantum. The implication, therefore, is that someone with a "4/4" Navajo blood quantum should not be presenting themselves in any way that could ambiguously be coded as anything other than Navajo. This, despite the fact that the Hopi Nation is surrounded by the Navajo Nation and that the Hopi clan (Kiis'áanii), referenced earlier, is a prominent Navajo adopted clan. Thus, one way to interpret this meme is as a commentary on contemporary Diné boundary policing along the lines of tribal identity, adopted clans, and how these identifications are performed through dressing style, haircut, ceremonial practices, and blood quantum.

FIGURE 4. "Hopi Bangs." Courtesy of "Diné Rights and Politics," copyright 2017.

As Joanne Barker has noted about the all-too-common exchange in which a non-Native meeting an American Indian for perhaps the first time in a public space asks them immediately "how much Native" they are in order to assess their Indigenous authenticity, "Questions and remarks about blood and appearance are not merely breaches in decorum—a faux pas of social etiquette or arrogance. They are interpersonal instances of deeply entrenched social ideologies and identificatory practices of race within the United States" (2011, 3). Similarly, in these Diné-created memes, we gain insight into the central roles of kinship, blood quantum, social ideologies, and the politics of authenticity in contemporary Diné identity formation, as well as the role that phenotype, hair color, and even hairstyle play not only in dating practices but also in assessments of political and social belonging.

Kinship Today: New Clans?

Today, while possibilities for formal clan incorporation are more constrained, the practice of clan adoption continues in a variety of ways. On an informal, family-by-family basis, author and nurse practitioner Ursula Knoki-Wilson has adopted non-Navajos into her family (Schulz, Knoki, and Knoki-Wilson 1999), and many non-Native anthropologists working on the Navajo Nation tell of being "given" a clan, although typically this is a clan belonging to the bestower rather than a new clan created for that outside person (Marshall 2016b; Mitchell and Frisbie 2001). In other cases, Navajo speakers use kinship terms such as mother, daughter, son, and father (*shimá, shitsi'/shich'é'é, shiye'/shiyáázh,* and *shizhé'é*) to address non-Navajos to whom they are not technically related but feel close or connected to in some way as a way to establish kinship.

More formally, singer, activist, and former Miss Navajo Radmilla Cody has advocated for the renaming and active creation of a new clan for African American people. Cody, the first biracial Navajo / African American Miss Navajo, now uses a new term for her paternal clan, Naahiłii, which was given to her by a Diné medicine man and is now being used more broadly across the reservation (Lapahie 2001; Jacobsen-Bia 2014; Jacobsen 2017). As she notes on her website, "The term Naahiłii is a new term that was passed down to Radmilla from a Dine' practitioner when she inquired about a more positive, respectful, and empowering term to identify those whom she is born for, the African Americans. The following is a Dine' description of the term Naahiłii/Nahiłii: 'Na(a)'—Those who have come across. 'hił'—dark, calm, have overcome, persevered and we have come to like. 'ii'—oneness" (Cody 2017). Cody is now actively working to change language use on the reservation, encouraging Diné citizens to use the term Naahiłii rather than the more disparaging and racially charged term that also refers to African Americans, Naakai Łizhiinii.[35] By providing a new name that stems from a ceremonial context, Radmilla as a Diné woman is in effect arguing for a new adopted clan—and a new form of relationality through descent, or *k'éí*—for African American people on the Navajo Nation.

We find legacies of mixture between Diné and non-Diné peoples not only on the Navajo Nation but also away from Navajo land. Today, in present-day New Mexico, there is growing acknowledgment and awareness of communities known as *genízaros*: Native and Navajo war captives assimilated as slaves into New Mexico Hispanic communities between the 1740s and 1790s (Avery 2008; Chavez 1979; LaMadrid and Gonzales 2017; Gonzales 2014; Silverman 2011; Burnett 2016).[36] As this recent scholarship reveals, cultural mixture and incorporation in the Southwest and among Diné communities are indeed defining aspects of Diné and southwestern experience, but these relationships are defined differently within various southwestern Indigenous communities. In fact, the practice of slave taking was so prevalent that by the late 1700s, one-third of the population of New Mexico were *genízaros* (Burnett 2016). As folklorist Enrique LaMadrid notes about the commonality of slave taking and the trafficking of Indigenous children in Spanish households, "In the 1770s, if you were going to get married, one of the best wedding presents you could get is a little Indian kid who becomes part of your household. They took on your own last name, and they became part of the family" (LaMadrid in Burnett 2016). As Moisés Gonzales notes, one thing the new *genízaro* scholarship does is "smash the conventional notion that New Mexican identity is somehow defined as either the noble Spaniard or the proud Pueblo Indian" (Gonzales in Burnett 2016); Diné histories of mixture are part and parcel of that same history.

Conclusion

Today what is perhaps most remarkable about Diné practices of adoption is how unremarkable it was, until at least the late 1800s, for Navajos to incorporate groups from elsewhere into the central fabric of Diné society. If kinship is "a set of concepts, beliefs, and attitudes about solidarity which are embodied in symbols," then these symbols are indeed still palpable and real today, embodied through memes, new clan names, and continued contemporary practices of adoption (Witherspoon 1975, 14). Navajos were an incorporative and inclusive polity, and this didn't make them less Diné, it made them more so. As historian William Lyon notes, "They (Diné people) recognized the contributions made by the Pueblos and Mexicans to Navajo life, realized that their relationships were often one of conflict, but they possessed societal mechanisms to incorporate these others into their own way of life" (2000, 147). Rather than Navajos being "cultural borrowers" (Bsumek 2004) who lacked a distinctly Diné cultural core, this openness and these extant categories for incorporation were (and are) uniquely Diné in their own right (Denetdale 2006). As our own Diné students from myriad clans,

Native nations, and ethnicities attest when they introduce themselves in Navajo, in English, and in Spanish in our classrooms, this history of mixture, albeit with a fundamentally Diné identity, continues today.

Adopted clans not only show us Diné historical inclusivity but also give us a unique window into the ruptures caused by US settler colonialism on Diné senses of self and how constructions of the "other" have changed relatively recently in Diné history (Iverson and Roessel 2002; Denetdale 2006; L. Lee 2012; T. Lee 2009). The institution both of a census and of BIA rolls created a freeze-frame of Diné society at a given moment in time that today, however inaccurate it may be, has in many ways become the litmus test for assessing Diné membership and belonging.

Diné poet Sherwin Bitsui (Tódich'íi'nii) makes this same point through another means, where primary identity is always through one's mother's clan and not through a more racialized identification with a people group known as "American Indian" or the biologized idea of blood quantum as the determinant for what makes one Native. For example, in a performance of the poem "Northern Sun" in Washington, DC, Bitsui described how he identified with his maternal clan over and above not only his name but also over identifying as American Indian or Diné. Leading by introducing your clans rather than your name also ensures that anywhere you go where there are other Navajos, you will always encounter a relative and thus be known: "The cab driver asks if I'm American Indian." Refusing the categorization and racialization implied in the very question posed, Bitsui responded: "And I said, 'No, I'm of the Bitterwater People'" (Bitsui 2003).

KRISTINA JACOBSEN is a cultural anthropologist, ethnographer, and songwriter who teaches classes on country music, Diné expressive culture, and the anthropology of music and language at the University of New Mexico. Her primary Navajo language teacher is the late Shirley Ann Bowman.

Originally from Tohatchi, New Mexico, the late **SHIRLEY ANN BOWMAN** is of the Tsénahabiłnii (Sleep Rock People), Bit'ahnii (Within His Cover), Áshįįhí (Salt), and Tódich'íi'nii (Bitterwater) clans. She was an esteemed teacher of Navajo language and culture in Navajo Nation's eastern agency, mentoring students at Diné college, Crownpoint, and in the public school system in Crownpoint for much of her rich and diverse teaching career.

Notes

The authors wish to thank Paul Zolbrod, Bidtah Becker, Paul Spruhan, Lloyd Lee, and Kerry Thompson for their feedback on this article and stimulating conversations on this topic over the years. We also wish to thank the anonymous authors of "FUNNY Navajo MEMES" for their permission to reprint their memes here and graduate assistant Renata Yazzie for bringing our attention to these memes.

This article engages with the Fourth Part of the Diné Journey Narrative, the Gathering of the Clans, stories typically told orally during the winter months. If it is outside the winter season, you may want to wait to read this article until the appropriate time of year.

Fieldwork for this project was permitted through a Class C Ethnographic Permit issued by the Navajo Nation Historic Preservation Department (Jacobsen) under the guidance of Ron Maldonado and Ora Marek-Martinez. This research was also supported through a Wenner-Gren dissertation fieldwork grant (Jacobsen).

1. James June and Ernest Tsosie III. See https://search.yahoo.com/yhs /search?p=james+and+ernie+youtube&ei=UTF-8&hspart=mozilla&hsimp=yhs -002, accessed November 27, 2015.

2. Traditionally, marrying someone who shares a first or second clan is considered a form of incest, so establishing that you aren't related often occurs fairly early on in dating situations. This clan name is pronounced "Kee-uh-aw-nee," Towering House clan, one of the four original clans. This comment implies that Towering House should be the man's primary, or maternal, clan.

3. "Adopted" is the local terminology used to describe the ways in which individuals and groups outside of Diné society have been incorporated into Diné kinship structures and social worlds. To be clear, this article focuses on a set of practices completely separate from the twentieth-century practice of non-Natives claiming they have been "adopted" by a Native American tribe or being given a so-called Indian name (Deloria 1998; Green 1988; Strong 1998; Sturm 2011).

4. According to the 2010 US census there are 332,129 enrolled citizens of the Navajo Nation. Of this number, 173,667 (52.3 percent) are residents of the Navajo Nation, or 158,512 enrolled citizens who live *off* the Navajo Nation (this includes the three satellite reservations). The largest population of Navajo Nation residents is under the age of twenty (37.4 percent), and the smallest populations are age groups 60–69 (7.1 percent) and 70–85+ (6.5 percent). Given these data, the outlook for language retention is unclear (see footnote 35 in Jacobsen and Thompson forthcoming, taken from Navajo Division of Health and Navajo Epidemiology Center 2013).

5. In general, if you are related to someone by clan you might refer to them as *shik'éí,* or "my relative." There are different forms of address depending on precisely how you are related to someone else by clan and also determined by age and gender. (Keep in mind that some people are related through more than one clan.) For example, two persons who share a first clan (maternal parallel

cousins) and are of the same generation would refer to one another as brother or sister.

6. One needs to be enrolled in a federally or state-recognized tribal nation in order to be considered a citizen of that nation; criteria for membership are determined by tribes themselves and therefore vary widely.

7. Spanish period (1539–1821), Mexican period (1821–48), American military period (1846–68), American period (1868 to the present) (timeline taken from Thompson 2009). As Zolbrod notes, "The Athabascans of the Southwest, rather than being warlike, were more inclined to trade and carry on fairly heavy commerce with the sedentary Pueblos, who relied on them for hides to be used for blankets and clothing. The Apaches and Navajos seem to have cultivated their aggressive ways only as a reaction to Spanish oppression and atrocities" (1984, 413n14). Allotments were given only to male heads of household.

8. The number seventy is disputed. Some say there are as few as thirty-five active clans, while others say there are as many as ninety (Bowman 2016; Lapahie 2001; Lee 2016). For example, Witherspoon (1975, 119) lists sixty active clans; Matthews (1897) recorded fifty-one; the Franciscan Fathers (1910) recorded fifty-eight; Reichard (1928, 13) identified forty-nine; and Lapahie (2001) identifies ninety. Navajo clans are divided into nine major clan groupings, each with its own characteristics: (1) Kinyaa'áanii (Towering House clan), (2) Honágháahnii (One Who Walks Around clan), (3) Tódích'íi'nii (Bitterwater clan), (4) Hashtł'ishnii (Mud clan), (5) Tábąąhá (Water's Edge clan), (6) Táchii'nii (Red Running into Water clan), (7) Tsé Níjíkiní (Cliff Dwelling clan), (8) Tó'aheedlíinii (Water Flows Together clan), and (9) Tsi'naajinii (Black Streaked Wood People) (Lapahie 2001).

9. Towering House clan (one of the four original clans) originated in Crownpoint, New Mexico, and is named after a structure on the east side of town called Kin Ya'á.

10. For example, Bowman introduces her clans as Tsénahabiłnii nishłį́ (I am born to the Sleep Rock People), Bit'ahnii báshíshchíín (I am born for the Within His Cover clan), Áshįįhí dashicheii (my maternal grandfather is of the Salt clan), and Tódich'íi'nii dashinálí (my paternal grandfather is of the Bitterwater clan).

11. From a kinship and belonging perspective, having a Navajo mother (the primary clan one is born to) holds greater weight than having a Navajo father (the second clan one is born for). One is born *to* one's mother's clan and born *for* one's father's clan.

12. From one perspective, giving your name to someone gives them power over you and hence gives the potential for someone else to bring harm upon you. This is why, in her Navajo language introduction, Jacobsen was encouraged by Bowman to say, "Kristina Jacobsen dashijiní," or "they call me Kristina Jacobsen," rather than using the first-person verb for "I am called" and saying "Kristina Jacobsen yinishyé."

13. We have also seen this extend to kinship recognition—based on acknowledged, shared adopted clans—with other Pueblo and Apache groups.

14. Prior to the American occupation, Diné people had significant clout in

the Southwest vis-à-vis other Native nations. Since the Navajos are the second largest tribe in the United States, this continues to be the case today.

15. Following scholar Lloyd Lee (2012, 279), to foreground the complexity of these oral narratives and to emphasize their equivalence with written texts such as the Christian Bible, we also refer to these stories as Journey Narratives and Creation Scriptures. There are as many versions of the Journey Narratives as there are clans, and the variations between the stories are substantial (e.g., some clan groups believe there are five worlds, while others believe there are four). For our discussion of the Gathering of the Clans, we rely primarily on Zolbrod's published synthesis of these narratives gathered from practitioners in Northern and Eastern Agencies in his monumental work *Diné Bahane': The Navajo Creation Story* (1984).

16. Zolbrod's point is to emphasize the diversity of Diné culture and the ways that it presages the diversity of US society at large. However, it is also important to note that among Indigenous tribes in the United States, Diné people were certainly not the only ones to intermarry and adopt people from other tribal nations.

17. Lapahie (2001) notes, "As the years passed, most of the people of Dinétah started moving around from place to place, and other American Indian tribal bands were adopted into the Navajo tribe. When the Diné moved back from Hwéeldi (Ft. Sumner), New Mexico, in the 1860s, some newcomers joined them on their walk back home. These people had also been imprisoned and now formed their own clans, the Chíshí Dine'é (Chiricahua Apache Clan) and Naashgalí Dine'é (Mescalero Apache Clan)."

18. Although it is the specific word for "Hopi," Kiis'áanii is also an umbrella term used to refer to all Pueblo peoples in Navajo.

19. As Thompson and others have pointed out, "adoption" may be misleading as a term here, since many of these processes occurred gradually and not through a set, fixed, and demarcated event with a clear before and after (Thompson 2017).

20. This includes the Athabaskan (Dené) languages spoken by Hupa, Eel River, Mattole (Bear River), and Tolowa citizens.

21. The Indian Health Service (IHS), an agency within the Department of Health and Human Services, is responsible for providing federal health services to American Indians and Alaska Natives. The IHS provides comprehensive health care for approximately 2.2 million American Indians and Alaska Natives who belong to 573 federally recognized tribes in thirty-six states. It is also arguably the only form of large-scale socialized medicine offered in the United States (https://www.ihs.gov/aboutihs/).

22. Census numbers are not automatically assigned; rather, the parents of the child must affirmatively apply for enrollment with the Office of Vital Records and Identification to receive a census number (Spruhan 2017).

23. Enrolled members and descendants of enrolled members are eligible to receive services from Indian Health Services facilities located on the Navajo Nation (email communication with an IHS employee in Chinle, November 6, 2017).

24. Known as roll 272 and listed as "Navajo: (Moqui Pueblo, or Hopi, and Navajo Indians)."

25. For example, the National Archives online database states that "only persons who maintained a formal affiliation with a tribe under federal supervision are listed on these census rolls" (https://www.archives.gov/research /census/native-americans/1885-1940.html). The first Indian census was taken shortly before the passage of the Allotment or Dawes Act (1887–1934), a law legislating the privatization of Indian land and drastically reducing Native landholdings nationwide. Allotments were only given to male heads of household (Deloria and Lytle [1985] 1998; Iverson and Roessel 2002), and one had to be listed on an Indian census roll in order to be considered "competent" enough to be allotted land or given the ability to vote. Unlike in most other contexts, allotment was not used on the Navajo Nation to break up existing landholdings but to provide land rights to landless off-reservations Navajos who were seen as "squatting" on public land (Spruhan 2017). In theory, American Indians gained suffrage nationwide in 1924. In practice, in the Southwest and on the Navajo Nation, many citizens were first able to cast their vote after World War II, in 1948.

26. Nationalities are often substituted for clans when non-Navajos or those of "mixed" Navajo/non-Navajo descent are learning to introduce themselves in Navajo.

27. CNIBs for new enrollees refer specifically to the 1940 roll (Spruhan 2017).

28. These different processes of incorporation are often oral-formulaic and employ repetitive devices throughout the text to demonstrate continuity between one story and another.

29. Throughout the Journey Narrative, there are multiple references to "Apaches." In some cases, specific tribes are mentioned—Mescalero and Jicarilla in particular—but in many cases they are referred to as simply Apache.

30. No specification is made here as to which band of Paiutes these might have been.

31. The Franciscan Fathers also created the orthography still used for the Navajo language today.

32. The Navajo Tribal Council formed in 1923 for the purpose of signing oil and gas leases for off-reservation entities.

33. "Memes" are images and videos combined with pieces of often-humorous text that are copied (often with slight variations) and spread rapidly via social media by Internet users.

34. Our thanks to Renata Yazzie for pointing out the connection between hair and Hopi ceremonial practices.

35. Often shortened to "zhinii," this is a stigmatizing term in Navajo for African Americans, comparable to English use of the n-word.

36. "Taken from the Spanish term, 'janissary,' in the 18th and 19th centuries, Native American women and children captured in warfare were bought, converted to Catholicism, taught Spanish and held in servitude by New Mexican families. Ultimately, these nontribal, Hispanicized Indians assimilated into New Mexican society" (Burnett).

Works Cited

Austin, Raymond D. 2007. "Navajo Courts and Navajo Common Law." PhD diss., University of Arizona.

Avery, Doris S. 2008. "Into the Den of Evils: The Genízaros in Colonial New Mexico." Master's thesis, University of Montana.

Barker, Joanne. 2011. *Native Acts: Law, Recognition, and Cultural Authenticity.* Durham, NC: Duke University Press.

Begay, Yolynda. 2011. "Historic and Demographic Changes That Impact the Future of the Diné and Developing Community-Based Policy." PhD diss., University of New Mexico.

———. 2014. "Historic and Demographic Changes That Impact the Future of the Diné and the Development of Community-Based Policy." In *Diné Perspectives: Revitalizing and Reclaiming Navajo Thought*, edited by Lloyd L. Lee, 105–28. Tucson: University of Arizona Press.

Berard, Father, OFM. 1932. Review of *Social Life of the Navajo Indians* by Gladys A. Reichard. *American Anthropologist* 34: 711–17.

Bitsui, Sherwin. 2003. "Northern Sun." In *Shapeshift*, 52. Tucson: University of Arizona Press.

Bond, C., M. Brough, and L. Cox. 2014. "Blood in Our Hearts or Blood on Our Hands? The Viscosity, Vitality and Validity of Aboriginal 'Blood Talk.'" *International Journal of Critical Indigenous Studies* 7, no. 2: 2–14.

Bowman, Shirley Ann. 2009. Interview. Crownpoint, Navajo Nation. July 23.

———. 2009. Personal correspondence. September 15.

———. 2010. Personal correspondence. October 1.

———. 2011. Personal correspondence. December 15.

———. 2016. Personal correspondence. June 15.

Bsumek, Erika. 2004. "The Navajos as Borrowers: Stewart Culin and the Genesis of an Ethnographic Theory." *New Mexico Historical Review* 79, no. 3: 319–51.

Burnett, John. 2016. "Descendants of Native American Slaves in New Mexico Emerge from Obscurity." *All Things Considered.* Podcast audio, December 29. http://www.npr.org/2016/12/29/505271148/descendants-of-native-american-slaves-in-new-mexico-emerge-from-obscurity/.

Chavez, F. A. 1979. "Genízaros." In *Southwest*, edited by Alfonso Ortiz, 198–200. Vol. 9 of *Handbook of North American Indians*, edited by William A. Sturtevant. Washington, DC: Smithsonian Institution Press.

Cody, Radmilla. 2016. Personal correspondence. July 9.

———. 2017. http://radmillacody.net/biography.html. Accessed November 23.

Deloria, Philip J. 1998. *Playing Indian.* New Haven, CT: Yale University Press.

Deloria, V., and C. M. Lytle. (1985) 1998. *The Nations Within: The Past and Future of American Indian Sovereignty.* Austin: University of Texas Press.

Denetdale, Jennifer. 2006. "Chairmen, Presidents, and Princesses: The Navajo Nation, Gender, and the Politics of Tradition." *Wicazo Sa Review* 21, no. 1: 9–28.

———. 2008. "Carving Navajo National Boundaries: Patriotism, Tradition, and the Diné Marriage Act of 2005." *American Quarterly* 60, no. 2: 289–94.

"Diné Rights and Politics." 2018. https://www.facebook.com/DineRights nPolitics/. Accessed June 13.

Forbes, Jack D. 1960. *Apache, Navajo, and Spaniard.* Norman: University of Oklahoma Press.

Franciscan Fathers. 1910. *An Ethnologic Dictionary of the Navajo Language.* St. Michaels, AZ: St. Michael's Press.

"FUNNY Navajo MEMES." 2017a. Facebook Messenger, personal communication, November 14.

———. 2017b. Facebook. https://www.facebook.com/FUNNY-Navajo-MEMES -163300343833676/. Accessed June 13, 2018.

Gardner, Johanna. 2015. "Mythological Story Structure and Neurology: Re-imagining the Floating Gap." Seminar paper written for Native Mythologies of the Americas, taught by Paul Zolbrod. Pacifica University.

Gonzales, Moisés. 2014. "The Genízaro Land Grant Settlements of New Mexico." *Journal of the Southwest* 56, no. 4: 583–602.

Green, Rayna. 1988. "The Tribe Called Wannabee: Playing Indian in America and Europe." *Folklore* 99, no. 1: 30–55.

Hall, Kira, and Mary Bucholtz, eds. 2012. *Gender Articulated: Language and the Socially Constructed Self.* New York: Routledge.

Hall, Stuart. 2000. "New Ethnicities." In *Writing Black Britain 1948–1998: An Interdisciplinary Anthology,* edited by James Procter, 441–49. Manchester: Manchester University Press.

Indian Census Rolls, 1885–1940. National Archives. https://www.archives.gov /research/census/native-americans/1885-1940.html.

Iverson, Peter. 1994. *When Indians Became Cowboys.* Albuquerque: University of New Mexico Press.

Iverson, Peter, and Monty Roessel. 2002. *Diné: A History of the Navajos.* Albuquerque: University of New Mexico Press.

Ives, John W. 2003. "Alberta, Athapaskans, and Apachean Origins." In *Archaeology in Alberta: A View from the New Millennium,* edited by J. W. Brink and J. F. Dormaar. Medicine Hat: Archaeological Society of Alberta.

Jacobsen, Kristina. 2017. *The Sound of Navajo Country: Music, Language, and Diné Belonging.* Chapel Hill: University of North Carolina Press.

Jacobsen, Kristina, and Kerry Thompson. Forthcoming. "'The Right to Belong': Navajo Language, Translanguaging, and Diné Presidential Politics." *Journal of Sociolinguistics.*

Jacobsen-Bia, Kristina. 2014. "Radmilla's Voice: Music Genre, Blood Quantum, and Belonging on the Navajo Nation." *Cultural Anthropology* 29, no. 2: 385–410.

Kauanui, J. Kehaulani. 2008. *Hawaiian Blood: Colonialism and the Politics of Sovereignty and Indigeneity.* Durham, NC: Duke University Press.

LaMadrid, Enrique, and Moisés Gonzales. 2017. *Genízaro Nation.* Albuquerque: University of New Mexico Press.

Lapahie, Harrison. 2001. "Diné Dóone'é / Navajo Clans. http://www.lapahie .com/dine_clans.cfm. As of June 12, 2018, this website is no longer accessible.

Lee, Lloyd L. 2007. "The Future of Navajo Nationalism." *Wicazo Sa Review* 22, no. 1: 53-68.

———. 2012. "Gender, Navajo Leadership and 'Retrospective Falsification.'" *AlterNative: An International Journal of Indigenous Peoples* 8, no. 3: 277.

———, ed. 2014. *Diné Perspectives: Revitalizing and Reclaiming Navajo Thought.* Tucson: University of Arizona Press.

———. 2016. "Traditional Navajo Identity Markers in a 21st Century World." *American Journal of Indigenous Studies* 1: B1—B8.

Lee, Tiffany S. 2009. "Language, Identity, and Power: Navajo and Pueblo Young Adults' Perspectives and Experiences with Competing Language Ideologies." *Journal of Language, Identity, and Education* 8, no. 5: 307—20.

Littleben, Thomas. 2010. "Navajo Language 201." Diné College, Tsaile. Course materials.

Lomahaftewa, Gloria. 2018. "Hopi Butterfly Dance." In *Circle of Dance*, October 6, 2012—October 8, 2017. National Museum of the American Indian in New York. Curated by Cécile R. Ganteaume. http://nmai.si.edu/exhibitions/circleofdance/hopi.html.

Lyon, William H. 2000. "Americans and Other Aliens in the Navajo Historical Imagination in the Nineteenth Century." *American Indian Quarterly* 24, no. 1: 142—61.

Marshall, Kimberly. 2016a. Personal correspondence. December 15.

———. 2016b. *Upward, Not Sunwise: Resonant Rupture in Navajo Neo-Pentecostalism.* Lincoln: University of Nebraska Press.

Matthews, Washington. 1894. "Songs of Sequence of the Navajos." *Journal of American Folklore* 7, no. 26: 185—94.

———. 1897. *Navaho Legends.* Boston: Houghton Mifflin and Company.

McAllester, David P., and Charlotte J. Frisbie. 1992. *Navajo Songs: Recorded by Laura Boulton in 1933 and 1940.* Smithsonian Folkways.

McAllester, David P., and Douglas F. Mitchell. 1983. "Navajo Music." In *Southwest*, edited by Alfonso Ortiz, 605—23. Vol. 10 of *Handbook of North American Indians*, edited by William A. Sturtevant. Washington, DC: Smithsonian Institution Press.

Mitchell, Rose, and Charlotte Johnson Frisbie. 2001. *Tall Woman: The Life Story of Rose Mitchell, a Navajo Woman,* circa *1874—1977.* Albuquerque: University of New Mexico Press.

Navajo Division of Health and Navajo Epidemiology Center. 2013. *Navajo Population Profile: 2010 U.S. Census.* Window Rock: Navajo Nation Planning and Development.

Paquette, Peter. 1915. Census of the Navajo Reservation-with letter by Peter Paquette. Film no. 579,683. Microfilm Division, Harold B. Lee Library, Brigham Young University, Provo, UT.

Perdue, Theda. 2010. *Mixed Blood Indians: Racial Construction in the Early South.* Athens: University of Georgia Press.

Reichard, Gladys A. 1928. *Social Life of the Navajo Indians: With Some Attention to Minor Ceremonies.* New York: Columbia University Press.

Ruhlen, Merritt. 1998. "The Origin of the Na-Dene." *Proceedings of the National Academy of Sciences* 95, no. 23: 13994–96.

Schilling, Vincent. 2014. "Natives & the Military: 10 Facts You Might Not Know." *Indian Country Today*, January 9. https://indiancountrymedianetwork.com /news/veterans/natives-the-military-10-facts-you-might-not-know/.

Schulz, Amy, Faye Knoki, and Ursula Knoki-Wilson. 1999. "'How Would You Write about That?': Identity, Language, and Knowledge in the Narratives of Two Navajo Women." In *Women's Untold Stories: Breaking Silence, Talking Back, Voicing Complexity*, edited by M. Romero and A. J. Stewart, 174–91. New York: Psychology Press.

Silverman, Jason. 2011. "Indian Slavery: The Genízaros of New Mexico." *Native Peoples Magazine*, July–August: 50–53.

Spruhan, Paul. 2006. "Legal History of Blood Quantum in Federal Indian Law to 1935." *South Dakota Law Review* 51, no. 1: 1–31.

———. 2007. "The Origins, Current Status, and Future Prospects of Blood Quantum as the Definition of Membership in the Navajo Nation." *Tribal Law Journal* 8, no. 1: 1–17.

———. 2017. Personal correspondence. December 19.

———. 2018. "CDIB: The Role of the Certificate of Degree of Indian Blood in Defining Native American Legal Identity." *American Indian Law Journal* 6, no. 2: 169–96.

Strong, Pauline T. 1998. "Playing Indian in the 1990s: Pocahontas and the Indian in the Cupboard." In *Hollywood's Indian: The Portrayal of the Native American in Film*, edited by Peter Rollins and John E. O'Connor, 187–205. Lexington: University Press of Kentucky.

Strong, Pauline T., and Barrik Van Winkle. 1996. "Indian Blood: Reflections on the Reckoning and Refiguring of Native North American Identity." *Cultural Anthropology* 11, no. 4: 547-76.

Sturm, Circe. 2002. *Blood Politics: Race, Culture, and Identity in the Cherokee Nation of Oklahoma*. Berkeley: University of California Press.

———. 2011. *Becoming Indian: The Struggle over Cherokee Identity in the Twenty-First Century*. Santa Fe, NM: School of Advanced Research Press.

TallBear, Kimberly. 2003. "DNA, Blood, and Racializing the Tribe." *Wicazo Sa Review* 18, no. 1: 81–107.

———. 2013. *Native American DNA: Tribal Belonging and the False Promise of Genetic Science*. Minneapolis: University of Minnesota Press.

Thompson, Kerry. 2009. "Ałk'idą́ą́dą́ą' hooghanę́ę (They Used to Live Here): An Archeological Study of Late Nineteenth and Early Twentieth Century Navajo Hogan Households and Federal Indian Policy." PhD diss., University of Arizona.

———. 2016a. Personal correspondence. August 5.

———. 2016b. Personal correspondence. December 5.

———. 2017. Personal correspondence. November 16.

———. Forthcoming. "The Landscape of Navajo Identities." In *Engaged Archaeology in the Southwest/Northwest: Interdisciplinary Perspectives*, edited by

Kelley Hays-Gilpin, Sarah Herr, and Patrick Lyons. Boulder: University of Colorado Press.

Tom, Orlando. 1997. "Sense of Identity." *Navajo Times*, December 23.

Tribal Employee Blogspot. 2015. "Blood Quantum." http://tribalemployee.blog spot.com/search/label/language%20and%20culture.

Vansina, Jan. 1985. *Oral Tradition as History*. Madison: University of Wisconsin Press.

Villazor, Rose C. 2008. "Blood Quantum Land Laws and the Race versus Political Identity Dilemma." *California Law Review* 96, no. 3: 801–37.

Webster, Anthony. 2015. *Intimate Grammars: An Ethnography of Navajo Poetry*. Tucson: University of Arizona Press.

Whyte, Don. 2010. Personal correspondence. Chaco Culture National Historic Park. July 15.

Wilson, C. Roderick. 1970. "Navajos, Apaches, and Western Canada—Introduction." *Western Canadian Journal of Anthropology* 2: 176.

Witherspoon, Gary. 1975. *Navajo Kinship and Marriage*. Chicago: University of Chicago Press.

Young, Robert W., and William H. Morgan. 1987. *The Navajo Language: A Grammar and Colloquial Dictionary*. Albuquerque: University of New Mexico Press.

Zolbrod, Paul G. 1984. *Diné Bahane': The Navajo Creation Story*. Albuquerque: University of New Mexico Press.

———. 2016. Personal correspondence. December 19.

THOMAS BIOLSI

Racism, Popular Culture,
and the Everyday Rosebud Reservation

HOW DO WE MAKE SCHOLARLY (and political) sense of the *everyday* lives of people living in Native communities? By "everyday" I do not mean the episodic moments (and movements) of critical consciousness or resistance (e.g., protest against the Dakota Access Pipeline) or of heightened awareness of racial or colonial oppression (e.g., the Idle No More Movement).[1] Instead, I mean the mundane, habituated, and taken-for-granted daily routines that compose most of Native experience. This is not at all to say that the everyday is not power laden or that the personal is not political for Native people. Far from it; there is no question that this everyday world is "structured" by settler colonialism and capitalism in determinate ways, including what we might aptly call "everyday racism."[2] But that does not exhaust the everyday world of Native people. Both individuals and the everyday worlds they actively take part in making have what Chris Andersen insightfully calls *density*— a complexity (and a politics) not reducible to a single subject position. Even if we recognize that the Native subject is complicated by "intersectionality," this does not approach the full complexity of Native density. Andersen quotes Robin Kelley on the density of Black being, which Kelley insists is "not just political struggle but the struggles of everyday life . . . : fighting, dancing, begging, cajoling, teaching, thinking, loving." Andersen forces us to recognize the "more serious and infinitely less schematic *livedness*" of Native life.[3] Indeed, Andersen's argument is that theorizing the politics of colonialism and racism—which, given the nature of structural accounts, runs the risk of schematization—will be *deepened* by careful attention to the everyday. After all, most Native people do not *theorize* settler colonialism or racism or explicitly engage in anticolonial or antiracist action in their everyday lives. Nevertheless, they live both within and against oppression. How do they do it? By examining the everyday world of Native people—and taking the role of *embodiment* seriously, as Brendan Hokowhitu urges us to do—we can bring to light Native ways of being that have escaped scholarly attention.[4] In pursuit of the everyday on Rosebud Reservation, I begin with two South Dakota scenes.

Scene one. From 1910 to 1997 a mural titled *The Spirit of the West*, created by New York artist Edwin Blashfield, graced the governor's office in the

South Dakota Capitol in Pierre (Figure 1). State historian Doane Robinson described the mural at the time of installation: "South Dakota is represented as a beautiful woman, in the spotlight, with the figure of hope floating over her and pointing forward. Trappers and settlers are beating back and overcoming the Indians who are clinging to her garments, attempting to impede her progress. Outlawry, represented by a dark and hooded figure is scuttling away into the darkness. In the background the prairie schooners of the early settlers are to be seen making their way across the prairie."[5] After a long controversy beginning at least as early as the 1970s, in which the mural was severely criticized by Lakota people as racist because of its negative and exclusionary—even genocidal—depiction of Indians, it was walled over by Governor William Janklow (R) in 1997 after he had long resisted making any changes.[6] The mural clearly fell into line with a persistent settler-colonial imagination of Indian people as the antithesis of civilization, with no contribution to make to, or modern place in, South Dakota. In the present, white imaginings of incompetent tribal governments that cannot be trusted to dispense justice to non-Indians on the reservation or traveling through it, of lazy people (including "welfare queens") living on "government handouts," and of Indian children who are a menace to white children in public schools are alive and well.[7] In 2006 a group of Rosebud Sioux schoolchildren and their parents and guardians sued the off-reservation Winner School District in federal court for creating a "racially hostile educational environment." The plaintiffs claimed that "Caucasian students frequently call Native American students racially derogatory names, such as 'dirty Indian,' 'Black boy,' 'Indian bitch,' or 'prairie nigger,' and tell them to 'go back to the reservation.'" School administrators were alleged to "routinely accuse Native American students of engaging in gang-related activities when they walk, talk, or stand in a group of three or more, wear bandanas, or write 'Native Pride' or draw medicine wheels on their notebooks."[8]

I want to focus on the pervasive presence of a racist gaze—or the reasonable presumption of such a gaze—that Lakota people confront in habitual, anticipated, or imagined interactions with whites. I want to distinguish quotidian experience from "crisis" moments when Lakota people confront demonstrable instances of racism and respond with protest and resistance. The "level" I want to identify is the *taken-for-granted background experience* of the individual, not the more outrageous and egregious experiences of blatantly racist actions and representations. The latter are egregious and outrageous precisely because they reflect a deeper and more systemic racism. This deeper and more systemic racism is what Lakota people—adults and children—live within and against every day. It is even possible that this background experience of pervasive racism is preconscious, part of

FIGURE 1. *The Spirit of the West* by Edwin Blashfield. Source: State Archives, South Dakota Historical Society, Pierre.

the *habitus* (see more on this concept below) of Lakota people, and closely aligned to how we commonly think of microaggression harming people without necessarily being recognized. How, in fact, *do* Lakota people live with the taken-for-granted background experience of racism?

Scene two. Lenora Kills Enemy attended the prom in 1957 at the St. Francis Mission Boarding School (Jesuit) on Rosebud Reservation (Figure 2). From a 2010 interview with her at a nursing home operated by the Rosebud Sioux Tribe, I learned that her mother made her prom dress and bought the sweater ready-made. Ms. Kills Enemy recalled that when she was young she liked to listen to rock and roll—"Oh, I loved Buddy Holly"—and country-and-western music on the radio. She also recalled enjoying movies, including *Gone with the Wind, Titanic, Shane,* and *Bambi.* Liz Taylor and Rod Taylor were among her favorite movie stars. She made her *style* of performing popular culture a *project* and actively made her appearance at the prom and in other places on the reservation as a fashionable and music- and dance-loving young woman. In a personal story to which many Americans of her generation can relate, she went to the prom with the young man she would eventually marry. Ms. Kills Enemy's immersion in popular American culture is hardly unusual among Sičaŋġu Lakota (also known as Rosebud Sioux) people on Rosebud Reservation, since they have eagerly participated in it from very early on in reservation history.[9] This is clear from a series of remarkable photographs of Catholic Indian people and from interviews I conducted with thirty Lakota elders (aged sixty or older) in 2010 and 2015. Magazines, newspapers, movies, music and other radio programs, records, local bands, and "white" dances were all popular to varying degrees among people on Rosebud Reservation. So were "white" fashions, home-sewn fashionable (and sometimes not-so-fashionable but "country" style) clothes, and catalog shopping (even when only "window" shopping, as it were).

This article focuses on how the performance of popular culture allowed Lakota people to address the systemic racism of settler colonialism in everyday life. Their uptake of popular culture cannot be written off as mimicry or "assimilation" in the sense of somehow becoming "less Indigenous" but must be understood in more nuanced terms. It was the skilled and creative performance of popular culture that enunciated clearly, loudly, and indisputably in public space that Lakota people are fully contemporary or *coeval*, perfectly (even exceptionally) at home in modernity and inescapably belonging to the partly imagined, partly real consumer *public* of modern life that encompasses us all.[10] The openness of Lakota people to mass media and popular styles—a stunning example of their density—can be fully understood only by seeing it against the background of the racial harms they faced daily. I focus on their active engagement with two mediascapes that were most important in this project of Lakota self-fashioning: mail-order catalogs and radio.[11] I will show how the *race-neutral hailing* of both catalogs and radio offered Lakota people an avenue

FIGURE 2. Lenora Kills Enemy at the St. Francis High School prom, 1957. Photographer unknown. Source: St. Francis Mission, St. Francis, SD.

for full presence in modernity (or cultural citizenship or "belonging").[12] I also show that the particular cultural forms of fashion in music and clothing—based on heterosexual physical attractiveness—were particularly resonant for people who daily faced defamation as "backward" or even as insufficiently attentive to personal appearance and hygiene.

My argument is not about "weapons of the weak" or "everyday forms of resistance," understood *as conscious challenges to power or domination*.[13] What I examine here is something more subtle, perhaps best understood as "preconscious," that had to do with *expanding the density of the self* beyond ascribed racialized identities. Radio and catalogs offered new "territories of feeling," as Nigel Thrift describes the aesthetics of "glamour," territories not available—or necessary—previously for Lakota people. The new mediascapes enabled "the creation of worlds of virtual self-difference which allow[ed] 'extra-yous' to thrive," "extra-yous" that replace or *implicitly* "answer"—by creating alternatives—elements of the racist gaze directed at Native people.[14] I am suggesting that the colonized do use the "master's tools" in projects of forming the (Native) self, and they use those tools in ways that amount to what Brendan Hokowhitu describes as *subversion* (more on this below), even if it is not consciously recognized or explicitly theorized as such by people in a colonial situation.[15] It would thus be a mistake to consign either radio or mail-order catalogs simply to the "colonial" category.

Chris Andersen and Aileen Moreton-Robinson, in dealing with a different question, persuasively argue how much we ignore about Native subjectivity when we are too hasty to parse the supposed "endogenous" from the equally supposed "exogenous" in Native studies.[16] It would be a grave error to write off what will be described here as "assimilation" (an extremely dirty word in Native American studies), for that would be to ignore the daily life of real Lakota people or to consign it to the categories of "collaboration" or "false consciousness." It is clearly not the case that traditional Lakota ways of being and knowing were automatically or necessarily "replaced" by their uptake of American popular culture, any more than learning a second language means forgetting the first.[17] The question is how colloquial ways of being are actively practiced by real historical people in a settler colonial context saturated with racist oppression. It might be remembered that Native peoples have *never* not been cosmopolitan—a term in need of democratization if ever there was one.[18] Trade and intermarriage continually mixed cultures (material and ideational) and language. Among the earliest studies ethnographers conducted on recently established reservations in the early twentieth century were "diffusion" studies of the movement of ceremonies and dances across what we would distort by calling them "tribal boundaries."[19]

The difference that settler colonialism and late capitalism make is that the conditions under which Native peoples "borrow" culture have changed in critical ways—for better and for worse, no doubt. It is cultural "borrowing" in the colonial context that is the central focus of this article.

Racism and the Reservation Everyday

By the turn of the twentieth century, and in the wake of the Ghost Dance movement on western reservations and the Wounded Knee Massacre on Pine Ridge Reservation (just west of Rosebud) in 1890, a colonial system for (ostensibly) benevolently civilizing Indians was instituted—a system that penetrated deeply into, and complexly shaped, the everyday lives of Native people. It was based on the idea of the educability of Indians (it was surprisingly free of eugenic premises) and was modeled to some extent on practices of tutelage both in and out of reservation schools.[20] But, critically for present purposes, it was founded on the legal presumption of wardship, in turn grounded in the premise of the *incompetence* of Indian people—both as tribes and as individuals—to manage their own affairs. Only the secretary of the interior could determine when an Indian was "competent and capable of managing his or her affairs."[21] The administrative apparatus of the reservation was meant both to subject Indian people to (claimed) benevolent surveillance in their daily lives and to thereby judiciously discipline them into civilized habits of mind and action.[22]

While the Indian Reorganization Act of 1934 and the "Indian New Deal" were meant to repudiate the older policy of civilizing Indians by encouraging tribal self-determination and guaranteeing the protection of the rights of individual Indians (e.g., the constitutional freedom to practice Native religion, which had been formally banned), no scholar—not to mention any Native American who lived on a reservation in the twentieth century—doubts that Indian people continued to be subject to various forms of intrusive (and harmful) supervision—as individuals and as tribes—well after the 1930s. Winnie Burnette from Rosebud Reservation wrote to Congressman Karl Mundt (R-SD) in 1943, "I think it would be a good thing to turn us loose and let us live like the rest of the people in America." Among other things, she complained about the restrictions on the expenditure of money in individual Indian bank accounts (known as Individual Indian Money in BIA terminology) held in trust by the BIA: "They give us purchase orders and they think we don't know how to spend cash" because of the fear that Indians would use cash to buy alcohol. She pointed out that Indians could buy alcohol while serving in the military, but not when they returned home to the reservation. "Us Indians are sure under dictatorship and this is supposed to be a free county but we are not free."[23] Chief Steven Brave Bird wrote to Mundt,

> I think that we Indians should be made free. . . . Most of our young people have fair to good schooling and there are no reasons why we should be dictated to like we are child, by people who know less than we do. If we happen to get a little lease money [from renting allotted land to non-Indian ranchers], we have to beg for it and they tell us what to buy with it. I believe that my people will all be glad to have the Indian Bureau investigated and I think we would be better off if we did not have any Indian Bureau.[24]

We could usefully summarize the formula of the colonial gaze here by recognizing that because of their presumed backwardness, Indian people were deemed not to have agency, not to be agents in a legal, practical, or moral sense. As Beth Piatote describes it, the BIA agent (and ultimately the secretary of the interior) would hold agency for individual Indians in executing his formal role as trustee, while Indian people would be deemed not yet competent for agency.[25] We should also draw the lesson from these quotes that Lakota people were hardly resigned to bureaucratic supervision and in fact deeply resented it.

The colonial situation in which Lakota people lived entailed a stunningly penetrating hierarchal gaze. They were repeatedly *examined* in a Foucauldian disciplinary sense and often—usually—found wanting.[26] Figure 3 is an image of a survey conducted on Rosebud Reservation in 1906. The men were surveyed by the local day school teacher and the women by the local housekeeper, who was usually the teacher's wife. Reading the list of characteristics assessed and recorded on the right-hand side (beginning with "Age of patron"), men were encouraged to—and assessed in their success at—working steadily; going to church and becoming members; avoiding (traditional) dances; not drawing rations; marrying legally and having only one wife; taking an interest in their school and visiting it for entertainment, (modern) medicine, advice, etc.; owning and giving personal attention to livestock, harvesting hay, milking cows, fencing their land, and providing sufficient food and clothing for their families; and learning to read and write English. Also included were metrics more directly related to bodily appearance: the wearing of "citizen" clothes and keeping one's hair short.

It will come as no surprise that the colonial metrics for women differed from those for men (Figure 4). Each woman was assessed on her home—its type; number of rooms and windows; number of occupants; ventilation; and whether she had tables, chairs, and a cupboard. Women were encouraged to join a sewing club and own a sewing machine; to attend and become a member of a church; to be progressive; like men, to avoid Indian dancing; and to take an interest in their children's school and to seek medicine and

NAME OF PATRON.	Age of patron.	Wear citizen clothes?	SCHOOL ATTENDED.	No. of years at school.	Progressive?	Hair long or short?	No. days worked.	Patronize church?	Member of church?	Patronize dance?	Draws rations?	Married legally?	Takes interest in school?	No. of times visited school.
Atkinson, John	29	Yes	Genoa, Neb.	6	yes	S	300	yes	yes	yes	yes	yes	yes	0
Iron Bull	65	No	None	0	no	L	0	No	No	yes	yes	No	No	0
Hawk, Luke	38	No	None	0	yes	S	300	yes	yes	yes	yes	yes	yes	5
Jackson, Joseph	57	Yes	None	0	Yes	S	300	yes	yes	yes	yes	yes	yes	2
Kills Two, Samuel	38	Yes	None	0	yes	S	312	yes	yes	No	yes	yes	yes	10
Kills Alive, Thos.	44	Yes	None	0	yes	S	300	yes	yes	yes	yes	yes	yes	1
Moore, Henry	31	Yes	Lincoln Inst. Phila.	9	Yes	S	312	yes	yes	No	No	yes	yes	5
Pawnee, John	57	Yes	None	0	yes	S	300	yes	yes	yes	yes	yes	yes	3
Ronkideaux, Chas. E.	35	Yes	Genoa, Neb	3	yes	S	300	yes	yes	No	yes	yes	yes	3
Whirlwind Soldier, George	34	Yes	Yankton, S.D.	2½	yes	S	30	yes	yes	No	yes	yes	yes	40
White Boy, Henry	36	yes	Genoa, Neb.	½	No	S	250	yes	yes	No	yes	No	No	1

FIGURE 3. Survey of men, 1907. Source: National Archives and Records Administration, Kansas City, MO.

NAME OF PATRON.	Age of patron.	SCHOOL ATTENDED.	No. of years at school.	Wear citizen clothes?	CLEANLINESS (good, poor, or bad).				HOME.					No. times visited school.	No. times visited school for medicine, advice, etc.
					Of home.	Of beds.	Of children.	Of women.	No. rooms.	Kind (log, etc.).	No. windows.	Ventilation (good, poor, or bad).	No. occupants.		
Mrs Annie Bordeaux	29		0	yes	Poor	poor	poor	Poor	1	log	2	gud	6		
Mrs Mary Bordeaux	31		2	yes	Poor	Poor	poor	Poor	1	log	4	gud	7		
Mrs Poor Man	51		0	No	Poor	por	gud	Poor	1	log	2	por	6		
Mrs Nellie Red Shirt	38		0	yes	gud	gud	gud	gud	2	log	4	par	6		
Mrs Rattling Leaf	40		0	yes	par	por	gud	por	1	tent		par	4		
Mrs Side Hill	51		0	No	par	par	gud	par	1	log		par	3		
Miss Syrie W. Buffalo	29		0	yes	por	par	gud	por	1	tent		par	2		
Mrs Hattie White Wing	26		0	yes	par	par	gud	par	1	tent		par	0		
Mrs Jack	39		0	No	por	por	gud	Poor	1	log	2	poor	3		
Mrs Lucy Standing Elk	40		0	yes	gud	gud	gud	gud	2	log	4	gud	5		
Mrs Thompson	39		0	yes	gud	gud	gud	gud	2	log	4	gud	7		

FIGURE 4. Survey of women, 1907. Source: National Archives and Records Administration, Kansas City, MO.

Soldier Day School, Rosebud Reservation, S.D., made by

No. of times visited school.	No. of times visited school for medicine, advice, etc.	Read and write?	Working knowledge of English?	NAME OF PHYSICIAN CALLED ON.	No. of cattle owned.	No. of horses owned.	No. of domestic fowls owned.	No. of cows milked.	Tons hay harvested.	Acres fenced.	Employed by a show?	Give personal attention to cattle?	No. school entertainments attended.	Distance from school. Miles	No. of wives.	Sufficient food?	Sufficient clothing?	No. of visits made to each home.
0	8	yes	yes	Agency Physician	36	18	0	3	20	0	no	yes		1/4	1	yes	yes	5
0	5	no	no	None	0	4	0	0	0	0	no	no		1/4	1	no	yes	10
5	25	yes	yes	Agency Physician	21	4	0	0	11	0	no	yes		1/4	1	yes	yes	4
2	10	no	yes	Agency Physician	20	15	12	2	50	18	no	yes		1/4	1	yes	yes	10
10	40	yes	no	Agency Physician	10	5	0	0	10	0	no	no		1/4	1	no	yes	15
1	20	no	no	Agency Physician	20	7	0	0	8	0	no	yes		1	1	yes	yes	3
5	25	yes	yes	Agency Physician	17	3	0	2	11	0	no	yes		1/4	1	yes	yes	10
3	10	no	no	Agency Physician	46	5	0	0	12	0	no	yes		1/4	1	yes	yes	15
3	5	yes	yes	Agency Physician	15	60	0	1	11	1	no	yes		1/4	1	yes	yes	10
40	20	yes	yes	Agency Physician	20	4	0	0	12	160	no	yes		18	1	yes	yes	10
1	3	yes	yes	Agency Physician	3	0	0	0	0	0	no	no		1	1	yes	yes	2

Day School, Rosebud Reservation, , made by

No. times visited school for medicine, advice, etc.	Belong to sewing society?	NAME OF PHYSICIAN CALLED ON.	Children had vermin?	Took interest in school?	Progressive?	Member of any church?	Attend church?	Attend dance?	CHILDREN				FURNITURE					No. of visits made to each home.
									No. born.	No. living.	No. attending school.	No. excused.	No. beds.	Use tables.	Use chairs.	Have sewing machine?	Have cupboard, etc.?	
			yes	no	yes	yes	yes	no	6	4	1		2	yes	yes	yes	yes	1
			yes	no	yes	yes	yes	no	7	4	3		2	yes	yes	yes	yes	1
			yes	no	no	yes	yes	yes	9	5	3		8	yes	no	no	no	1
			yes	no	yes	yes	yes	no	5	4	2		3	yes	yes	yes	yes	1
			yes	no	no	yes	yes	yes	10	2	1		0	0	0	no	no	1
			yes	no	no	yes	yes	yes	5	1	1		2	0	0	no	no	1
			yes	no	no	yes	yes	yes	1	1	1		0	0	0	no	no	1
			yes	no	no	yes	yes	no	4	3	2		0	0	0	no	no	1
			yes	no	no	yes	yes	yes	12	6	1		2	0	0	no	no	1
			no	no	yes	yes	yes	no	5	3	2		2	yes	yes	yes	yes	1
			yes	no	yes	yes	yes	no	6	5	2		3	yes	yes	yes	yes	1

advice there. They were also assessed on the cleanliness of their home, beds, children, and themselves and were charged with responsibility for keeping their children vermin-free.

It was not only the BIA that was hard at work uplifting, surveilling, and disciplining Indians. Missionaries made great inroads among the Lakota people, many of whom quickly became devout Christians (especially Catholics and Episcopalians) while not at all necessarily giving up on traditional Lakota religion.[27] Mission personnel were no less colonial agents than were BIA personnel, and there was plenty of talk among missionaries about the problem of Indian *paganism*. The Bureau of Catholic Indian Missions sought evidence from the field in 1934 of "defections to paganism" that could be attributed to John Collier's "Indian New Deal" policies of religious freedom (particularly the protection of the religious use of peyote and of other traditional Native practices).[28] The BIA worried that Collier and BIA personnel were acting as "pagan missionaries."[29]

Beyond the disciplinary-institutional context of the reservation, which imposed the default status of *incompetence* or *primitivity*, Lakota people also faced a racialized gaze in the face-to-face interactions of commercial dealings with ranchers (over land leases) and small business owners, in interactions with teachers in public schools attended by Indians, and literally "on the street" and in stores, cafés, and theaters in local towns both on and off the reservation. Indians became a numerical minority on the reservation as "surplus" lands were opened to non-Indian homesteading in the early twentieth century. Indian people went to town just like their white neighbors to shop and for entertainment, and some Indian children attended public schools with white children. Furthermore, many Indian people traveled off the reservation to "border towns" for shopping, work, and other purposes. What kind of reception did Lakota people receive in public and commercial spaces? There is no simple answer to this question. While there was never anything approaching the racist segregation of African Americans (e.g., Indian-white intermarriage was common, and *formally* there were no impediments to Indian participation in local publics and public [or private] institutions), a racist gaze is not difficult to locate in the everyday world of Lakota people.

In 1952, for example, the South Dakota State Commission of Indian Affairs distributed "A Message to Our Friends, the Dacotah People." "Recogniz[ing] the fact that Indian people encounter certain types of discrimination," the message assured them that "this discrimination is not against them as a race but because of certain conditions under which they live," "conditions which have had a tendency to cause discrimination." The commission recommended the following as a prescription for Indians to avoid racial discrimination: "obeying laws pertaining to marriage and divorce"; "honesty in all dealings, integrity in repaying loans, and meeting other financial obligations"; "develop the old saying 'The Lord helps those who help themselves'"; "cleanliness is next to Godliness"; "planning and hard work is necessary for righteous living." "Being a member of the Indian race does not in itself create discrimination," the commission optimistically explained; instead, "discrimination results from . . . [l]ack of personal cleanliness and neatness. Lack of assurance they are free from: . . . [h]ead and body lice . . . [t]uberculosis . . . [s]kin disease . . . [v]enereal disease . . . [t]rachoma. . . . As soon as the Dacotah people conform to accepted standards of health, personal cleanliness and good work habits, there will be few problems of social acceptance."[30]

While the commission no doubt saw this "message" as a sincere invitation to assimilate and appear in public without any impediment from white racial bias, the message would have been received by Indian people as a concise outline of the racial stereotypes that attributed to them backwardness and deeply personal—bodily—undesirability in white South Dakota on the basis of their race.

Prominent in the racist imaginary projected onto Lakota people is what Hokowhitu calls *physicality*: the body is both a key racist sign of Native deficiency and the content of much of the deficiency. The Native is too physical, too bodily (*distance* from the merely bodily as a sign of civilization, of course, has a long history in Western thought).[31] Frantz Fanon's concept of "the racial epidermal" is apt here. In *Black Skins, White Masks,* he famously elucidated "the fact of blackness" by describing the existential situation of the *Black* self. Fanon rejected the supposedly universal case for the emergence of the self (in the sense of a phenomenological level common to all human beings and at a level at which race supposedly does not matter). The Black subject emerging into consciousness, Fanon insisted, is "called on for more" than the white, unraced subject.[32]

> I had to meet the white man's eyes. An unfamiliar weight burdened me. The real world challenged my claims. In the white world the man of color encounters difficulties in the development of his bodily schema. *Consciousness of the body is solely a negating activity.* I was responsible at the same time for my body, for my race, for my ancestors. I subjected myself to an objective examination, I discovered my blackness, my ethnic characteristics; and I was battered down by tom-toms, cannibalism, intellectual deficiency, fetishism, racial defects, slave-ships, and above all else, above all: "Sho' good eatin'."[33]

Fanon thus articulates the "racial epidermal schema" at the core of the colonial situation worldwide for Black people. Such racial visibility—how one appears in public—is clearly at work in South Dakota.[34] It is not difficult to understand how Indian people might feel called on for something more—to own up to and be battered down by the deep and enduring presumption of their savagery reflected in the Blashfield mural and South Dakota's message to "our friends, the Dakotah people."

Hailed Otherwise

But the reservation everyday includes not *only* colonial forms of surveillance and discipline or only racialized forms of slander or stigma. Broadly, the reservation everyday entails all the elements of experience that constitute the individual's *density*. We can think of the everyday metaphorically as the path (not only spatial but also social and cultural, material and imaginary) that an individual follows as she navigates daily life. The path involves tasks the individual hopes or is compelled to complete (cooking, eating, praying, interacting with others, going to work or school, entertaining oneself and others, caring for oneself and others) and larger projects of work on the self (learning how to pray with the pipe, being a good relative, learning to play a musical instrument, learning to dance or sing, learning to sew or bead, learning to have a personal style, learning how to read and write one or more languages, learning arithmetic, learning to drive and to operate other technologies). It helps to think of the individual's experience of the path as if she were encountering a landscape in her daily journey, but the landscape is experienced only through what she is "equipped" with—her physical body, of course, but also her language(s), forms of practical and reflective knowledge, and sense(s) of self in relation to others (we can, if we like, call this the individual's *habitus*, the taken-for-granted framework and equipment for living).[35] Clearly, all of this is complex and difficult to describe empirically (this difficulty in "totalizing" a person in language is precisely part of the density of the human being itself). This level of everyday experience is not easily or directly known—perhaps even by the subject herself—and it is even more difficult to put into words. While macrotheory has its place, the everyday and lived experience cannot be easily fitted into a priori theoretical slots. Indeed, the study of these phenomena directly requires our being open to possibilities of density not conforming to dominant theoretical grids in Native American studies or critical theory.

None of which suggests that it is necessary to avoid recognizing patterns or structures or, better, "formations" such as we have laid out regarding colonialism and racism in the previous section. Racism and colonialism are as real as any physical landscape a Lakota person encounters in her everyday path. What else looms large in the reservation everyday? Popular culture surely comes to mind to anyone who has spent much time on a reservation. Here we consider the ambient presence of both mail-order catalogs and radio in the everyday of Lakota people. As I mentioned above, we should consider mediascapes (akin to landscapes) in the reservation everyday, but in conformity with our openness to the unexpected densities of Lakota people, we should avoid reducing radio or catalogs to "colonialism," "capitalist penetration," or the haunting ghost of "assimilation" (as that term is commonly used in Native studies), at least as an initial method in making sense of the everyday.[36]

While most Lakota families could not afford newspaper and magazine subscriptions, they could afford another kind of periodical—the Sears Roebuck and Montgomery Ward catalogs, which were sent free by the companies. Of course, from the merchants' perspective, the catalogs were meant to be commercial "wish books" that generated the desire among recipients to order from the companies. While most Lakota people actually purchased little mail-order merchandise (see below), the catalogs did tutor Lakota people to recognize *fashion* itself as an inescapable part of living in the modern world, of which they had become very much a part in their own commonsense thinking and daily activity—at least by the 1930s. Lakota people arguably learned as much from catalogs (and movies and radio) as from the "civilization" programs and formal schooling for reasons we will examine. To open the catalog and peruse the illustrations was to glimpse not primarily an array of commodities to buy—at least not for most Lakota people—but a compelling visual representation (often in color) of "what people are wearing"—people who were both conscious of fashion and practical and economically minded (this was the market at which Sears and Montgomery Ward aimed their catalogs). The rhetoric—both textual and paratextual (including the illustrations)—of the catalogs and the way in which they were "read" had as much in common with the logic of news reporting as it did with advertising: the reported fact (in Mary Poovey's sense of a modern, produced, and mediated fact, which is not the same as a falsity) that "a well-dressed woman" or "young American" was wearing a particular style, or that a particular item is "the fastest selling _____ in America" or "the _____ that everybody wants" (the quotes are all from the Sears catalog) came across powerfully as credible and important *social knowledge* of real people and what they do (a public), as much as an obvious sales pitch.[37] Indeed, in an age before American consumer subjects—especially rural ones—had learned to read advertising claims with a skeptical eye, the catalogs were probably experienced more as compelling *news* than as commercial speech that needed to be taken with a grain of salt. And more than the kind of news to be read in a newspaper, the catalogs harnessed the visual; the text mattered, but mainly as brief captions to *images* that went beyond the merely symbolic level of intellection.

Radio, too, opened up new sensory attention to what was transpiring "beyond" the reservation, as well as beyond South Dakota, among Lakota listeners. Radio was as much a fixture in Lakota households as were catalogs, and my interviewees had a lot more to say about radio in their lives. Local radio (WNAX, Yankton, South Dakota, in the southeastern part of the state) became technically available to people in the eastern part of the reservation in 1925, although it was not until the 1930s that relatively inexpensive radio sets could be purchased that ran on either special dry cells or car batteries. (These "farm radios" were offered in the mail-order catalogs and were necessary for Lakota people, since electricity did not reach rural homes until the late 1960s.) While it is not possible to determine how many Lakota families had farm radios, only three of my thirty interviewees reported not having had radio as part of daily life from a young age. In addition to WNAX, my interviewees reported receiving WSL from Chicago and KMOA in Oklahoma City in the evenings during the 1940s and 1950s, as well as KWYR, which began broadcasting from Winner, South Dakota, in 1957.

The late Ollie Napesni—well known as a Lakota language teacher when I began fieldwork on Rosebud Reservation in 1985—wrote in her memoir of listening to the radio run on a car battery from as early as 1936: "During the day I listened to soap operas but just for short periods, to save [the battery] for the night, because in the evening we'd listen to 'Bob Wills and his Texas Playboys' coming from Oklahoma. And then also 'Men in White,' they were prisoners in Texas someplace but they had a good band. And we used to listen to 'Amos & Andy' in the evenings. So that was our entertainment."[38]

One of my interviewees told me, "That's what I grew up with, listening to the radio." Her mother listened to *Your Neighbor Lady*, a homemaking program on WNAX, from which she gleaned recipes and sewing projects. She also recalled the children listening in the afternoons to *The Roy Rogers Show*, *Hopalong Cassidy*, and *The Lone Ranger*. These were followed by mysteries and in the evening by *Amos and Andy*. She recalled listening with her sisters, and in the evening her mother and father would play cards while the girls played with dolls, and everyone listened to the radio. She told me the girls went to bed listening to the radio. Another interviewee who was born in 1926 recalled that her parents "saved the juice for the news, and Saturday they had the barn dance" (the WNAX *Barn Dance*, which was modeled on *National Barn Dance* and featured country-and-western music), but her mother also listened to *Ma Perkins* (a daily fifteen-minute soap opera broadcast from 1933 to 1960) and *As the World Turns*. Bob Raymond (b.

1931) writes in his memoir that "listening to the top 10 songs on the 'Lucky Strike Hit Parade' on Saturday night was a major family activity" and that his family listened to radio news every day during World War II. He recalls specifically "sitting by the radio" the night after the attack on Pearl Harbor in 1941.[39] Bill Thunderhawk, born in 1937, remembers his sister listening to soap operas. Another interviewee who was born in 1938 also recalled the children in the household listening to *The Lone Ranger* and *The Squeaky Door* in the evening after chores were done.

While Lakota people enjoyed the full range of radio programs available, it was music that had center stage. Though a few of my interviewees either did not have a radio at home when they were young or did not pay attention to music, most of them recalled radio music with fond memories. The first radio music enjoyed by Lakota families on Rosebud was country and western. One of my music-loving interviewees explained: "That's all we listened to was country, and we knew all the country singers." As rock and roll appeared in the 1950s, many Lakota young people were quick on the uptake. One interviewee recalled his uncle listening to Elvis and other rock-and-roll performers at home on a battery-powered radio in the 1950s. Inez Scott recalled her brother giving her a transistor radio when she was a sophomore at St. Francis Boarding School. She became a fan (and she is still).

It is important to recognize that the reportage by print and radio (as well as film) of widespread national currents in fashion, music, and entertainment was a source of pleasure for Lakota people in and of itself in the same way that news can be. One inevitably thinks here of Benedict Anderson's evocative image of the "extraordinary mass ceremony" of reading the morning newspaper, in which "each communicant is well aware that the ceremony he performs is being replicated simultaneously by thousands (or millions) of others of whose existence he is confident, yet of whose identity he has not the slightest notion. . . . At the same time, the newspaper reader, observing exact replicas of his own paper being consumed by his subway, barbershop, or residential neighbors, is continually reassured that the imagined world is visibly rooted in everyday life." What results is a "remarkable confidence of community in anonymity."[40] We should not necessarily assume that Lakota people were, by this process, mobilized into a *US* nationalism. And while I think it is indubitable that at least some Lakota people from at least World War I took their American citizenship very seriously in precisely the terms Anderson describes, in a book published after *Imagined Communities* he recognized a very different kind of imagined community, beyond the bounds of the nation-state, a "quite new sense of 'world,' a horizontal universe of visible and invisible human beings." This world was "understood as one, so that no matter how many different social and political systems, languages, cultures, religions, and economies it contained," a category such as politics was understood as "a common activity . . . that was self—evidently going on everywhere."[41] I suggest that in addition to politics, fashion, style, and news quickly came to be understood as "self-evidently going on everywhere." The point to draw for present purposes is that imagined communities are flexible and may be national, subnational (such as "the countryside," which is in play here, as we will see), or indefinite (as in "modernity" or "the world," also at work in this case). The kind of belonging at work on Rosebud Reservation was in most cases not nationalist in Anderson's sense, except for such cases as news about World War II, but it was decidedly *indefinite* regarding formal boundaries or scale—it was just "the public," "people," "everybody," or "a well-dressed woman," "the modern world," or "the world," without explicit or implicit qualification. And yet these thoroughly *new* communities were *easy* for Lakota people to imagine because of radio and catalogs. These media had the sensory capacity to command attention—they *hailed* listeners and readers among Lakota on Rosebud Reservation, much as they hailed a larger public.[42]

While many Americans were attracted to such new mass-mediated affiliations, my argument is not that Lakota people modernized themselves just as their white neighbors or other Americans did.[43] The racialized colonial hailings of Lakota people as backward, inferior, or otherwise undesirable, described above, fundamentally differentiated their standpoint in the process of receiving mass media. The affirmatively welcoming and (potentially) race-neutral address of both catalogs and radio was experienced by Lakota people as a truly authentic invitation to a "free" people "who live like the rest of the people in America," to quote Winnie Burnette again. Indeed, we need to take seriously the likelihood that the captivating public address in catalogs and radio may have had at least as much to do with how Lakota people came to understand the concept of *equality* and even *citizenship* as did their civics lessons in BIA and mission schools, which must have rung hollow, indeed. As Michael Warner describes the logic of *public* address: "No matter what particularities of culture, race, gender, or class we bring to bear on public discourse, the moment of apprehending something as public is one in which we imagine—if imperfectly—indifference to those particularities, to ourselves. We adopt the attitude of the *public subject*."[44]

The Lakota public subjects—personified in the knowledge that they were indeed as welcome as anyone else to consume radio and mail-order catalogs, to buy, and to participate in popular culture (all "consumers" of radio and catalogs understood that commercial hailing is meant to be as wide, inclusive, and nondiscriminatory as possible)—are fundamentally distinct from the racialized subject described in the first section of this article. It is an "extra-you" to which racism and colonialism have no claim, indeed, by which they are eclipsed. In the case at hand, what is critical is the open invitation in the catalogs and on the radio to become a "public" subject—not a "special" subject, much less an abjected subject deserving of exclusion, pity, or uplift—through the rural mediascapes that knitted the reservation to something larger. While Warner warns that this utopian moment in publicity has a structural tendency to fail in the case of minority members of the public—the price they pay for becoming public subjects is that their *particularities* are erased (clearly a critical flaw in political publics)—we cannot ignore what this utopian opening may offer to people who are the objects of racialized colonial hailings in everyday life and who would find *studied inattention* to their all-too-salient particularities an exhilarating new "self" to inhabit and a continuous project to work on in "freedom." This hailing was not just palliative or a balm—or "resistance"—but an opportunity to participate equally and practice modernity in undeniable ways.

When I first began doing ethnographic fieldwork on Rosebud in the 1980s, I was intrigued with the popularity of TV soap operas and assumed that the Indian viewers saw the programs as (specifically) "about white people." It came as a surprise to me that Indian people enjoyed soap operas in *much the same ways* as non-Indians and that they do not see the characters and situations as racially or culturally "alien," which I had expected because of my presumption of their marginalized standpoint relative to white privilege and racial hierarchy. They are able see white (and other non-Indian) mass-mediated characters as *generalized* (or *public*) characters, part and parcel of the *same world* that Indian people inhabit on a level of everydayness; in colloquial terms, they *identify* with the characters in ways that can only fairly be called *unraced*, provided we realize that it may be their racialization that makes the appearance of unraced hailings enticing in particular to Lakota and other Native American people.

The lesson to draw for present purposes is that Lakota people looked, for example, at the illustrations of *specifically white models* in the mail-order catalogs and nevertheless imagined *fashion and mainstream convention, from which they were not excluded and in which they directly and concretely were invited to participate.* The Lakota reader was, or could be, "a well-dressed woman," part and parcel of "young America" or in tune with "everybody" (to quote Sears again). This, after all, is the abiding pragmatics of *commercial* speech. While one might reasonably doubt the credibility of high school civics lessons for Indian people in a settler-colonial society, the whole point of commercial speech in the era of Fordist mass production was that the message was meant (in profit-seeking earnest) for everyone, and the wider the audience the better. This pragmatics of commercial speech was understood by Lakota people early on in reservation history—the fact that commercial speech was *truly* aimed at "democratic" inclusion that did not discriminate (on the basis of race, anyway) and that approached the ideal of equality in ways that racialized people seldom experienced in everyday interactions with whites. The same is true about radio, particularly music broadcasts, but also the soap operas, variety, news, and other shows that were mentioned by my interviewees. Participation in commercially mediated publics held out the possibility for belonging that participation in civic publics (even voting, which Indian people did from 1924 onward) could not come close to for Indian people.

Enacting Modernity

How were mail-order catalogs and radio used by Lakota people? While some purchases were made from the catalogs—especially items such as shoes and outerwear that were difficult to make at home—most clothing worn on the reservation from the 1930s into the 1960s was not purchased ready-made but was made by Lakota women with reference to the styles in the catalogs. Both the Rosebud Boarding School (operated by the BIA) and the St. Francis Mission Boarding School (a Jesuit institution established in 1886) taught girls how to make clothes on treadle sewing machines, and of course they also learned from older women relatives. Several of my interviewees recalled that women made clothes for the family without patterns; instead, they referred to illustrations in the mail-order catalogs. One recalled that her sister had been "the seamstress" in the family home: "She used to make dresses that were like store-bought. . . . She didn't have patterns. She just looked at the book [as the catalog was commonly called nationwide] and if we said we like that dress, she'd look at it, cut it out, and sew it." Another interviewee also remembered as a child picking out an illustration of a desired item from the "wish book" and her mother making a newspaper pattern and constructing the garment from flour-sack cotton.[45]

Many of my interviewees insisted that fashion was not something with which everybody could afford to be concerned, even if they wanted to be. Many espoused a rural style—bib overalls, denim shirts, "Levi's and T-shirts"—that they attributed to their families' lack of disposable cash. This, too, of course, was inevitably a distinct fashion style, a rustic or "country" style, and one just as apparent in the pages of the catalogs as were the more "fashionable" styles. Most of these people probably wore more dressy clothes for special occasions (such as going to a dance, to church, or to a Catholic or Episcopal convocation).

For others among my interviewees, a more fashionable personal style beyond jeans and T-shirts was avowedly important. The photographs in Figures 5–10 were taken by Jesuit priests over the course of three decades. They depict students at the boarding school, as well as Catholic parishioners. One can easily see the evolution of fashion in conformity with the larger history of style (especially for women), including the attention to hairstyle and accessories (shoes, jewelry) and even pose (hand on hip, arms crossed). One interviewee told me that while she herself had never been picky about clothes as a teenager, her mother "was fashion-minded, so she always bought us clothes that were fashionable. She always looked at catalogs, and if she thought that's what we needed, she'd buy it." In this case, it was a parent contemplating what is best for an adolescent daughter that motivated fashion consciousness. Inez Scott recalled in an interview:

> I wanted to be like Twiggy. She was so nice and skinny, and I wanted to be like her, . . . and I was like her. I didn't eat much, and me and my friend . . . ordered our go-go boots out of the catalog. So we wore those long white boots. . . . We had to wear our dresses below our knees [at the St. Francis Boarding School], but when we had socials [dances] they let us wear whatever we wanted, so we could go to socials with miniskirts. . . . I was into . . . fixing my own hair. I always liked short haircuts.

Clearly, all this is far beyond mere "consumption" understood as a passive process. Lakota people were actively and skillfully performing personal style.[46] Radio was also far from simply consumed; instead, it was actively received as an incitement to song and dance. Local "white dances" (attended mostly by Indian people but nevertheless mixed) were as popular as radio music on Rosebud. We touched on Ollie Napesni's enjoyment of dances above. In 1942 and 1943 she and some friends organized square dances to raise funds for the Mother's Victory Club in St. Francis.[47] Sam High Crane recalls square dances in the traditional community (with a high concentration of Lakota speakers) of Spring Creek from as early as 1951 or 1952. But it was not just rural folk dancing that was popular, and one of my interviewees recalls that "everybody did the Jitterbug in those days" (1940s). From my interviews, I could detect no difference between people from traditional communities and those from nontraditional families in terms of interest in popular culture. While not everyone was equally interested, the interest does not appear to have been correlated one way or the other with Lakota "culture" or language, and being modern did not lead one to become more or less "traditional." The process seems to have been one of biculturation, not acculturation or assimilation.

Along with the race-free hailing of catalogs and radio, it is important to recognize how actively performing modernity would have been particularly attractive to Lakota people. As we have seen, the racial epidermal schema

FIGURE 5. Two sisters, date unknown. Photographer probably Eugene Buechel, SJ. Source: St. Francis Mission, St. Francis, SD.

FIGURE 6. 1932. Photographer probably Eugene Buechel, SJ. Source: St. Francis Mission, St. Francis, SD.

FIGURE 7. At a mass given at a Lakota home, 1933. Photograph by Eugene Buechel, SJ. Source: St. Francis Mission, St. Francis, SD.

FIGURE 8. Fourth of July celebration, Spring Creek, 1942. Photo by Eugene Buechel, SJ. Source: St. Francis Mission, St. Francis, SD.

FIGURE 9. St. Francis prom, 1957. Photographer unknown. Source: St. Francis Mission, St. Francis, SD.

FIGURE 10. St. Francis prom, 1957. Photographer unknown. Source: St. Francis Mission, St. Francis, SD.

of settler colonialism has long entailed imaginaries of the personal unattractiveness of Indian people—their personal backwardness, dependence, and lack of a moral compass, certainly, but, more specifically, their "looks": their "lack of personal cleanliness," as the South Dakota Commission on Indian Affairs put it in 1952. It should come as no surprise that young people subjected to this racist gaze would be attracted to performing their (modern, public, even "universal") personal attractiveness in compelling, undeniable ways. The other characteristic of popular culture that would have made it particularly attractive to people considered "backward" or "tradition bound" was the temporality that Walter Benjamin called "the eternally up-to-date."[48] Zygmunt Bauman describes the tempo of "liquid modernity" as "*pointillist* . . . [or] *punctuated* time, . . . marked as much (if not more) by the profusion of *ruptures* and *discontinuities*, by intervals separating successive spots. . . . Pointillist time is broken up, or even pulverized, into a multitude of 'eternal instants'—events, incidents, accidents, adventures, episodes."[49] This aptly describes the temporal logic of fashion, music, and dance. We might want to add the *speed-up* of time through fashion and music. In terms of the experience of time in modernity, this amounts to an increasing differentiation between present and past, which we experience as things coming to our attention as clearly "cutting edge" or "current" or, conversely, as "out of date," "outmoded," or simply old. As Ulrich Lehman describes it, "fashion endows human beings with a much stronger feeling of the present than does any other social phenomenon."[50] This happened on Rosebud Reservation, even as Lakota traditions were reproduced.

Both the photographs and the interviews offer strong evidence of the self-conscious practices of at least some Lakota people to "stay up to date"—in fashion, music (and even "the news")—in the increasingly faster-moving world in which the reservation, like all places, is situated. My interviews also suggest that Lakota people, like all of us, have learned to recollect their lives in terms of the punctuations of which Bauman writes. One of my interviewees described to me a modernist moment if there ever was one, and one we can all relate to. Her parents had a wind-up phonograph at home with records from the 1920s through the 1940s. The children would play the records in the 1950s and 1960s and "laugh and laugh" at the "old" music. Such "ruptures" and "discontinuities" are not necessarily disorienting—as Bauman seems to presume—but are sources of pleasure (and reinforcement of the uniqueness of the present) in themselves. Ted Standing Cloud enjoyed the fact that "music changed with the times," that "almost every year . . . there'd be new songs."

But it was not *just* a matter of enjoying the present because of its novelty. Practicing accelerated, pointillist time must have been a particular source of pleasure or, better, affirmation and affiliation for people long subjected to a racial epidermal associated with their supposed backwardness: *being "up-to-date" on music, fashion, and news belied the stereotype of the backwardness and tradition boundedness of Indians.* Indeed, it was possible for Lakota people to *outpace* local non-Indians—BIA personnel, white farmers, ranchers, business owners, and missionaries—on the measures of fashion, music, and popular culture and news in general. Like all American teenagers by the mid-twentieth century in the United States, they no doubt saw institutional authorities as "squares" or "hayseeds"—the evidence of fashion and musical taste (or lack of it) must have been stunning. It is not difficult to recognize how Lakota performance of their modernity would belie white racial discourses about Indian backwardness in fundamental ways, making it difficult to accuse of backwardness people who wear the latest fashions, listen and dance to the latest music, and are up on the latest news, perhaps in ways that even put the relative "modernity" of the white spectator into doubt. I think this gives deeper meaning to Chief Steven Brave Bird's 1943 criticism of BIA staff as "people who know less than we do." Might he have been thinking of his educated and fashionable grandchildren? Again, however, my argument is not that this was an everyday form of resistance, and when I asked interviewees why music, for example, was so appealing, people did not raise the idea of besting white people or talking back to racism.

The Density of Lakota Being

My argument up to this point has been that engaging with and enacting popular culture have been responses to racism and colonialism by Lakota people in two ways. First, performing modernity has created new spaces of self-making that are separate from and inconsistent with the racialized selves Lakota people regularly encounter as they see themselves as seen by white people. Fanon described the awareness of the white gaze by Black people as a constitutive—and deeply undermining—part of the Black subject. The significance of popular culture for Lakota people is that it eclipses the content of the white racist gaze by disclosing to anyone with eyes and ears the contemporaneousness and even heterosexual attractiveness of Lakota people on a par with everyone else. Popular culture enables "extra-yous" that, in this case, stand dramatically apart from racialized self-images of backwardness and unattractiveness (the self as felt through the awareness of the white racist gaze). This does not eliminate white racism, of course, but it creates alternative spaces for knowing one's self. These are not "safe spaces," since performance in public is always risky (see below), especially in the realm of heterosexual attractiveness, but these spaces offer the possibility of active "selves" that are inescapably part of the subject as a whole. Even if Foucault disabused us of the idea of a "coherent subject," his work on "technologies of the self" encourages us to pay attention to how individuals make themselves or "work on" themselves in the everyday. It may be that different technologies of the self, or alternative spaces of self-activity, "speak" to each other. Does it not seem likely that the "modern" (now an outdated word, perhaps) or "fashionable" Lakota self *addresses* at some preconscious level the abjected (the backward, unattractive) self offered by racism?

Second, I would like to suggest that beyond what is happening to the sense of self of Lakota people themselves, the performance of popular culture may actually change the (racist) gaze of whites. This requires a brief theoretical detour that sets the stage for an existential insight into the Lakota everyday.

Sovereignty, resistance, refusal. These are clearly among the key words of Native American studies. No one doubts the depth of their critical purchase on our subject matter or the rich paradigmatic intellectual and political vision they have contributed to the field over the last four decades. These concepts cannot, however, offer much insight into the modes of everyday Lakota life (and, yes, everyday politics) examined here. I hasten to add that my point is not to critique the critical categories of Native studies—for we clearly cannot continue to do our work without them—but to suggest the value of additional critical "tools." If sovereignty amounts to a conceptual focus on the *autonomy* of and *boundaries* between nations, the concept cannot help us understand the mediascapes and publics described here, which dissolve boundaries. If resistance (including everyday resistance) is about conscious opposition to power, it does not seem to apply here where my consultants never discussed the politics of popular culture—and never brought up racism or white people—even when I prompted them to. For them, music and fashion are just facts of life. I would not have been surprised to hear them ask, "How else would you have expected us to dress?" or "Did you think we only listen to powwow music or Sundance songs?" If refusal is about saying no to the "slots" the larger (settler) society offers to Native people, the case here seems rather to run in the opposite direction.

What *can* shed light on popular culture on Rosebud Reservation is a focus grounded in what Hokowhitu calls "Indigenous existentialism." I would like to engage that focus by considering Hannah Arendt's theorization of *appearance*. Her interest is on how human beings "*make their appearance* like actors on a stage set for them."[51] For Arendt, appearance refers to the elementary—phenomenological or existential—condition of the *subject coming to be perceived by* others; the human condition is inherently public. Now, my reader might well ask, isn't the public appearance of the (racialized) subject precisely what Fanon was at pains to show in all its agony? Doesn't Arendt's "appearance" threaten to be just another racialized examination that Native people are at risk of failing? Why should her concept of "appearance" interest us? Arendt's concept might also seem suspiciously similar to "recognition," which has been so effectively critiqued from the standpoint of Indigenous people by, for example, Glen Sean Coulthard and Audra Simpson.[52] But Arendt did not understand public appearance as the emerging human subject simply being dependent upon those who gaze upon her performance, as if it was simply a matter of public ratification, nor was the master/slave dyad—or power generally—part of her theorization of public appearance (such power would have been a distortion for Arendt). Appearance is much more a two-way street than is recognition. Her vision of human appearance in public has much in common with Emmanuel Levinas's theory of the other and his analysis of the individual's ethical obligation and faith toward the other flowing out of the mutuality of language.[53] In Arendt's thinking, in other words, the "witness" to another's appearance is not free to ignore what is thus disclosed to her. In appearance, the individual—even a previously abjected individual—is enabled to take *action* in the world—action that potentially *changes* how others perceive her. This is clear in Arendt's related concept of natality, which emphasizes the *fact of one's presence making a difference in the larger scheme of things*. Thus, the refugee *introduces a new presence, a new demand or necessity*, that cannot be denied by others without denying the humanity of the refugee. Though such denial may be common enough, it is ultimately self-defeating, since it is a motivated denial of a disclosed phenomenological presence. In other words, Arendt opens a horizon of optimism: as new "kinds" of subjects emerge into public(s), new demands are made on the other participants not only by the rhetoric of the new subjects but also and perhaps more forcefully by the simple fact of the new subjects' concrete (including their race) human existence. Natality is the phenomenological origin of the right to have rights in Arendt's famous argument.

Appearance thus has a meaning for Arendt closer to the idea of a legal appearance—*having standing*, or *compelling others to take account of oneself*. Natality emphasizes "the constant influx of newcomers who are born into the world as strangers," each "newcomer possess[ing] the capacity of beginning something anew, that is, of acting" and changing the status quo.[54] Even though Arendt cited the dramatic stage as a metaphor, we need to avoid understanding performance here in its colloquial sense, as in the performer (narrowly conceived as an actor, poet, musician, or comedian) consciously struggling to get the desired *reaction* out of her audience. "Acting" and performance in the sense intended by Arendt are much more of an incitement in the sense of creating the *unprecedented*, outside the audience's expectations, and actually *changing the audience's expectations.* Acting in this sense has to do with *disclosing something real*, in this case, the fact of Lakota being fully coeval people, even as they live in their cultural and racialized specificity. Lakota appearance in public, I am arguing, has the effect of changing—for the better—how at least some whites think about Lakota people at least some of the time.

We have seen how Lakota people have made their appearance in public, understood as active, unprecedented action (Indians being not just civilized but modern and in sync with the present). They have appeared to concrete others—BIA personnel, mission staff, local whites, farmers, and businesspeople—and we must not underestimate the potential of this performance of modernity to pose "difficulties" for the white taken-for-granted expectations about "Indians." The witnesses are forced to adapt to the newly disclosed phenomenon. In Hokowhitu's terms, there is a lot of *subversion* of racist imagery at work here, even if it is not exactly conscious or easy to express in words by most people. Can we imagine a young Lakota man or woman visiting the BIA office or a local store to conduct business, dressed in fashionable clothes, and might this have altered not only the nature of the interaction but also the settled expectations of the white interlocutor? Might it have put the white communicants off guard or undermined their confidence in their habitual way of "dealing with Indians"?

Appearance is not the same thing as "resistance," but it does entail initiative and action—erupting into Lakota (and white!) being, in this case, making a difference for both. "The space of appearance comes into being wherever men are together in the manner of speech and action." It is quintessentially transparent, in the sense that "everything that appears in public can be seen and heard by everybody." This transparency is critical for human beings because it is only "the presence of others who see what we see and hear what we hear [that] assures us of the reality of the world and ourselves."[55] Critically, this would apply as much to whites as to Native people in the realm of what we might call "Indian-white relations": in spaces of appearance that include both "races" (more common than might be imagined in reservation communities), whites cannot easily write off what appears transparently for everyone present. Arendt is primarily concerned with *political* publics—in which equals gather to discuss political issues of a public nature—and her paradigmatic case of a political institution built on the basis of this space of political appearance is the Greek *polis*. But Arendt makes it clear that "the space of appearance . . . predates and precedes all formal constitution of the public realm and the various forms of government."[56] In fact, the *polis* is an apt example for present purposes, since the whole point of the *polis* was that each individual can, and does, make a difference in that public, has the capacity to change the discussion, and can alter the public mood on a level playing field guaranteed by the transparency of the pubic setting. If this is also true of other publics—and Arendt seems to be saying that "prepolitical" publics are not qualitatively different—we should read the practice of modernity by Lakota people as weighty, as potentially making a difference in the reservation everyday.

Conclusion

In the end, we must admit that Lakota people's appearance in public is indeterminate in its outcome as far as racism is concerned, no matter how modern or cosmopolitan they are. There are no guarantees, and that is why public appearance is always a risk. This is because the racial epidermal has endured in the reservation everyday and beyond. Recall that Fanon insisted that "consciousness of the body is solely a negating activity" for people of color in racist society. This is one of the key premises of settler-colonial studies in understanding the situation of Native people. But this is only part of the story of Native appearance in public. The other part is the formidable inciting power of appearing itself, understood in an Arendtian sense, to intrude into the racial epidermal and to alter how a group of people appear (in the conventional sense) to others. Racism and white supremacy very much persist, and one of the sources of their durability is their ability to "adapt" to challenges to the racial epidermal status quo by updating the particular white racial imaginaries at work.[57] Thus, at a time when Lakota young people—wired up as they are through the internet and sundry devices—cannot reasonably be accused of not being up-to-date or "contemporary," even "sophisticated," it is noteworthy that a new white racial mythology of savagery about "gangs" (perhaps not that different from "tribes" in the white imagination) would emerge to name the school subculture of Indian students (as we saw in the case of the Winner School District). Nevertheless, the conceptual point to take from the material examined here is the inherently unstable and fundamentally contested nature of racism at the existential or phenomenological level. We risk losing sight of this if we only examine settler-colonial "structure" and only explicit, self-conscious political "resistance" on the part of the colonized. The everyday feelings and practices described here operate at a level that we might call "the politics of experience." By focusing on those feelings and practices, we gain insight into how the racialized live within and against white supremacy in ways that make a difference for them and for all of us.

We cannot end without an honest recognition of the "costs" of the Native performance examined here and of the need to answer questions I did not ask my consultants but that are necessary in pursuing our goal to make sense of the Native everyday. Two come readily to mind. First, the popular culture described here is saturated with heteronormativity. How and when did Lakota people become straight—and did they? Mark Rifkin might aptly ask.[58] And how did this affect *winkte* and possibly other gender identities in Lakota communities? Relatedly, how did the heteronormativity of popular culture affect gender relations between straight men and women? More than fifty years ago Marshall McLuhan urged us to ask how media enable "a world of people living in their own movies and listening to their own soundtracks," as described by Lewis Lapham.[59] Did Lakota people come to see their love lives and personal lives generally in terms of country music lyrics or of movies? And if so, what does that mean?

Finally, the activity described in this article clearly amounts to "body projects," or at least projects of work on the self that were never far from the body.[60] Again, given the physicality Hokowhitu locates at the center of the colonial situation of Indigenous peoples, this is perhaps only to be expected. But could we develop a more general theory of Native embodiment in colonialism? There is much remarkable work out there—on Native gender and sport, for example. What if we put that work together with another well-known Native American activity that we generally do not think of as a body project: military service? Could we learn something if we put military service in a category related to what I have described here? *Hasn't military service served as bodily performance of public belonging*—a body project with a vengeance (where the body is put at great *risk* in combat; one thinks of Lakota code talkers in particular, but the risk was generalized) and with deep and long-lasting consequences (both good and bad) for the individuals serving? Historically, it was mainly Native men who pursued this route (or were conscripted), and men from Rosebud Reservation volunteered as early as World War I for military service (in return they received US citizenship; women volunteered significantly from World War II on). The image in Figure 11 was shot on neighboring Pine Ridge Reservation circa 1940. Does it not offer a powerful lesson about Lakota women's and men's *different* body projects in earlier generations?[61] Are we looking at heterosexual allure and military service as two gendered avenues to self-respect that are part of the colonial situation?

FIGURE 11. A couple on Pine Ridge Reservation (Holy Rosary Mission) about 1940. Photographer unknown. Source: St. Francis Mission, St. Francis, SD.

THOMAS BIOLSI is a professor of ethnic studies at the University of California at Berkeley.

Notes

I am deeply indebted to the people of Rosebud Reservation who allowed me to interview them. For those who were comfortable with being named, I acknowledge their time and generosity: Catherine Clairmont, Audry Cordry, Sam High Crane, Ann Moran, Bob Raymond, Sherry Red Owl, Inez Scott, Earl Siers, Ted Standing Cloud, Bill Thunder Hawk, the late Lorraine Walking Bull, Tim White Bird, and Phyllis Yellow Eagle. I also thank the Tribal Health Board (which acted as the tribal Institutional Review Board) and the Rosebud Sioux Tribal Council for granting me permission to interview tribal members on the reservation. I thank the St. Francis Mission for permission to publish photographs from its collection. Special thanks to Marcia Poole, Mark Thiel, David Wing, and Ray Bucko for their help in identifying the photographers. I am also indebted to Tria Andrews, Shari Huhndorf, Miyako Inoue, David Nugent, Beth Piatote, and Lani Teeves for very helpful commentary and advice and for being so generous with their time. And thanks, as always, to my *huŋka* sister, Rose Cordier, for putting me up and putting up with me and for sage advice on my work.

1. See, for example, Glen Sean Coulthard, *Red Skins, White Masks: Rejecting the Colonial Politics of Recognition* (Minneapolis: University of Minnesota Press, 2014).

2. Philomena Essed, *Everyday Racism: Reports from Women of Two Cultures*, trans. Cynthia Jaffé (Alameda, CA: Hunter House, 1990), 31.

3. Quoted in Chris Andersen, "Critical Indigenous Studies: From Difference to Density," *Cultural Studies Review* 15, no. 2 (2009): 92.

4. Brendan Hokowhitu, "Indigenous Existentialism and the Body," *Cultural Studies Review* 15, no. 2 (2009): 101–18.

5. Doane Robinson, "Capital and Capitol History of South Dakota," *South Dakota Historical Collections* 5 (1910): 245.

6. For a history of the Blashfield mural, see South Dakota Bureau of Administration, "South Dakota State Capitol: The Decorated Capitol," https://boa.sd.gov/divisions/capitol/CapitolTour/blashfield.htm.

7. I do not mean to suggest that white imaginaries of Native people have not changed historically, but there is nonetheless a durable pattern of othering Native people in negative (and romanticized, "positive") terms. Both images construe Native people as uncivilized or nonmodern. See Robert F. Berkhofer, *The White Man's Indian: Images of the American Indian from Columbus to the Present* (New York: Knopf, 1978); see also my "Race Technologies," in *A Companion to the Anthropology of Politics*, ed. David Nugent and Joan Vincent (Malden, MA: Blackwell Publishing, 2004), 400–417.

8. Antoine v. Winner School District, United States District Court for the District of South Dakota, Central Division, Civ. 06-3007, Complaint, 2006.

9. I render Lakota words in the orthography officially adopted by the Rosebud Sioux Tribe in 2012, although any spelling errors are mine. See

"Sicangu Lakota Orthography," http://www.rst-education-department.com/sicangu-lakota-orthography/.

10. For "coeval," see Harry Harootunian, *Overcome by Modernity: History, Culture, and Community in Interwar Japan* (Princeton, NJ: Princeton University Press, 2000), xvi–xviii.

11. I borrow the term "mediascapes" from Arjun Appadurai, who defines a mediascape as both the stretching of message distribution across cultural and other boundaries (he has in mind global mediascapes) and "the images of the world created by these media" (*Modernity at Large: Cultural Dimensions of Globalization* [Minneapolis: University of Minnesota Press, 1996], 35).

12. Renato Rosaldo, "Cultural Citizenship, Inequality, and Multiculturalism," in *Latino Cultural Citizenship: Claiming Identity, Space, and Rights*, ed. William Flores and Rina Benmayor (Boston: Beacon Press, 1996), 97–123.

13. James Scott, *Weapons of the Weak: Everyday Forms of Peasant Resistance* (New Haven, CT: Yale University Press, 1985).

14. Nigel Thrift, "The Material Practices of Glamour," *Journal of Cultural Economy* 1, no. 1 (2008): 11, 13.

15. Hokowhitu, "Indigenous Existentialism," 113, 115.

16. Andersen, "Critical Indigenous Studies"; Aileen Moreton-Robinson, *The White Possessive: Property, Power, and Indigenous Sovereignty* (Minneapolis: University of Minnesota Press, 2015), xiv–xvi.

17. The classic source rejecting the "replacement" theory of "acculturation" is Malcolm McFee, "The 150% Man, a Product of Blackfoot Acculturation," *American Anthropologist* 70 (1968): 1096–1107.

18. While we certainly want to go about provincializing Europe (Dipesh Chakrabarty, *Provincializing Europe: Postcolonial Thought and Historical Difference* [Princeton, NJ: Princeton University Press, 2000]), we also need to see Indigenous peoples as much more in tune with translocal flows and travel— cosmopolitan—than the word "tribal" seems to suggest.

19. See, for example, Clark Wissler, "General Discussion of Shamanistic and Dancing Societies," *Anthropological Papers of the American Museum of Natural History* 11, pt. 12 (1912).

20. See Thomas Biolsi, *Power and Progress on the Prairie: Governing People on Rosebud Reservation* (Minneapolis: University of Minnesota Press, 2018), chap. 2.

21. See the Burke Act of 1906, in *Kappler's Indian Affairs: Laws and Treaties*, 3:182, https://dc.library.okstate.edu/digital/collection/kapplers/id/25235/rec/2.

22. See Thomas Biolsi, "The Birth of the Reservation: Making the Modern Individual among the Lakota," *American Ethnologist* 22, no. 1 (1995): 28–53. See also Frederick E. Hoxie, *A Final Promise: The Campaign to Assimilate the Indians, 1880–1920* (1984; Lincoln: University of Nebraska Press, 2001); Mark Rifkin, *When Did Indians Become Straight? Kinship, the History of Sexuality, and Native Sovereignty* (New York: Oxford University Press, 2011); Beth Piatote, *Domestic Subjects: Gender, Citizenship, and Law in Native American Literature* (New Haven, CT: Yale University Press, 2013).

23. Winnie Burnette to Congressman Karl Mundt, 22 April 1943, microfilm reel 104, Karl E. Mundt Archives, Karl E. Mundt Library, Dakota State University, Madison, SD.

24. Chief Steven Brave Bird to Congressman Karl Mundt, 5 April 1943, microfilm reel 104, Mundt Archives.

25. Beth Piatote, "The Indian/Agent Aporia," *American Quarterly* 37, no. 3 (2013): 45–92.

26. Michel Foucault, *Discipline and Punish: The Birth of the Prison*, trans. Alan Sheridan (1975; New York: Vintage Books, 1979), 184–94.

27. See Harvey Markowitz, *Converting the Rosebud: Catholic Mission and the Lakotas, 1886–1916* (Norman: University of Oklahoma Press, 2018).

28. See Thomas Biolsi, *Organizing the Lakota: The Political Economy of the New Deal on Pine Ridge and Rosebud Reservations* (Tucson: University of Arizona Press, 1992), 63–64.

29. Director to All Indian Missionaries, 27 June 1934, St. Francis Mission Records, General Correspondence, Special Collection, Raynor Memorial Libraries, Marquette University, Milwaukee, WI.

30. South Dakota State Commission on Indian Affairs, "A Message to Our Friends, the Dacotah People" (1952), Indian Affairs Commission Records, Archives, South Dakota State Historical Society, Pierre. By "Dacotah" the commission meant all of the Očeti Šakwiŋ, Seven Council Fires, or "Great Sioux Nation."

31. Hokowhitu, "Indigenous Existentialism," 108–11.

32. Frantz Fanon, *Black Skins, White Masks*, trans. Charles Lam Markmann (1952; New York: Grove Press, 1967), 111. See also Nigel Gibson, "Losing Sight of the Real: Recasting Merleau-Ponty in Fanon's Critique of Mannoni," in *Race and Racism in Continental Philosophy*, ed. Robert Bernasconi with Sybol Cook (Bloomington: Indiana University Press), 129–50.

33. Fanon, *Black Skins, White Masks*, 112, emphasis added.

34. I do *not* mean that South Dakota is a *particularly* racist place, indeed, no more so than where I live and work in the San Francisco Bay Area. Settler colonialism is a structurally collective and spatially continental formation, and settler-colonial racism is *not* best theorized as a matter of offenses attributable to specific perpetrators. See my *Deadliest Enemies: Law and Race Relations on and off Rosebud Reservation* (2001; Minneapolis: University of Minnesota Press, 2007).

35. Pierre Bourdieu, *Outline of a Theory of Practice*, trans. Richard Nice (1972; New York: Cambridge University Press, 1977), 78–87. I depart here from the formal definition of *habitus*, which focuses on the preconscious—that which is not learned or directly expressible in language. In my use, the *habitus* may include conscious elements.

36. In understanding a mediascape as the communicative and sensual topography encountered by the individual, I am departing from Appadurai's emphasis upon media stretching or flowing across institutionalized (national) borders.

37. Mary Poovey, *A History of the Modern Fact: Problems of Knowledge in the Science of Wealth and Society* (Chicago: University of Chicago Press, 1998).

38. Ollie Napesni, *Salt Camp,* recorded, transcribed, and edited by Dianna Torson (Victoria, BC: Trafford Publishing, 2003), 89.

39. Robert G. Raymond, *Scouting, Cavorting and Other World War II Memories* (privately published, 1994), 20, 49.

40. Benedict Anderson, *Imagined Communities: Reflections on the Origin and Spread of Nationalism*, rev. ed. (London: Verso, 1991), 35, 36.

41. Benedict Anderson, *The Spectre of Comparisons: Nationalism, Southeast Asia, and the World* (New York: Verso, 1998), 31, 32.

42. Louis Althusser brought hailing to the attention of critical theory by arguing that the subject seems to have no choice but to recognize himself being hailed and turning to face the police officer who shouts, "Hey, you there!" But it is important to recognize that Althusser saw the police officer's hailing—of a potentially guilty party—as but one "quite 'special' form" of an "everyday practice." In other words, we should be open to a wide range of situations in which subjects are interpellated by recognizing themselves through the process of being hailed. Louis Althusser, *Lenin and Philosophy and Other Essays*, trans. Ben Brewster (1971; New York: Monthly Review Press, 2001), 118; see also Judith Butler, *The Psychic Life of Power: Theories in Subjection* (Stanford, CA: Stanford University Press, 1997), 5.

43. See, for example, Lizbeth Cohen, *Making a New Deal: Industrial Workers in Chicago, 1919–1939* (1990; New York: Cambridge University Press, 2008), chap. 3.

44. Michael Warner, "The Mass Public and the Mass Subject," in *Habermas and the Public Sphere,* ed. Craig Calhoun (Cambridge, MA: MIT Press, 1992), 377, emphasis added.

45. Flour sacks were commonly manufactured in patterned cotton so that the material could be used at home to make clothing.

46. See John Fiske, *Understanding Popular Culture* (1990; New York: Routledge, 1998), 11–19.

47. Napesni, *Salt Camp*, 144, iii.

48. Walter Benjamin, *The Arcades Project*, trans. Howard Eland and Kevin McLaughlin (1972; Cambridge, MA: Harvard University Press, 1999), 543; see also Susan Buck-Morss, *The Dialectics of Seeing: Walter Benjamin and the Arcades Project* (Cambridge, MA: MIT Press, 1999); Ulrich Lehmann, *Tigersprung: Fashion in Modernity* (Cambridge, MA: MIT Press, 2000); Andrew Benjamin, *Style and Time: Essays on the Politics of Appearance* (Evanston, IL: Northwestern University Press, 2006).

49. Zygmunt Bauman, *Consuming Life* (Malden, MA: Polity Press, 2007), 32.

50. Lehman, *Tigersprung*, 180.

51. Hannah Arendt, *The Life of the Mind* (1971; New York: Harcourt, 1978), 21.

52. Coulthard, *Red Skins, White Masks*; Audra Simpson, *Mohawk Interruptus: Political Life across the Borders of Settler States* (Durham, NC: Duke University Press, 2014).

53. Emmanuel Levinas, *Totality and Infinity: An Essay on Exteriority*, trans. Alphonso Lingis (Pittsburgh, PA: Duquesne University Press, 1969); *Otherwise Than Being, or Beyond Essence*, trans. Alphonso Lingis (1981; Pittsburgh, PA: Duquesne University Press, 1998).

54. Hannah Arendt, *The Human Condition* (Chicago: University of Chicago Press, 1958), 8.

55. Ibid., 199, 50.

56. Ibid., 198, 199.

57. On how racial formations and in particular white supremacy adaptively persist, see Michael Omi and Howard Winant, *Racial Formation in the United States*, 3rd ed. (1986; New York: Routledge, 2015), chaps. 7–8.

58. Rifkin, *When Did Indians*.

59. Lewis H. Lapham, "Introduction to the MIT Press Edition," in *Understanding Media: The Extensions of Man*, by Marshall McLuhan (1964; Cambridge, MA: MIT Press, 1994), xix.

60. Joan Jacobs Brumberg, *The Body Project: An Intimate History of American Girls* (New York: Vintage Books, 1997).

61. Lakota women have also volunteered for military service since World War II. Until recent decades, however, they have not been in combat or high-risk roles.

CRISTINA STANCIU

Americanization on Native Terms: The Society of American Indians, Citizenship Debates, and Tropes of "Racial Difference"

"America"

IN OCTOBER 1911 local newspapers in Columbus, Ohio, reported on an unprecedented gathering of Native Americans. The Society of American Indians (SAI) met strategically in Columbus on Columbus Day, an irony the local newspapers failed to notice; but they did report on meetings with local and national dignitaries, as well as an evening of entertainment consisting of "Indian songs and dances and the portrayal of scenes from Indian life."[1] The SAI was also greeted by local chapters of patriotic organizations such as the Ohio Daughters of Pocahontas and the Improved Order of Red Men, which presented the attendees with small American flags as souvenirs. This effervescence of American patriotism reached its peak when the SAI members were reported singing the song "America" on top of a mound, followed by "an impromptu war dance on the same elevation."[2] As the SAI grew in the following years, it went on to stage its own Native pageants, a growing national attraction, as US nativism was also on the rise.[3] But why would a group of professional, articulate Native men and women, wearing citizens' clothing, intone "My Country, 'Tis of Thee," a song so antithetical to the scope of the SAI—"the revival of the natural pride of origin, the pride of the race"—as penned by its first president, Reverend Sherman Coolidge?[4]

For students of Native history, it is hard, although not impossible, to imagine a few Native men doing a war dance on top of a sacred mound during the SAI's first meeting in Columbus, Ohio. But the Native men and women gathered on the campus of Ohio State University in 1911 had different wars to wage with white America, and their decision to sing a patriotic song before dancing a traditional dance was perhaps indicative of their strategic use of public spaces and their performance on multiple local and national scenes. Contemporary Native critics like Osage literary critic Robert Warrior find this image troublesome, and rightly so; in a special issue dedicated to the SAI's one hundredth anniversary, Warrior argued that, "[a]propos their widely shared belief in the passing by the wayside of older forms of Indianness, we could caption this photo, ironically, 'The End of History.'" Granted that such concerns are warranted, especially when raised by contemporary Native intellectual historians working through the legacy of an older Native organization for contemporary Native communities, not all the Native people present at the first meeting of the SAI shared the belief in the passing of "older forms of Indianness." Oneida SAI founding member Laura Cornelius Kellogg claimed unambiguously, "I'm not the new Indian; I'm the old Indian adjusted to new conditions" in an attempt to bridge the Old with the New.[5]

If we think about this episode in the larger context of the early twentieth-century ideological pressures of the Americanization movement, we may also read the irony of this performance and strategic use of Americanness in less apocalyptic terms than Robert Warrior. Yes, the patriotic local societies welcomed the Native intellectual elite to Columbus by presenting them with American flags. However, if we consider the growing numbers of national patriotic societies and nationalist pageants in the first decades of the twentieth century, flag exercises, and other public displays of patriotism triggered by the so-called immigrant invasion and an exacerbated nativism, we could construe this episode as a necessary *simultaneous* reaffirmation of American nationalism and emergent Native nationalism in the SAI members' performance of both American and Native allegiances—a form of what historian Jeffrey Mirel calls "patriotic pluralism," which I interpret to mean competing nationalisms in a Native context: on the one hand, a deep commitment and allegiance to Native nations; on the other, a strategic commitment to the settler nation.[6]

As I show throughout this article, the Red Progressives used the immigrant analogy as a common strategy to argue for Indian citizenship: The immigrant can easily become a citizen; why not the Indian? The most politically active and savvy members of the SAI argued for political integration rather than an erasure of Native identities and sovereignty through a blind replication of the imagined model of immigrant Americanization. I say "imagined" for two reasons: first, because of the distance between the ideological tenets of Americanization, scripted in legal and cultural institutions (the school, the factory, and the newspaper), and the immigrants' willingness to Americanize; second, because of the little evidence we still have about the SAI's intimate familiarity with sociological data warranting this analogy, as we will see toward the end of the article. Not only were the Red Progressives more critical of Americanization than scholars have credited them, but by subverting and rewriting the mainstream discourses on "racial difference" as well as assimilation and acculturation they appropriated, they also *authored* Americanization on Native terms. I propose that two competing nationalisms, American and Indian—often overlapping—were at the heart of these spirited debates over American citizenship. This is a gap in SAI scholarship my study seeks to fill.

This article considers the cultural work and print culture of the Society of American Indians, the first pan-Indian national organization with an agenda for the political and intellectual future of Native communities nationally at the beginning of the twentieth century.[7] I read both the activist and print work of the SAI (zooming in on several of its key figures) to show how American Indian intellectuals negotiated rhetorical practices to educate readers about Native history, culture, and resilience against the pervasive trope of the "vanishing Indian," which had dominated nineteenth-century print and visual culture. In particular, the nuanced yet central debates over citizenship in the SAI's *Quarterly Journal of the Society of American Indians*, later titled the *American Indian Magazine*, show that despite the procedural disagreements and tension in the organization (Carlos Montezuma quit the SAI, Laura Cornelius Kellogg was ousted), a constant element on the SAI print agenda was the question of what American citizenship meant for Native people.

I argue that reading these debates over citizenship in the larger national pro-Americanization context raises further questions about both the SAI members' relative procitizenship stance and Native communities' more critical views of American citizenship. Perhaps the best-known case of Indigenous rejection of US citizenship at this time was that of the Haudenosaunee, or Six Nations Iroquois Confederacy, who offered a written dissent after the passing of the Indian Citizenship Act (ICA) in 1924. Their Grand Council sent letters to the US president and Congress *declining* US citizenship, rejecting dual citizenship, and emphasizing that the act was passed without their consent.[8] In his autobiography, Tuscarora chief Clinton Rickard described the Iroquois resistance to the ICA, which he called unambiguously a "violation" of Native sovereignty: "The Indian Citizenship Act did pass in 1924 despite our strong opposition. By its provisions, all Indians were automatically made United States citizens whether they wanted to be so or not. This was a violation of our sovereignty. *Our citizenship was in our own nations.* We had a great attachment to our style of government. We wished to remain treaty Indians and preserve our ancient rights."[9] Unlike many of the SAI members, Rickard saw the passage of the ICA in 1924 as another way of controlling Indigenous people. He expressed what many other Native people were also voicing when the SAI was advocating for citizenship as an end to wardship: the imposition of US citizenship was a threat to tribal status and to Indigenous sovereignty. These two views are not necessarily diametrically opposed, as K. Tsianina Lomawaima has rightly argued: American citizenship and Indigenous sovereignty were not mutually exclusive.[10] Citizenship would also allow Native people to argue their cases in US courts.[11]

Throughout this article I argue that a reexamination of the SAI publications as an archive mapping the SAI's rhetorical changes over the years affords a new opportunity to trace Indigenous arguments about "racial difference" and citizenship. In particular, this archive illuminates how Native writers and intellectuals used both the race rhetoric of the day and analogies to contemporary ethnic groups—especially the new wave of immigrants from southern and eastern Europe—as they argued for citizenship and the end of wardship for Native people in the United States. A closer examination of how the SAI journal indexed the rhetorical changes on the issue of citizenship among the SAI members over the years offers a powerful counterpoint to the Americanization campaigns led by white Progressive organizations and showcases both Indigenous assent and opposition to citizenship.

The SAI: "An Unfinished Experiment"

Initially called the American Indian Association, the SAI (1911–23) was the first pan-Indian national organization. Its platform expressed high hopes for the political and intellectual future of Native communities nationally.[12] Recent scholarship in American Indian and Indigenous studies has examined the SAI in the context of pan-Indianism, federal Indian policy, and American Indian intellectual history, from the groundbreaking work of Hazel Hertzberg, which remains a classic in the field, to more recent work by Robert Warrior, Lucy Maddox, K. Tsianina Lomawaima, David Martinez, Kiara Vigil, and Kevin Bruyneel.[13] Problematic as the SAI may appear in its optimism for progress and uplift, it differed from other Indian reform organizations in its responses to the paternalism of white reformers. Whereas Indian reform organizations like the Lake Mohonk Conference framed citizenship as a "gift," a culmination of the Americanization campaigns, the intellectuals of the SAI were interested in the effects of American citizenship on tribal citizenship and Native sovereignty. Native historian of education K. Tsianina Lomawaima, for instance, has shown how we can begin to understand citizenship and sovereignty as mutually constitutive rather than mutually exclusive categories: "From our twenty-first century perspective, the SAI's actions and imagination inspire possibilities of multiple, layered, mutually enriching citizenships, as well as multiple, layered partner sovereigns." Adding to Lomawaima's analysis, I propose that for some SAI intellectuals, citizenship was the answer to questions about Indian status, the promise of participatory democracy, a way out of federal paternalism, and the promise of a voice in determining Native future; for others, it was a strategic use of contemporary patriotic pluralist discourse to address and express indigeneity.[14] From its inception in 1911, the SAI gathered an exceptional Native membership from various professions and tribal backgrounds: Marie Bottineau Baldwin (Ojibwe), Sherman Coolidge (Arapaho), Charles Eastman / Ohiyesa (Sioux), Carlos Montezuma / Wassaja (Yavapai), Charles Daganett (Peoria), Thomas L. Sloan (Omaha), Laura "Minnie" Cornelius Kellogg (Oneida from Wisconsin), Arthur C. Parker (Seneca), Gertrude Bonnin / Zitkala-Ša (Yankton Sioux), Henry Standing Bear (Lakota Sioux), Henry Roe Cloud (Ho-Chunk), and others (Figure 1).[15]

The SAI's agenda, published and republished over the years in the SAI journal, aimed to promote Native "enlightenment"; to provide a forum for addressing the welfare of Indian people through conferences; "to present in a just light the true history of the race" and to preserve its records; to promote and fight for citizenship and the rights of citizen Indians; to establish a legal department to investigate Indian problems; "to exercise the right to oppose any movement that may be detrimental to the race"; and to "provide a bureau of information, including publicity and statistics."[16] The SAI, therefore, was concerned with producing and disseminating *accurate* information about Native tribes to both mainstream American readers and to Native readers, with an emphasis *on the true history of the race*, in opposition to the popular representations of *Indians* as either savage or vanishing. One main platform over which the SAI argued consistently was the issue of citizenship: American citizenship alongside tribal citizenship and the end of wardship, with an emphasis on Native rights. Less programmatically, the SAI wanted to show white America that Native values, epistemologies, and philosophies were as complex as those of people of European ancestry.[17]

FIGURE 1. "Some of the Indian Members" at the first conference of the SAI in Columbus, Ohio, 1911. Source: *Report of the Executive Council on the Proceedings of the First Annual Conference of the Society of American Indians* (Washington, DC, 1912), 2.

When the SAI met for the first time on the campus of Ohio State University in 1911, Arthur C. Parker—SAI founding member, secretary, and longtime editor of the SAI's journal—called the organization "an unfinished experiment . . . an acid test . . . a demonstration of the qualities of the race."[18] Parker frequently meditated on the contributions of both the SAI and its journal to the formation of what he called the "modern Indian": "The very fact that we exist as a Society and that we publish a periodical is an answer to the question of what the modern Indian is."[19] Defining the "modern Indian" for the modern American readership was vital, in Parker's view, to enlisting support for Native political causes. Michelle Patterson sees the SAI members' actions—rhetorical and otherwise—as an exploitation of non-Native interest in Native culture to advance Native goals, where SAI members "carefully tread a line between pandering to a white image of 'the Indian' and advancing their own model of the acculturated Indian American."[20] After all, modern (and modernist) Americans were already exploiting Indian tropes in search of an "authentic" life that rapid modernization and city life could no longer offer.[21] But perhaps a strategic use of non-Native resources and human capital characterizes better the SAI agenda and method rather than the mere "exploitation" Patterson diagnoses. Vocal SAI founding members like Carlos Montezuma and Laura Cornelius Kellogg opposed the pandering to the Indian of the white imagination and offered sustainable, albeit at the time controversial, models of what Kellogg called "[old Indians] adjusted to new conditions." Adjustment, not pandering to white Progressives, characterizes the work of the SAI. Presenting the image of the confident Progressive American Indian to the world in the first issue of the *Quarterly Journal* in 1913, the SAI introduced readers to a drawing epitomizing the SAI's vision of the modern Indian (Figure 2).

Drawn for the journal by non-Native artist Harold Bierce, *The Progressive Indian American* appeared strategically at the end of a section titled "The Indian in Caricature," which reproduced caricatures of Native people from national newspapers. In contrast to the duped, poor, neglected "Indian" of the national press—and the national imagination—*The Progressive Indian American* shows a confident Native man who is dressed in citizens' clothes and who wears the emblem of the SAI on his lapel, "the star of hope" and "the new beacon of light for the race."[22] Read against the caricatures of the period, which included a host of iterations of the stereotypical "Lo, the Poor Indian," this representation of the Progressive American Indian was perhaps the SAI's subtle version of the imagined modern Indian, although SAI members often disagreed on what modernity was or should be for Native communities.

Although the SAI's definition of "the modern Indian" changed over the years and often created tensions between the members—between those who argued for a quick leap into "civilization," those who advocated that indigeneity and modernity were not incompatible, and those who maintained strong ties with their communities—in one way or another, most SAI members engaged modernity and its discontents, often in the pages of the SAI journal.

The SAI Journal

At the second national conference in 1912, the SAI resolved to publish a journal devoted to the history of Native people and their place in American culture and history. A Native journal was certainly no aberration at the time; between 1826 and 1924, over two hundred Native newspapers and periodicals were published by nonsectarian and sectarian presses, government-supported presses, and the American Indian and Alaska Native press.[23] The journal displayed the SAI's political and cultural commitments, making literature a secondary—or even tertiary—interest, although some of

The Progressive Indian American
Drawn by Harold Bierce for the *Journal*.

FIGURE 2. *The Progressive Indian American, Quarterly Journal of the Society of American Indians* 1, no. 1 (April 15, 1913). Image courtesy of the Newberry Library.

its members were published writers. For the first time on a national scale, a Native journal was devoted to issues like "race ethos," wardship, education, autonomy, the assertion of Native leadership and agency, and citizenship.

If we focus our attention on the SAI's radical (yet equally complicated) visions of Native modernity in the context of an unprecedented push for Americanization, what do we learn about this new era in Native representation?[24] As Arthur C. Parker, the journal's first editor, explained in the first issue of the journal, published in 1913, "Never before has an attempt been made on the part of a national Indian organization to publish a periodical devoted to the interest of the entire race."[25] Although one organization could not represent the interests of all Native communities, the SAI's journal was committed to bringing "the interest of the entire race" to national readership. The SAI motto, inscribed on the official stationery, professed that "the honor of the race and the good of the country shall be paramount." Initially titled the *Quarterly Journal of the Society of American Indians* (1913–16), the journal changed its name to the *American Indian Magazine* (1916–20) to reflect the SAI's interest in reaching a larger (and non-Indian) readership but continued to include the original journal title on the title page in a smaller font. The journal presented itself throughout its publication life as "the official organ of the Society of the American Indians." The SAI motto, slightly revised, accompanied the journal's title pages: "For the Honor of the Race and the Good of the Country." Published by "the American Indian Magazine Publishing Committee of the Society of the American Indians," the journal was edited by three prominent SAI members—Arthur C. Parker (1913–18), Gertrude S. Bonnin (1918–19), and Thomas L. Sloan (1919–20)— and was devoted to the "immediate needs relating to the advancement of the Indian race in enlightenment."[26] Prominent SAI members were contributing editors, and they were listed on the journal's first pages throughout its publication.[27] The journal's subtitle also saw a subtle change in January 1917, under Parker's editorship, from the *American Indian Magazine: A Journal of Race Ideals* to the *American Indian Magazine: A Journal of Race Progress.*[28] This transition from "race ideals" to "race progress" reveals an awareness of the print medium's potential to document and enact change, from aspiration ("race ideal") to action ("race progress").

As correctives, articles by Native writers of various backgrounds in the SAI journal offered Native-centered views of Native cultures. For instance, Chauncey Yellow Robe's "The Menace of the Wild West Show" (1914) decried the artificial, offensive representations of Native people in a popular and low-brow form of entertainment. Poems and short fiction also made their way into the journal after 1916, when it grew more eclectic in both vision and politics.[29] This interest in new genres showed readers another facet of Native writers the journal had heretofore neglected: the literary.[30]

Archival evidence reveals the SAI members' desire to write about Native communities and some of the challenges they faced. Gertrude Bonnin's work on reservations in the West also shaped her vision of the SAI journal, which she had criticized in the past for "concentrating too much on the abstraction of theory and policy," thus limiting its reservation audience. In 1916, writing from Fort Duchesne, Utah, to Parker, Bonnin proposed that "someone should write an *Uncle Tom's Cabin* for the Aborigine. Every Indian Agent is a 'Legree,' the slave killer. The task would be too difficult for an Indian. The perspective, entirely too close. I can hardly write a few pages of a report on conditions in one agency without being nearly consumed with indignation and holy wrath."[31] Bonnin expressed the Native writer's affective impasse in her difficulty to detach emotionally from the lived reality. We should also understand this less explored (affective and otherwise) dimension

Vol. VI. No. 4

THE
AMERICAN INDIAN
MAGAZINE
A JOURNAL OF RACE PROGRESS
EDITED BY GERTRUDE BONNIN
WINTER NUMBER
1919

DR. CHARLES A. EASTMAN (Sioux)
President of The Society of American Indians

PUBLISHED BY THE
AMERICAN INDIAN MAGAZINE PUBLISHING COMMITTEE
OF THE SOCIETY OF AMERICAN INDIANS
$1.00 A Year   25c A Copy.

FIGURE 3. Cover of an issue of the journal from 1919, under the editorship of Gertrude Bonnin, featuring then SAI president Charles Eastman on the cover.

of the SAI writers and intellectuals in the context of the publishing industry at the time, the reading public, the expectations of mainstream readers of what Native writing should be, and the control Indian agents exerted on reservations.

Another Native activist and female writer, SAI founding member Laura Cornelius Kellogg, professed in 1903 that "literature shall be my life work, and its aim shall be to benefit my people."[32] After many disappointments, including the factionalism within the SAI that led her to part ways with the organization in 1913, she dedicated her life to social work, deferring her literary plans: "Later, *when my people are happier*, I hope to show that the quality of the Indian imagination has a place among the literatures of nations."[33] Although Kellogg devoted most of her life to political and activist work for the Six Nations land claims, she was a passionate writer, and, had she had the leisure and disposition, she might have rivaled Bonnin's literary accomplishments.[34]

In the early 1910s, few Native writers had access to the columns of mainstream newspapers and magazines, and the SAI journal offered an alternative forum for voicing concerns over issues such as citizenship, racial justice, and the future of American Indians.[35] Besides articles on these subjects and conference proceedings, the SAI journal also published editorials, letters, announcements, and reprints from national and international newspapers.[36] Published by the Arthur H. Crist Company in Cooperstown, New York, and owned by the SAI, the journal was not published as "a money-making scheme," it carried no advertisements, its editors and mailing clerks received no salary, and it received no help from the government.[37] Appeals to subscribers were published periodically, sometimes in poem form—"I'll send the S.A.I. a dollar, I'll send one often too, / And when I can I'll make it ten, to show my colors true"—documenting the organization's fund-raising efforts. The same issue of the journal also documents the journal's financial and distribution efforts since its inception: "To write, print and circulate our literature requires a large amount of time and money. . . . The grand total of our circular printed matter is 69,000." The journal's circulation since 1911 is listed at a total of 207,300 copies of individual essays, information booklets, annual platforms, conference announcements, posters, and copies of previous journal issues disseminated from 1911 to 1916. As Arthur C. Parker intimated, "This amount of literature poured into the minds and hearts of the American public cannot have helped but to effect a change in sentiment toward the Indian."[38]

The run of the SAI journal coincided with contemporaneous weekly and monthly publications of government schools like Carlisle Indian Industrial School (Pennsylvania), Hampton Institute (Virginia), Haskell Institute (Kansas), Chilocco Indian School (Oklahoma), and others. Occasionally, the SAI journal advertised the boarding school publications; a rubric in the June 1916 issue, "With Our Contemporaries," praised the work of publications like the *Native American* (published at the Phoenix Indian School in Arizona), the *Indian Leader* (at Haskell Institute), and the *Red Man* (at Carlisle Indian Industrial School).[39] In an attempt to promote other Native publications, the *American Indian Magazine* also advertised the publication of Dr. Carlos Montezuma's *Wassaja,* which started in Chicago in 1916.[40] For the first time in Native history, in the SAI meetings and publications, the SAI had a forum from which to voice and disseminate ideas nationally and internationally, and to embrace and challenge Progressive ideas. A letter from a Danish writer to Arthur C. Parker documents the journal's popularity in northern Europe. The vast correspondence in the SAI papers also points to the journal's popularity internationally.[41] The choice of the journal's masthead and the SAI emblem—an eagle on the left and a lighted torch on the right—changed very little over the years. Ho-Chunk artist Angel DeCora chose the copper eagle as an emblem to symbolize "the reawakened activity of the race and its determination through wisdom, courage, and foresight."

According to an editorial comment, the eagle was both an object of veneration by ancestors and a symbol of wisdom and courage: "The Old Indians say that the eagle is the only bird that can fly in the face of the sun and look into its blazing countenance without closing its eyes; the *eagle can face the light, unafraid.*"[42]

After six years as the SAI journal's editor, Arthur C. Parker stepped down, and Gertrude Bonnin took over for a brief stint, expressing a strong belief in the power of print to influence public opinion.[43] Under her editorship, the winter 1917 issue of the journal was an Indigenous-centered issue, described as a "Special Sioux Number" (advertised as such on the cover) and featuring essays by the Sioux intelligentsia of the day, including her work and essays by Chauncey Yellow Robe, S. M. Brosius, and Charles Eastman. This strategic focus on Indigenism was balanced by a larger national focus in the following year. In the autumn 1918 issue, published also under Bonnin's editorship, Chauncey Yellow Robe wrote an impassioned plea for Americanization as he extolled the patriotism of Native soldiers, many of them not yet American citizens, who were fighting in the Great War: "We must Americanize our glorious America under one government, one American language for all, one flag, and one God." Yellow Robe's patriotic appeal in 1918 is consistent with the journal's and the organization's work in 1918 of advocating for American citizenship for Indigenous people as an end to wardship; the same issue of the journal published the text of the proposed Indian citizenship bill (which would not pass for six more years), as well as excerpts from the *Congressional Record*.[44] Thomas Sloan took over his one-year editorship in 1919 with renewed faith in the publication's appeal to a national audience. In a letter to General Hugh L. Scott in June 1920, Sloan described the journal as "a monthly publication . . . devoted entirely to the interests of the North American Indian, and which in literary and artistic quality will rank as the equal of such publications as *Harper's*, *Century*, *Scribner's*, *National Geographic*, *Asia* and other periodicals appealing to the highest type of reader."[45] In a 1916 editorial, Arthur C. Parker had reaffirmed the idea of the journal's appeal: "We are reaching outward as well as inward. . . . If the universities and libraries of civilization find within our pages real contributions to science, literature, history, sociology, education, and philosophy, these centers of culture will radiate a greater respect for the Red race." Although it went through three different editorships, the SAI journal maintained a vision for a national readership and an awareness of its potential to instill in its readers "a greater respect for the Red race."[46] Despite Sloan's and Parker's hopeful visions, the SAI journal soon published its last issue.[47]

What distinguished the SAI journal from publications controlled by the federal government, however, was the SAI intellectuals' control of their meaning as they presented themselves to the world by carefully crafting their message as they addressed a predominantly white readership. Ojibwe scholar Scott R. Lyons calls this strategy "rhetorical sovereignty": "the inherent right and ability of peoples to determine their communicative needs and desires . . . to decide for themselves the goals, modes, styles, and languages of public discourse."[48] The SAI journal—a politically savvy and activist forum—was also part of a long tradition of Native writing in English since the late eighteenth century.[49] One of the SAI's aspirations was to mediate between white and red America, to "give to each an understanding of the other."[50]

To be sure, the SAI journal was in high demand, and the presentation of the issues of the *Quarterly Journal* in nicely bound royal morocco attests to the imagined legacy of an organization that put print culture and its preservation and dissemination at the center of its campaign to reform its readership and change public opinion.[51] To position itself within a national context, the SAI used Americanism strategically in the marketing of the SAI journal. In 1915 the editor described the issues of the *Quarterly Journal* as "Books of Unquenchable Americanism" (Figure 4).

The bound volumes, with the title page displaying the writing plume and the copper eagle as the SAI emblem, reveal the Native intellectuals' idea of permanence not only in the American imaginary but also in American print culture and literature. If the primary goal of the SAI was to "develop and organize men and women of Indian blood as wise leaders of their race," how did Americanism fit into their plan?[52] What made it especially unquenchable? Like this statement, the meaning of Americanism itself is historically contingent, grounded in the sociopolitical moment of the 1910s, and addressing an audience sensitive to the nuances of nationalist discourse. The putatively genuine Americanism of the 1910s was premised on hostility to non-Americans and foreigners: either one was an American, or one was not welcomed into the nation.[53] To position themselves in the national debates—especially over citizenship and rights—the SAI intellectuals appropriated the rhetoric of American patriotism to convey, perhaps, an equally "unquenchable" Indigenism.

The Print Debates over Citizenship and Americanization in the SAI Journal

The arguments over citizenship presented in the SAI journal were shaped by their political moment—before, during, and after World War I—and by the editorial vision of each of the three journal editors (Parker, Bonnin, and Sloan). In 1917, as Native men started fighting in the Great War as Americans—

FIGURE 4. "Books of Unquenchable Americanism." *Quarterly Journal of the Society of American Indians* 3, no. 3 (September 1915): 240. Image courtesy of the Newberry Library.

as noncitizens de jure, as the ICA was not signed into law until 1924—the Native intellectuals' attention was galvanized, as never before, around the issue of citizenship. As they positioned themselves within the debates over racial uplift alongside their African American peers (the American Negro Academy, founded in 1897, of which W. E. B. Du Bois was a prominent member), the SAI intellectuals also made Indian reform and citizenship their central goals on their own terms.[54] As Kyle Mays has argued persuasively, during the Progressive Era "partial citizenship affected both Black Americans and Native Americans," which translated into multiple forms of exclusion from the public sphere.[55]

In the early years of the journal, the issues tackled ranged from religious exhortations about good citizenship (Sherman Coolidge's address started with the motto "Use Your Citizenship Worthily of the Gospel of Christ"), to Progressive arguments for "standing on a par with the best intellects of other races" (Fred E. Parker) and making way for "competent" and "efficient" citizenship (Arthur C. Parker), to the perceived incongruence of reservation life with modern citizenship (Carlos Montezuma), and legal arguments and roadmaps toward citizenship (Arthur Parker, Hiram Chase).[56] Other key terms in these discussions included "real independent citizenship" (Richard Henry Pratt, founder of the Carlisle Indian Industrial School), full citizenship, to the transformation of *potential* into *actual citizens* (Bonnin).[57] In an editorial from 1914, "The Road to Competent Citizenship," Arthur C. Parker argued that Native people needed *preparation* for US citizenship; he also argued for the formation of a presidential commission that would "study existing laws," demanding Indian representation at the negotiation table. The same journal issue reprinted a letter from President Howard Taft in which he expressed his support for an Indian "voice" yet cautioned readers that citizenship came with responsibilities.[58]

Besides original essays and speeches by SAI members, the journal also reprinted essays on citizenship from national journals, newspapers, and magazines to insert the SAI conversation into the national debate. Before the SAI meeting in Cedar Rapids, Iowa, in 1916, one local paper included an article titled "Citizenship Is the Theme of Talks by Indians."[59] When Native soldiers started fighting in World War I, the rhetoric of the SAI journal changed to patriotic appeals ("Make Them Citizens"). The contributors offered detailed reviews of proposed legislation—such as the three citizenship bills introduced in Congress—and the Indian Citizenship Campaign, a series of lectures undertaken by the SAI president, Charles Eastman, in 1919.[60] In a letter to members, Eastman decried the overwhelming control of the Indian Bureau; with renewed faith in the mission of the SAI in 1919, Eastman declared: "We are not a 'dying race;' we are alive and asking for our share of the liberty and democracy that we have fought for."[61] The SAI's eighth conference, held in Minneapolis in 1919, went so far as to use the slogan "American Citizenship for the Indian."[62] Even after the last issue of the journal saw print in August 1920 and the SAI soon thereafter disintegrated, SAI intellectuals continued to advocate for citizenship, eventually granted to all Native people through the blanket ICA of 1924.

Why was citizenship one of the SAI's most powerful platforms? For one, it addressed consistently and forcefully over the years the incongruity between the nationalist fervor toward Americanization and the incomplete citizenship model imagined for Native people. In the preface to the *Proceedings* of the SAI's first meeting, published in 1912, the SAI called for unified action to fight dependence, wardship, and poverty. In this early twentieth-century Indigenous manifesto, "the thinking Indian of today" asked that "he [sic] be treated as an *American*" in order to rise "to positions of the highest honor and responsibility . . . to develop normally as an American people in America."[63] This seeming erasure of indigeneity from the SAI plea may ring false to contemporary readers, who may dismiss this claim too easily as "assimilationist" or pro-Americanization. This is also one of the main critiques of the SAI in our own time, as it was in theirs. As Lucy Maddox has argued, "The effort of Native Progressive Era intellectuals to insert Indian history and local Indian issues into a universal framework anticipated the kind of questions scholars of American Indian histories and cultures are still asking about the American public's resistance to taking American Indian intellectualism seriously."[64] As we saw in the previous section, Arthur C. Parker's vision of the journal in his long tenure as secretary and editor shows a clear sense of the journal's audience. Sherman Coolidge's presidential address at the second conference, "The Indian American—His Duty to His Race and to His Country, the United States of America," also called attention to Native civic responsibility by subtly changing the terms and privileging one identity over the national category ("the Indian American") and by appealing to white America's Christian beliefs to call attention to the incompleteness of Native citizenship.[65]

Despite some occasional procedural disagreements and later factionalism surrounding issues such as the Indian Office, peyote, and the SAI's handling of specific complaints raised by tribes, SAI members were more or less united by the idea of citizenship, although many were concerned whether a uniform US citizenship would allow retention of federal protection of Indian lands and other rights and were questioning whether citizenship would bring an end to wardship. American citizenship, yet another colonial imposition, did not restore Native land when it was eventually granted to Native people in 1924, nor did it erase Native people's status as wards of the federal government. Whereas the blanket naturalization offered by the ICA in 1924 may be read as a corrective to earlier *exclusionary* legislation, Native naturalization proved to be an afterthought in US naturalization law. Not only was there no uniform policy in place until 1924, but the ICA passed in 1924 *after* the Quota Act / Immigration Act, just as Native soldiers who fought in World War I were naturalized months *after* their immigrant peers who fought in the same war.[66] Considering that, at the time, about two-thirds of American Indians were already citizens, naturalized through previous treaty provisions, land allotments, and statutory measures, the question remains: Why did the SAI intellectuals continue to advocate for citizenship?[67]

To begin to answer this question, we may consider first the lack of Indigenous participation and agency in determining American Indians' consent to becoming US citizens (consent being a key tenet of naturalization). At the same time, as David Martinez has shown, the SAI sought universal citizenship for Indians "as a way of alleviating the perennial problems caused by the reservation system."[68] And since American citizenship was the goal of Progressive organizations nationwide to Americanize and homogenize its citizenry in the context of unprecedented immigration from southern and eastern Europe, citizenship soon became the main strategic discourse in SAI rhetoric as a Progressive Native organization. The Red Progressives could not only "talk back to civilization," as Frederick Hoxie put it, but also write back to civilization, often borrowing the rhetoric of "civilization" and "racial difference" to assert Native presence and sovereignty.[69]

The uncertain legal status of Native people was one of the driving forces of the SAI citizenship debates. A pamphlet published in 1912, *The Indian and Citizenship*, by non-Native SAI founding member Fayette McKenzie, a sociology professor at Ohio State, and then reprinted in the *Quarterly Journal* after it appeared in the Carlisle publication the *Red Man*, called attention to Native people's lack of legal status, "perpetual inhabitant[s] with diminutive rights." This "condition of confusion in Indian affairs," McKenzie argued, was "intolerable."[70] The codification of Native people's legal status was a shared concern of SAI members. In 1912 the SAI drafted what became the Carter Indian Code Bill (H.R. 18334, 62nd Cong., 2nd sess.), introduced in the House of Representatives by Chickasaw congressman Charles D. Carter, which aimed at spelling out the terms of Indian citizenship. Arthur C. Parker also lobbied the Lake Mohonk Conference for support: "The Indian as neither citizen nor foreigner has occupied . . . a precarious position in our national life." Ultimately, he failed to gain support for the Carter bill in 1912.[71] In his correspondence with Carter years later, Parker revisited the issue of citizenship, noting that New York Indians might vehemently oppose it (given the possibility of dividing their lands, recognized as Six Nations lands through the Treaty of 1794). Nevertheless, Parker maintained that the revival of Carter's citizenship bill would offer Native people "the even chance to struggle into the life of the Nation."[72]

The early issues of the *Quarterly Journal* argued for the desirability of citizenship and the necessity of adjusting the legal status for "the Indian of the present," whose ability is "on a par with the best intellects of other races." Thus wrote Fred E. Parker (Seneca) in the article "The Indian as Citizen," also noting that "the Indian citizen of to-day is an honor to his race."[73] A year later, Gabe E. Parker called for abandoning tribal relations altogether as Indian people assumed the "responsibilities of American citizenship."[74] Most active SAI members remained ambivalent about the role of the reservation in advancing or stalling American citizenship. Carlos Montezuma became the reservation's most vocal enemy. In his speech to an SAI regional meeting in 1914 "The Reservation Is Fatal to the Development of Good Citizenship," Montezuma talked about Indian reservations as prisons, reiterating his belief that, just like foreign immigrants, Indians must learn to speak English, attend public schools, and immerse themselves in "civilization" to become American citizens.[75] In this line of argument, citizenship was, therefore, desirable for Native people, yet its terms were somewhat nebulous.

From its inception, the SAI promoted acquisition of citizenship "on a voluntary basis" yet continued to emphasize the disparity between Native rights and the rights of the naturalized new immigrants. In his address "The Law and the American Indian" (1912), Judge Hiram Chase argued that Indian citizenship acquisition should be voluntary. At the same time, Chase claimed that the naturalization of Native people could borrow from the immigrant model.[76] This idea was also rehearsed, over and over, in the Carlisle student publications and in Richard Henry Pratt's correspondence, especially with his longtime friend and protégé Carlos Montezuma. For the most part, the SAI publications endorsed Pratt's views and often printed his bombastic prose. In a provocative article from 1914 titled "Why Most of Our Indians Are Dependent and Non-citizens," Pratt blamed the Indian Bureau in his well-rehearsed rhetoric: "Can't you see that Indian civilization and real independent citizenship means death to the Indian system? The so-called 'Indian Problem' has always been the *Indian System*, never the Indian."[77] Many SAI members agreed. Yet Native activists like Charles Eastman, Arthur C. Parker, and Gertrude Bonnin envisioned a political future for Native nations different from Pratt's.[78] Nevertheless, Pratt's argument for the transformation of the Indian into a self-supporting individual American, ready to engage with the competitive market and capital, was a favorite topic of at least two SAI members: Carlos Montezuma and Arthur C. Parker.

Although Parker's incursion into procitizenship arguments in his SAI editorials become more and more pronounced over the years, by 1915 the SAI had not made much progress toward citizenship and changes in government policies. In a 1916 issue of the *American Indian Magazine*, Parker reprinted Theodore Roosevelt's piece "Indian Citizenship," in which the former president (who had left the White House in 1909) called for "preparing" the Indian for citizenship and cautioned that this process would take time.[79] Roosevelt's anti-Indian rhetoric and policy were consistent with his legacy as an "Indian-hater" president. His vision of Americanization—while seemingly inclusive and welcoming of all ethnicities into a great American melting pot—was one of "forced Americanization." For Native people, it meant forced Christianization, education, the breaking up of reservation land into individual allotments, and American citizenship.[80]

In 1917, when Congressman Carl Hayden of Arizona introduced a new Indian citizenship bill in Congress (a rather controversial one, with stipulations for gradual taxation), editorials about citizenship continued to take center stage in the *American Indian Magazine*. When the United States entered World War I, the tenor of the journal was more patriotic than ever before, as thousands of Native soldiers were drafted or volunteered to fight in the war. In their correspondence, then president Arthur C. Parker and Secretary Gertrude Bonnin planned that the program of the 1917 SAI conference would include the slogan "The American Indian in Patriotism, Production, Progress." However, after intense preparations, the SAI conference, projected to take place at the University of Oklahoma in 1917, was postponed because of the war.[81] Nevertheless, a renewed interest in and fervor for the citizenship bill permeated later issues of the journal (under Bonnin's editorship, now using many exclamation marks, reflecting her increasing frustration with both the SAI and her reservation constituents).

As they debated American and Native citizenship, SAI members also presented arguments about "racial difference" to position Native people in the growing contemporary landscape of Indigenous, racial, and ethnic groups, using both the rhetoric of racial difference of the day and analogies to American ethnic groups as they argued for citizenship for Native people. As we have seen, a common strategy in the SAI's argument for racial difference in the early twentieth century was the comparison of Native civic and racial status with that of European immigrants. This idea did not, however, originate with the SAI members; it found its most acerbic advocate and supporter in Carlisle's mastermind, Richard Henry Pratt.

In his many published and public addresses and private letters, including letters to his disciple Carlos Montezuma, Pratt insisted ceaselessly that the "Indian problem" and its solution—total assimilation—could be addressed by adopting the model of immigrant assimilation and Americanization. In his paternalistic tone Pratt invoked often the success of Anglicizing and citizenizing African Americans and European immigrants and called for the immediate subjection of "our Indians" to the same treatment: "Encouraging foreigners of all lands to come and settle among us has in every instance, where we have avoided the congesting of them in separate and large communities, led them to abandon their past and become thoroughly American."[82] Pratt called for Native people to abandon their past in order to "become thoroughly American." So influential was Pratt on the SAI agenda of Americanization that some members went so far as to propose that Pratt be adopted as an Indian.[83] Under Bonnin's editorship, Pratt's photograph was again featured prominently in the SAI journal after a short hiatus, and his contributions to Native Americanization were praised.[84] SAI members of the pro-Americanization faction rehearsed Pratt's arguments on different occasions, stressing the importance of the work ethic to both immigrant and Native survival. Francis La Flesche (Omaha) opined: "If the Indian were to go to work, do like the Immigrants who come here . . . , he will have solved this problem that seems so difficult to us. . . . So, I say, tell the Indian to go to work."[85] In other words, labor would make an Indian into an American during the Progressive Era.

Labor and industry were virtues touted by Progressive Era reformers, including Commissioner of Indian Affairs Robert G. Valentine, whose prescription for Indian progress was based on an Indian ideal who was "first, a solid, healthy human being, and second, a good laborer or other workman." In an article published in *Sunset* in 1910 titled "Making Good Indians," Valentine opined that Indians did not work because they didn't have to: "They are often lazy just as you or I would be lazy if we had no great worry as to where our means were coming from."[86] Native Progressives like Fred E. Parker soon appropriated Valentine's prescription for Native progress based on the Protestant work ethic. In 1913 he offered a solution for the putative Indian laziness by appealing to both Anglo-Saxon values and the immigrant analogy: "If the Indian were to go to work, do like the immigrants who come here—build houses, such as the German does that comes from Europe, till the soil as the native that comes from Sweden, he will have solved this problem that seems so difficult to us and to the white people. . . . So, I say, tell the Indian to go to work."[87] He attributed Indians' lack of industry to a "disinclination to work," as well as a fondness for liquor, at the same time that he appropriated, like many contemporary Native peers, a detached persona, a non-Native voice—"Tell the Indian to go to work"—ventriloquizing Progressive Era rhetoric and its glorification of the Protestant work ethic. Fred E. Parker's provocative statement about Indians and work foreshadows changes in both the conception of and the rhetoric around Native labor, materialized in the next few decades during the administration of John Collier at the Bureau of Indian Affairs (BIA), and the Indian New Deal. *Indians at Work* (1933–45), a BIA publication started in 1933 by Collier, served his political agenda, which included, among other things, promoting vocational education in community day schools on reservations.[88] Labor, in Collier's vision, would help Native people thrive on reservations during the Indian New Deal era.

Nevertheless, the SAI intellectuals continued to use the immigrant analogy to signal a lack in the Native community, especially around two pressing issues: education and health. Laura Cornelius Kellogg, founding member of the SAI and chairman of its Division of Education, was a declared enemy of the boarding school system, which removed Native children from families with the mission of making Americans of them in the quickest way. In her report to the SAI at the second conference, "Some Facts and Figures on

Indian Education," Kellogg looked back on over twenty-five years of federally funded Indian education, tracing the contradictions of misused government funds and their consequences for Native children.[89] She pointed out the importance of Indigenous self-determination in the process of education and saw the future of Indian education as a meeting ground of tribal knowledges and epistemologies with "Caucasian" education.[90] As someone educated at white institutions, Kellogg expounded: "We want education, yes, we want to know all the educated Caucasian knows but we want our self-respect while we are getting his knowledge." She invoked the "power of abstraction in the Indian mind" and described the merits of Indian oratory in its "profound thought, literary merit and logic." Kellogg further criticized the Office of Indian Affairs for failing to include funds for Native students' health care, called for a transition from off-reservation schools to local public schools "where feasible," and asked for appropriations for Indian students pursuing higher education: "Our future is in the hands of the educational system of today. Those of us who have come thus far know how our youth have longed to reach the summit of the mountain. Let us not forget our own yearnings and the prayers of our ambitious young for opportunity. Let us climb the highest mountain, without looking back till we have reached the top."[91] Kellogg ultimately criticized the irresponsibility of the Indian Office (OIA) personnel in handling resources appropriately and suggested future directions for congressional appropriations to benefit Native education and health.

Whereas the link between public health and immigrants served American nativist claims for racial purity at the beginning of the twentieth century (keeping undesirable "races" out), Kellogg pointed to the ongoing extermination at home due to the nefarious epidemics Native students contracted at boarding schools and spread upon their return to reservations. In both scenarios, the discourse of eliminating the Native and the immigrant as threats to a healthy nation was based on fears of coexisting alongside groups who were not Anglo-Saxon Protestants, the putative threats to Americanism. Kellogg sanctioned this nativist fear as she continued to advocate for Indigenous rights. Although Kellogg ended her SAI speech on education on an optimistic note, she reminded the audience members how crucial education was for Indigenous self-determination. She argued that the crowded quarters of the boarding schools and lack of hygiene exposed Native students to trachoma and tuberculosis, the two most common diseases in Indian boarding schools. Alerting her audience to the danger of trachoma, she deplored what she considered a criminal lack of sanitation: "Why, no immigrant can land in New York who has trachoma, but here we are exposing the youth of the race to an incurable disease. If this were done by an individual to another, it would be a penitentiary offense."[92] Using the immigrant analogy strategically—she was, after all, a student of social work at Barnard College under Franz Boas—she referred specifically to yet another excludable category: persons affected by contagious diseases. This new category of exclusion was added through the Immigration Act of 1907, signed by President Theodore Roosevelt, which denied admission into the United States of the following categories of immigrants: "all idiots, imbeciles, feebleminded persons, epileptics, insane persons, and persons who have been insane within five years previous; persons who have had two or more attacks of insanity at any time previously; paupers; persons likely to become a public charge; professional beggars; *persons afflicted with tuberculosis or with a loathsome or dangerous contagious disease.*"[93] Kellogg noted that whereas immigration restriction laws responded to the exaggerated fear of alien contagion—what Alan Kraut has called "medicalized nativism"—Indian boarding schools continued to be loci of disease dissemination without any federal acknowledgment or regulation. Kraut documents that exclusions of immigrants for medical reasons peaked as never before in 1916, when they reached an unprecedented 69 percent. Only a few years before Kellogg's speech, Congress made a small appropriation to study and treat trachoma in Native communities. Yet around the time she gave her speech at the SAI annual meeting in 1912, public health physicians still argued that the trachoma epidemic on reservations was being spread by the government boarding schools, as historians Brenda Child and David W. Adams have shown.[94]

Unlike Kellogg, who raised awareness about the dire sanitation of the governmental boarding schools in the pages of the SAI journal, Arthur C. Parker expressed a more abstract concern with Native education as he also attempted to theorize rapid Americanization and Native people's place in what he called a "uniform civilization." He acknowledged—and thus agreed with Kellogg—that the public school, not the reservation or boarding school, was the greatest of all Americanization forces. In "The Editor's Viewpoint: What Makes the Indian a Problem?," published in the second issue of the *Quarterly Journal* in 1913, Parker, unlike many of his Native peers, claimed that the "Indian problem" no longer emerged from what he called "racial conditions"; instead, it was a social problem. He intimated, therefore, that there was no inherently biological deterrent to Native people's quick Americanization but that the "Indian problem" was larger, systemic. Like Carlos Montezuma—but in subtler rhetorical moves—Parker also directed his critique to the Office of Indian Affairs. On the one hand, Parker claimed that Native Americans should not be judged on racial terms as they entered modernity; on the other hand, he called for the creation of a "Bureau of Race

Development" to promote what he called "human efficiency" and to standardize "every racial element."[95] Why would Parker make a seemingly circular argument?

One of the growing concerns of the anti-immigrant sentiment in the 1910s—familiar to Parker and his SAI fellow members—was the centrality of the argument about certain groups' racial inferiority. This concern, aided by pseudoscientific reports (like those of the Dillingham Commission, produced between 1907 and 1911), led to immigration restriction policies in the 1920s. The reports of the commission, which ultimately recommended that Congress enact restrictions on immigration based on what it found to be the "unassimilable character of recent immigrants," also offered analogies between the perceived intellectual differences of new immigrants compared to the old: "The new immigration as a class is far *less intelligent* than the old."[96] Through a similar racist logic, the commissioner of Indian affairs had commented on Native Americans' intelligence just a few decades earlier: "We have within our midst two hundred and seventy-five thousand [Native American] people, *the least intelligent* portion of our population, for whom we provide no law, either for protection or for the punishment of crime committed among themselves."[97]

The SAI intellectuals were well aware of the work of scientific racists, which targeted in particular the "inferior" new immigrant groups (such as the Alpine Slavs and the Jews). Immigration restrictionists invoked Darwin's theory of evolution and Mendelian genetics to support racist arguments about racial inferiority, which led to immigration restriction policies. In 1920 Harry H. Laughlin, a leader of the eugenics movement in the United States, argued that the new immigrants were simply diluting the national racial stock and, therefore, had to be stopped.[98] In a 1916 essay, "The White Aryan and the Red American," the SAI journal's editor, Arthur C. Parker, critiqued the claims to supremacy of both European and American "Aryans" popularized by contemporary race scientist Joseph P. Widney, who referred to Native Americans as one of the "lower" and "passing" races, with little capacity to "join the work of civilization" in *Race Life of the Aryan Peoples* (1907). Parker maintained that "civilization"—a standard Indigenous nations were critiqued for not yet having attained—was not "the property of any race, any more than air or water or truth." In fact, according to Parker, in 1916 "more men and women of Indian blood in proportion to their number are doctors, lawyers, clergymen, and teachers, than the people of any other race in America." Parker ended his essay on a hopeful note: "The American Indian is in America to stay and to leave the indelible impress of his mind and blood."[99]

Like many Indigenous Progressives, Parker expressed dissatisfaction with the OIA and its regulation of Native life. He used yet another immigrant analogy: "If there is no Immigrant Bureau devoted to the *continual* care of foreigners seeking Americanization, there should be no special Indian Bureau" (emphasis in the original). Undoubtedly, Parker was aware of the history of the Bureau of Immigration, created in 1895. In fact, at the time of Parker's remarks in 1913, the Bureau of Immigration and Naturalization (created in 1906) had separated into two different branches: the Bureau of Immigration and the Bureau of Naturalization, both under the jurisdiction of the Department of Labor. In his emphasis on the "*continual* care" of Indians, he stressed the paternalism of the OIA, which kept the Native wards of the federal government under an unnecessarily prolonged panoptic gaze more than any other group, especially the immigrants. In Parker's view, "a sick man, a pauper, a drunkard, an ignorant man, and a foreigner" are all at a disadvantage; however, he claimed, it was the "human" element above all that made possible their transition from one stage of development to another, not their racial background. Take, for instance, the immigrant (and by that he meant the white European immigrant): "The immigrant from Italy and the immigrant from Finland each must learn the English tongue and take on the manners of the American. Neither one can come here and succeed in rearing children or continue in business life without learning the principles of American civilization, the English tongue, the ethics, the economy and the manners of the country. This means a complete entering into the social fabric of the people."[100]

In "Problems of Race Assimilation in America; with Special Reference to the American Indian," Parker compared the difficulties of assimilating Native people and new immigrants to those faced by African Americans. To address the central question of his essay—"Why has the Indian not been absorbed?"—Parker argued that "the conditions of assimilation" of the three groups were unequal but that immigrants had the easiest path toward assimilation, though Parker did not directly attribute it to the immigrants' whiteness or European descent. He held that, unlike some "foreign bloods" who encountered an even greater prejudice in the process of becoming American, the assimilated Indians posed "no grave social or racial problem" because "their aims and methods of thought are thoroughly American." Like other Red Progressive peers (Kellogg and Montezuma), Parker found the reservation system isolating. He intimated that, like African Americans, Native people had to prove themselves to the white world and had to overcome both racial and cultural prejudice. After examining several preconditions for assimilating immigrants (moral energy, capital, similar values, and "good stock"), Parker concluded that the European immigrant is "a white man from a civilized country" who only changes one kind of civilization for another. But Parker's vision did not account for the agricultural and preindustrial communities in southern and eastern Europe many new immigrants had departed from. He also noted the difficulty of "the American Negro" to assimilate because of systemic racism and prejudice. Troubling race-based categories, Parker ultimately placed the argument about Native inferiority in a national context of structural barriers of prejudice against non-Anglo-Saxons.[101]

Engaging the Americanizers' emerging theories of the melting pot—"In this great melting pot of nations, the races that are poured in will not all melt at the same degree of temperature"—Parker also called attention to the disparities of assimilation, a process he believed inevitable:

> To the European immigrant we say, "Come, we want you in this free country. In many respects you are like us." . . . To the Negro we say, "In many respects you are unlike us. . . . However, we will tolerate you for after all you are a convenient laborer." . . . To the Chinaman we say, "Stay away, we don't want you. You are vastly different from the rest of us and we dislike your looks." . . . To the Indians we say, "You were here first, that is true, and although we tried we could not kill you entirely. You must be segregated until you can understand us."[102]

Appropriating the ubiquitous rhetoric of contemporary white America ("we"), Parker ultimately cautioned against the incongruities of assimilation practices, which always privileged the white immigrants, by pointing to the exploitation of African Americans and the dispossession of Native Americans. Parker's somewhat problematic ventriloquism and racist rhetoric toward Chinese immigrants—"Stay away, we don't want you. You are vastly different from the rest of us and we dislike your looks"—illustrates his contemporaries' racial prejudice, materialized in the first Draconian immigration restriction legislation, the Chinese Exclusion Act of 1882.[103] Bringing together the various degrees of discriminatory practices based on racial and ethnic group provenance—European immigrants, African Americans, Asian Americans, and Native Americans—Parker recapitulated his white contemporaries' exclusionary history as he also ventriloquized their position of privilege by reiterating the language of exclusion ("we say" and "we don't want you") to point to the absurdity of his contemporaries' theories about the "melting pot."

In the racial hierarchies Parker describes, only European immigrants fulfilled the requirements of white Progressive assimilation. Gertrude Bonnin reacted to the absurdity of these hierarchies in the pages of the *American Indian Magazine* in 1919, disheartened that the OIA would not permit SAI members to speak on a reservation: "Though the riffraff of the people from the four corners of the earth may enter Indian lands and homestead them, thus permitting daily contact with *the very scum of other races*, the educated, refined, and patriotic Indian, teaching the highest ideals of democracy is forbidden to meet with his own race, even for a day."[104] Bonnin called attention to the disparity between unsanctioned immigrant encroachment on Native lands—using, strategically, an ethnic slur to refer to "the very scum of other races"—and the refusal of the BIA to let Native leaders speak to the reservation communities, implying that the Americanization of Native people by their Native peers on Native terms and grounds was shunned. Parker's and Bonnin's contradictory rhetoric expressed the many paradoxes of Progressive evolutionary thinking.

The evolutionary model informing race thinking during the Progressive Era held that each race would gradually pass through "similar structural changes of economic, intellectual and social organization"—what anthropologists described as a progression from savagery (hunting) to barbarism (pastoralism) and civilization (agriculture). This evolutionary model of social development influenced the design of both Indian policy and immigrant programs during the Progressive Era. Yet the assimilation of immigrants was more pressing, given the large numbers of immigrant arrivals, whereas Indigenous people were believed to be vanishing.[105] Hazel Hertzberg argued that in 1919 the new direction in the SAI included a growing hostility to immigrants and African Americans. Whereas some SAI members bought into the nationalist xenophobic rhetoric occasionally (Parker, Bonnin, Montezuma), I'd like to propose that SAI intellectuals used this rhetoric purposefully to establish an even starker contrast between the rights granted to immigrants and African American citizens that Native people did not yet enjoy, particularly the right to citizenship. Although the evidence I found in the SAI papers about the SAI hostility toward European immigrants and African Americans is not overwhelming, a common strand emerging in the SAI argument for Indian citizenship between 1917 and 1919 is the recurring analogy of the civic and racial status of the Indian to that of the European immigrant. As Native soldiers returned home from the war in 1919, new arguments about Indian humanity took center stage in the SAI journal: "The Indian . . . is entitled to his human rights. . . . This is not the democracy for which our soldiers fought and died!"[106] Both nationalist and Native visions of American citizenship—sometimes overlapping—permeated the pages of the *American Indian Magazine*, inflecting the arguments with competing visions and calling for the recognition of Native people as full citizens.

"America" Redux

In 1921, after the SAI had published its last journal issue and was slowly dissolving, Gertrude Bonnin wrote the policy brochure *Americanize the First*

American: A Plan of Regeneration for the General Federation of Women's Club. It included two circular charts comparing bureaucracy with democracy under two separate categories marked by two distinct circles: "What We Have" and "What We Want." Detailing the layers of bureaucracy (superintendents, supervisors, special agents), Bonnin called specifically for an Indian Citizens' Association that would work directly with a reservation executive committee—an idea that would inform her post-SAI project, the National Council of American Indians (NCAI), which she helped form in 1926. In *Americanize the First American*, Bonnin pleaded with the women of America on behalf of "the Red man and his children" to advocate for Indian citizenship and the termination of Indian wardship: "Revoke the tyrannical powers of Government superintendents over a voiceless people and extend American opportunities to the first American—the Red Man."[107]

When *Americanize the First American* was first published, its cover sheet included a picture of Bonnin framed by American flags. This presentation is not entirely accidental, given the choices she made throughout her career to serve both her Native community and the white America she was navigating, as well as her strategic performance of both her Native and American personas. Her visual representations in the press of the time range from photographs in Native regalia to the modern suit of the "New Woman" whom Bonnin herself both embodied and advocated for. In her published articles and stories at the beginning of the twentieth century, Bonnin wrote under a self-given Lakota name, Zitkala-Ša, which means "Red Bird." She advocated for change in *Americanize the First American* and demanded freedom for Native people "to do their own thinking; to exercise their judgment; to hold open forums for the expression of their thought, and finally permit them to manage their own personal business."[108] Pleading for the Americanization of "the First American," Bonnin offered a biting critique of federal Indian policy, which continued to relegate American Indians to the status of wards of the federal government. To Bonnin, this was not "The Red Man's America."

In 1917 Bonnin published a poem titled "The Red Man's America" in the *American Indian Magazine*, offering a timely revisionist take on the popular patriotic song "America" by Samuel Francis Smith, the unofficial American anthem for almost one hundred years that her SAI peers had intoned and danced to only six years before in Columbus, Ohio, at the SAI first meeting. Variations of this immensely popular political song have abounded in American cultural history, from the abolitionists' use of the song to contest the significance of Fourth of July celebrations for enslaved Americans, to uses of the song in Progressive Era struggles for women's rights, to rallies against capitalism. Its use during times of political upheavals served not only to reaffirm American patriotism but also to voice political concerns, such as the disenfranchisement of Native people described in Bonnin's poem. Rewritings of the song have occurred during times of crisis and have used rhetorical strategies such as parody and irony to call attention to key terms, such as "land of liberty" and "freedom," and their significance for the country's diverse peoples. In Robert Branham and Stephen Hartnett's reading, "patriotism, the song teaches us, is not only about supporting [the] nation's policies, but also about questioning them when . . . they need questioning."[109]

Bonnin was not the first to rewrite this immensely popular patriotic song, but she was the first Native American to do so. African American leader and intellectual W. E. B. Du Bois also tried his hand at revising this unofficial American anthem early in the twentieth century, praising his country in lines such as "late land of slavery" and "My country 'tis of thee, / Late land of slavery," while reminding the nation that it was built on the injustices of slavery.[110] Bonnin's "The Red Man's America" lamented Native disenfranchisement and used it as a political platform to advocate for citizenship. Instead of the singular lament in Smith's poem—"Land where my fathers died, / Land of the pilgrims' pride, / From ev'ry mountainside / Let freedom ring!"[111] Bonnin used the voice of a Native speaker to signal the equally important but unrecognized part Native death played in the making of America: "Land where OUR fathers died, / Whose offspring are denied / The franchise given wide." Bonnin's poem sanctioned American hypocrisy in its refusal to grant citizenship to "the Red Man": "My native country, thee, / Thy Red man is not free, / Knows not thy love."[112] Establishing a double audience in the poem's first two stanzas by imagining two addressees, an American and a Native one—"My country" and "My native country"—the speaker brings her many "pleas" to appeal for Native enfranchisement to the first, and responsibility to the second (Figure 5).

"THE RED MAN'S AMERICA"

My country! 'tis to thee,
Sweet land of liberty
   My Pleas I bring.
Land where *OUR* fathers died,
Whose offspring are denied
The franchise given wide,
   Hark, while I sing.

My native country, thee,
Thy Red man is not free,
   Knows not thy love; [. . .]

"AMERICA"

My country, 'tis of thee,
Sweet land of liberty,
   Of thee I sing;
Land where *my fathers* died,
Land of the Pilgrim's Pride,
From every mountain side
   Let freedom ring.

My native country, thee,
Land of the noble, free,
   Thy name I love; [. . .]

FIGURE 5. Selections from Gertrude Bonnin's "The Red Man's America" (1917) and Samuel Francis Smith's "America" / "My Country 'Tis of Thee" (1831). Emphasis mine.

Bonnin's rewriting of the poem "America" with an Indigenous-centric appropriation of the song's main iconic symbols becomes a political appeal for Native rights—especially the rights of American citizenship. When the poem was published, the United States had just entered World War I, and a new brand of patriotism permeated the Native and the mainstream American public spheres, as well as the pages of the SAI journal. Read in the context of Native participation in the war (many Native men enlisted or were drafted to fight as "American soldiers"), the poem "The Red Man's America" rallied the readers of the *American Indian Magazine* in the SAI's fight for citizenship.[113] Published alongside reprints of newspaper articles about North American Native men's and women's work in the war, "The Red Man's America," with its reassuring cadences, asked the "sweet land of Liberty" to recognize Native humanity and, most important, Native rights. This confluence of patriotism performance and Native expression speaks to the larger challenges of Progressive Era Native intellectuals of negotiating both national and local communities, thus positioning themselves at the intersection of patriotic songs like "America" and traditional Native dances performed on Native-marked spaces (such as the "Indian mound" discussed at the beginning of this article). Like Bonnin, who indigenized an iconic American patriotic song, the Native intellectuals of the SAI used their public performance of patriotism to signal their political agenda of indigenizing the American public sphere. As they negotiated multiple audiences and expectations, they also used print culture to spell out, *to author*, the Indigenous terms of Americanization, even as those terms were sometimes problematic.

The SAI Native intellectuals this article has examined—educated professionals of the intellectual elite who sought to advance political and social agendas—were drawn into what we might loosely call two competing nationalisms: American and Indigenous. As they sometimes seemed to advocate for the former at the expense of the latter, they also cannily performed patriotism to enable Native persistence and cultural expression, and sometimes they firmly rejected assimilation in the name of Native nationalism. This article has mapped out those strategies by looking at the work of the SAI intellectuals, the print culture they shaped, and the national debates their public and printed work engaged, from advocating for Native citizenship as an end to wardship, to critiques of the melting pot and Americanization, and to assertions—through their published work—of a continued Native presence and future.

CRISTINA STANCIU is an associate professor of English at Virginia Commonwealth University. She is a coeditor (with Kristina Ackley) of *Laura Cornelius Kellogg: "Our Democracy and the American Indian" and Other*

Writings (2015) and (with Anastasia Lin) of the *MELUS* journal special issue, "Pedagogy in Anxious Times" (2017). Her work has appeared in journals such as *American Indian Quarterly, Studies in American Indian Literatures, MELUS, Intertexts,* and *College English* and in edited collections. Her book from which this article is derived is forthcoming from Yale University Press.

Notes

I thank the *NAIS* editors, Jeani O'Brien and Robert Warrior, and the anonymous reviewers for an engaging review process. Special thanks to Siobhan Senier for reading an early draft with wit and wisdom and to Cathleen Cahill for her insightful feedback on subsequent drafts. Robert Dale Parker deserves many thanks for teaching me about the joys of archival research. Many thanks to the Newberry Library for a semester-long fellowship, the Monticello College Fellowship for Women, which allowed the completion of the research for this essay; I'm especially grateful to Brian Hosmer, Scott M. Stevens, Patricia M. Norby, A. LaVonne Brown Ruoff, and John Aubry. The following scholars have also heard or read drafts at some point, and I'm grateful for their support: Jacki Rand, Beth Piatote, K. Tsianina Lomawaima, Sabine Klein, J. B. Capino, Phillip Round, Chadwick Allen, David Martinez, and Ned Blackhawk.

1. "Indian Congress Opens Two Meetings to Local Public," *Columbus Citizen,* October 11, 1911, reel 10, Papers of the Society of American Indians, ten microfilm reels, ed. John W. Larner Jr., 1986, Newberry Library, Chicago.

2. "Columbus Red Men Entertain Indians," *Ohio State Journal,* October 17, 1911, 10, reel 10, SAI Papers.

3. At the Minneapolis meeting in 1919, some SAI members performed "The Conspiracy of Pontiac," written for the occasion by Charles Eastman, with performers also including Carlos Montezuma and Gertrude Bonnin. See Lucy Maddox, *Citizen Indians: Native American Intellectuals, Race and Reform* (Ithaca, NY: Cornell University Press, 2005), 51.

4. Sherman Coolidge, "The Function of the Society of American Indians," *Quarterly Journal* 2, no. 3 (July–September 1914): 186–90, quote on 186.

5. Robert Warrior quotes an article from the Columbus press in "The SAI and the End(s) of History," *American Indian Quarterly* 37, no. 3 (Summer 2013): 219–35, quote on 224. Unless otherwise noted, all quotations from Laura Cornelius Kellogg's work come from Kristina Ackley and Cristina Stanciu, eds., *Laura Cornelius Kellogg: "Our Democracy and the American Indian" and Other Works* (Syracuse, NY: Syracuse University Press, 2015). This quote appears on page 8.

6. On the pageantry craze at the beginning of the twentieth century, see David Glassberg, *American Historical Pageantry: The Uses of Tradition in the Early Twentieth Century* (Chapel Hill: University of North Carolina Press, 1990). Jeffrey Mirel defines "patriotic pluralism" in the context of the Americanization of immigrants during the same period. Acknowledging the unequal power

relations between new immigrant groups and the American government, he shows how new immigrant communities tried "balancing a deep commitment to the US with an unequally strong desire to maintain crucial aspects of their cultural backgrounds and their composite American identity" (Jeffrey Mirel, *Patriotic Pluralism: Americanization Education and European Immigrants* [Cambridge, MA: Harvard University Press, 2010], 11).

7. The joint issue of *AIQ* and *SAIL* from the summer of 2013 is a step forward in combining both historians' and literary historians' work recovering the legacy of the SAI one hundred years later. Hazel Hertzberg's *The Search for an American Indian Identity* (Syracuse, NY: Syracuse University Press, 1971) remains the main study in the field, and studies of individual SAI members and Native intellectuals complement this research (Peter Iverson's work on Carlos Montezuma, Joy Porter's study of Arthur C. Parker, P. Jane Hafen's and Julianne Newmark's work on Gertrude Bonnin, David Martinez's study of Charles Eastman, and Kristina Ackley and Cristina Stanciu's work on Laura Cornelius Kellogg).

8. Laurence Hauptman, quoted in Joy Porter, *To Be Indian: The Life of Iroquois-Seneca Arthur Caswell Parker* (Norman: University of Oklahoma Press, 2001), 127.

9. Clinton Rickard, *Fighting Tuscarora: The Autobiography of Chief Clint Rickard* (Syracuse, NY: Syracuse University Press, 1973), 53, emphasis added.

10. K. Tsianina Lomawaima, "The Mutuality of Citizenship and Sovereignty: The Society of American Indians and the Battle to Inherit America," *American Indian Quarterly* 37, no. 3 (Summer 2013): 331–51.

11. In a letter to Carlos Montezuma, Jane Gordon amplified this claim: "Give citizenship to all Indians with equal rights (to go into the courts) with any other race or people here in the United States" (April 26, 1921, box 1, folder 65, Edward E. Ayer Collection, Carlos Montezuma Papers, Newberry Library, Chicago).

12. The SAI limited membership to people with at least one-sixteenth "Indian blood," a problematic use of the blood quantum concept but a necessary measure, in the organization's view at the time, in an attempt to preserve an all-Indian membership. The SAI was not the first attempt at a national Native political organization; preceding it by a few years was the National Indian Republican Association, organized by Carlisle graduate Luzena Choteau in 1904.

13. Hertzberg, *The Search*; Robert Warrior, "The SAI and the End(s) of History," *American Indian Quarterly* 37, no. 3 (Summer 2013): 219–35; Lucy Maddox, *Citizen Indians: Native American Intellectuals, Race and Reform* (Ithaca, NY: Cornell University Press, 2005); Lomawaima, "The Mutuality"; David Martinez, *The American Indian Intellectual Tradition: An Anthology of Writings from 1772 to 1972* (Ithaca, NY: Cornell University Press, 2011); Kevin Bruyneel, *The Third Space of Sovereignty: The Postcolonial Politics of U.S.-Indigenous Relations* (Minneapolis: University of Minnesota Press, 2007); Kiara M. Vigil, *Indigenous Intellectuals: Sovereignty, Citizenship, and the American Imagination, 1880–1930* (London: Cambridge University Press, 2015).

14. Lomawaima, "The Mutuality," 338, 335.

15. Other prominent members of the General Committee of the SAI included Hiram Chase, William Holmes, Marie Baldwin, Frank Wright, Howard E. Gansworth, Dennison Wheelock, J. E. Shields, Emma J. Goulette, and Rosa B. LaFlesche. The annual conferences were held as follows: the first conference, Ohio State University, Columbus, October 12—15, 1911; the second, also at Ohio State, October 2—6, 1912; the third in Denver, Colorado, October 14—20, 1913; the fourth at the University of Wisconsin, Madison, October 6—11, 1914; the fifth at the University of Kansas, Lawrence, September 28—October 6, 1915; the sixth at Coe College, Cedar Rapids, Iowa, September 26—October 1, 1916; the seventh was cancelled (it would have taken place at the University of Oklahoma, Norman, October 9—13, 1917); the eighth, in Pierre, South Dakota, September 25—28, 1918; the ninth, in Minneapolis, October 2—4, 1919; the tenth, in St. Louis, Missouri, November 15—19, 1920; the eleventh in Detroit, October 25—29, 1921; the twelfth in Kansas City, Missouri, October 17—20, 1922; and the thirteenth, also the last one, in Chicago, September 27—30, 1923.

16. The SAI president, Thomas Sloan, read these objectives. See "Proceedings of the Second Annual Conference, Held at Columbus, Ohio, October 2—7, 1912, at Ohio State University," *Quarterly Journal* 1, no. 2 (April—June 1913): 115—255.

17. Tom Holm, *The Great Confusion in Indian Affairs: Native Americans and Whites in the Progressive Era* (Austin: University of Texas Press, 2005), 53—56. Hertzberg's study of the SAI remains the most comprehensive to date. See *The Search*, esp. 59—193.

18. "Editorial Comment," *American Indian Magazine* 4, no. 2 (April—June 1916): 107.

19. Ibid., 110.

20. Michelle W. Patterson, "Real Indian Songs: The Society of American Indians and the Use of Native American Culture as a Means of Reform," *American Indian Quarterly* 26, no. 1 (Winter 2002): 44—66, 45.

21. On Native and colonial nineteenth-century participation in the colonial process, with consequences for contemporary Indigenous communities, see Paige Raibmon, *Authentic Indians: Episodes of Encounter from the Late-Nineteenth-Century Northwest Coast* (Durham, NC: Duke University Press, 2005).

22. "The Indian in Caricature," *Quarterly Journal* 1, no. 1 (January—April 1913): 84—87. The drawing of *The Progressive Indian American* with its accompanying commentary is on page 87.

23. Daniel F. Littlefield Jr. and James W. Parins, *American Indian and Alaska Native Newspapers and Periodicals, 1826—1924* (Westport, CT: Greenwood, 1984), ix.

24. "Editorial Comment," *Quarterly Journal* 1, no. 1 (January—April 1913): 1. On the political work of Native intellectuals in the nineteenth century, see Maureen Konkle, *Writing Indian Nations: Native Intellectuals and the Politics of Historiography, 1827—1863* (Chapel Hill: University of North Carolina Press, 2004).

25. "Editorial Comment: The New Quarterly Journal," *Quarterly Journal* 1, no. 1 (April 15, 1913): 2.

26. It also declared that it would not publish fiction or historical accounts

"unless there shall be sufficient space" (*Constitution and By-Laws of the Society of American Indians* [Washington, DC: The Society, 1916], 17, Ayer Collection).

27. In 1916 (vol. 4, no. 2), as the journal was changing its title from the *Quarterly Journal* to the *American Indian Magazine,* the following contributing editors were listed: Sherman Coolidge, Henry Roe Cloud, John Milton Oskison, Gertrude Bonnin, Carlos Montezuma, and Dennison Wheelock. The April–June issue (vol. 5, no. 2) listed two more Native women on the editorial board (substituting for Montezuma and Wheelock): Grace Coolidge and Lina K. Brown. After Gertrude Bonnin became general editor, she added two women to the review board and editorial board: Margaret Frazier (Sioux) and Elaine Goodale Eastman (see *American Indian Magazine* 6, no. 4 [Winter 1919]: 1).

28. The subtitle change was introduced in volume 5, number 1 of the *American Indian Magazine* (January–March 1917).

29. The SAI journal started publishing poems in its fourth year after it underwent a change of vision and name (to the *American Indian Magazine* in 1916). The first poem published was Gertrude Simmons Bonnin's "The Indian's Awakening." Later poems included "The Red Man's America," "A Sioux Woman's Love for Her Grandchild," and "The Indian's Awakening" by Bonnin; "The Indian's Salute to His Country" by William J. Kershaw (Menominee); and "Pay Your Freight" by Roland A. Nichols (Potawatomie).

30. Arthur C. Parker also published poems in the SAI journal under pen names. As Gawasa Wanneh, he published the poem "Faith"; as Alnoba Wabunaki, Parker published "My Race Shall Live Anew" and "The Robin's Song." Arthur C. Parker's poems are also collected in Robert Dale Parker's edited anthology, *Changing Is Not Vanishing: A Collection of American Indian Poetry to 1930* (Philadelphia: University of Pennsylvania Press, 2011). Arthur C. Parker's essays in the SAI journal include "The Indian as a Warrior" and "The Red Man's Love of Mother Earth."

31. Gertrude Bonnin to Arthur C. Parker, December 19, 1916, reel 1, SAI Papers.

32. "One Indian Maiden: Her Literary Plans for the Uplifting of Her Race," *New York Tribune,* February 15, 1903, A5.

33. "The North American Indians: A Redskin Princess," quoted in Ackley and Stanciu, *Laura Cornelius Kellogg,* 18, emphasis added.

34. On Laura Cornelius Kellogg's work, both activist and literary, see the introduction to the volume recovering her work for the first time: Cristina Stanciu and Kristina Ackley, "Laura Cornelius Kellogg: Haudenosaunee Thinker, Native Activist, American Writer," in Ackley and Stanciu, *Laura Cornelius Kellogg,* 1–64.

35. Gertrude Bonnin published stories and essays in the *Atlantic Monthly* ("Why I Am a Pagan," 1901) and *Harper's Magazine* ("The Soft-Hearted Sioux," 1901). Her two published volumes are *Old Indian Legends* (1901) and *American Indian Stories* (1921). For a comprehensive list of Native writers before 1924, see Daniel F. Littlefield Jr. and James W. Parins, *A Bibliography of Native American Writers, 1772–1924* (Metuchen, NJ: Scarecrow Press, 1981).

36. Just as Richard H. Pratt had called the first meeting of the SAI "the most momentous event in all Indian history," he declared about the journal: "It rings true from cover to cover" ("The First Number of *The Quarterly Journal*," *Quarterly Journal* 1, no. 2 [April–June 1912]: 101–2). Over the years, the journal would garner national praise. In the late 1910s the *American Indian Magazine* started including international news in rubrics such as "What the Papers Say about Indians" and "Under the Sun: Clippings on World News." See *American Indian Magazine* 7, no. 1 (Spring 1919): 43, 48–50.

37. "A Plain Statement about the Quarterly Journal," *Quarterly Journal* 1, no. 4 (October–December 1913): 341–42.

38. "Send That Dollar Now," *American Indian Magazine* 4, no. 2 (June 1916): 167. "Our correspondence is heavy. Nearly 30,000 letters have been written, dictated, and signed by the Secretary while he has been in Office, not including 49,000 circular letters and about 20,000 announcements. The grand total of our circular printed matter (168) is 69,000." Volume 3 of the *Quarterly Journal* has the highest distribution, at six thousand copies, followed by volumes 1 and 2 at forty-five hundred copies, and the previous numbers of the *American Indian Magazine* (1 and 2) at three thousand. "Our Office Work," *American Indian Magazine* 4, no. 2 (June 1916): 167–68.

39. "With Our Contemporaries," *American Indian Magazine* 4, no. 2 (June 1916): 186.

40. "Dr. Montezuma's Wassaja," *American Indian Magazine* 4, no. 2 (June 1916): 168.

41. Reel 8, SAI Papers.

42. *Quarterly Journal* 1, no. 3 (July–September 1913): 304, emphasis added.

43. According to Maddox, Bonnin had suggested to Parker in 1916 that the SAI journal also publish a leaflet especially for reservation Indians. Parker took Bonnin's advice on some matters, as the *Quarterly Journal* transformed into the *American Indian Magazine*, publishing stories set on reservations, poetry, biographical sketches of less prominent members of the SAI, and notes from reservations. Maddox, *Citizen Indians*, 102, 107.

44. Chauncey Yellow Robe, "Indian Patriotism," *American Indian Magazine* 6, no. 3 (Autumn 1918): 129–30. In the same issue, the text of the Citizenship Bill is reprinted on pages 131–34, and excerpts from the *Congressional Record* are featured on pages 134–40.

45. Thomas Sloan to General Hugh L. Scott, June 25, 1920, reel 9, SAI Papers.

46. Arthur C. Parker, "Editorial Comment: A World Opportunity for the Society," *American Indian Magazine* 4, no. 2 (April–June 1916): 116.

47. The SAI journal had a short life, which is consistent with many of the period's many "little magazines" (*Blast*, one year; the *Crisis*, twelve years; the *Egoist*, five years).

48. Scott R. Lyons, "Rhetorical Sovereignty: What Do American Indians Want from Writing?," *College Composition and Communication* 51, no. 3 (February 2000): 447–68, esp. 450–51.

49. For a comprehensive bibliography of Native American writers of this

period, see Littlefield and Parins, *A Bibliography*; and Daniel F. Littlefield Jr. and James W. Parins, *A Bibliography of Native American Writers, 1772–1924: A Supplement* (Metuchen, NJ: Scarecrow Press, 1985).

50. "Making a White Man out of an Indian Not a Good Plan," *Quarterly Journal* 5, no. 2 (April–June 1917): 85. Kathleen Washburn rightly notes that this declaration was published on the inside cover of the inaugural issue ("New Indians and Indigenous Archives," *PMLA* 127, no. 2 [2012]: 380–84, 381).

51. An editorial note in 1915 urged the readers: "Keep your copies of the *QJ*, they are valuable. Of some issues only a few copies remain in the reserve stock, so that it is increasingly difficult to make up back volumes wanted by university and public libraries. We had difficulty in making up a set for the libraries at Yale and the University of Michigan recently and had to refuse a German library in Berlin. We advise keeping every number clean and in condition for binding" (*Quarterly Journal* 3, no. 3 [September 1915]: 229).

52. *Quarterly Journal* 1, no. 1 (April 15, 1913): 69.

53. See Desmond King, *Making Americans: Immigration, Race, and the Origins of the Diverse Democracy* (Cambridge, MA: Harvard University Press, 2000), esp. 14–24.

54. Lucy Maddox writes about the SAI in the context of the ideology of uplift during the Progressive Era, illuminating especially the differences between the "Indian question" and the "Negro question." See Maddox, *Citizen Indians*, esp. 10–16, 54–88.

55. Kyle T. Mays, "Transnational Progressivism: African Americans, Native Americans, and the Universal Races Congress of 1911," *Studies in American Literature* 25, no. 2 / *American Indian Quarterly* 37, no. 3 (Summer 2013): 243–61.

56. Sherman Coolidge, presidential address, "The Indian American—His Duty to His Race and His Country, the USA," *Quarterly Journal* 1, no. 1 (1913): 20; Fred E. Parker, "The Indian as a Citizen," *Quarterly Journal* 1, no. 1 (1913): 131; Gabe E. Parker, "The Great End: Citizenship," *Quarterly Journal* 2, no. 1 (January–March 1914): 60–63; Carlos Montezuma, "The Reservation Is Fatal to the Development of Good Citizenship," *Quarterly Journal* 2, no. 1 (January–March 1914): 69–74; R. H. Pratt, "Why Most Indians Are Non-citizens," *Quarterly Journal* 2, no. 3 (July–September 1914): 219–23; Arthur C. Parker, "Problems of Race Assimilation in America; with Special Reference to the American Indian," *American Indian Magazine* 4, no. 2 (April–June 1916): 282.

57. Editorial, "The Path to Citizenship," *Quarterly Journal* 3, no. 1 (January–March 1915): 74; Gertrude Bonnin, "A Bill Conferring Citizenship," *Quarterly Journal* 5, no. 3 (July–September 1917): 138.

58. Arthur C. Parker, "The Road to Competent Citizenship," *Quarterly Journal* 2, no. 1 (January–March 1914): 178, 182. Taft is quoted on page 196.

59. *Coe College Cosmos*, October 3, 1916, reel 10, SAI Papers.

60. "Make Them Citizens," reprinted from *Native American* in *the American Indian Magazine* 5, no. 3 (July–September 1917): 206; "A Declaration of Citizenship" and "Citizen Indians," *American Indian Magazine* 6, no. 1 (January–March 1918): 93; "Indian Citizenship Bill," *American Indian Magazine* 6, no. 2 (April–June 1918): 131; "The American Indian as an Equal Citizen," reprinted from the

Christian Science Monitor in the *American Indian Magazine* 7, no. 1 (January–March 1919): 46–47.

61. Charles A. Eastman to SAI Members, January 11, 1919, reel 4, Papers of Carlos Montezuma, M.D., Including the Papers of Maria Keller Montezuma Moore and the Papers of Joseph W. Latimer, nine microfilm reels, Ayer Collection.

62. Hertzberg, *The Search*, 184.

63. Preface to *Report of the Executive Council on the Proceedings of the First Annual Conference of the Society of American Indians* (Washington, DC, 1912), 3–5. The first SAI conference met in Columbus, Ohio, in October 1911. Initially envisioned as the American Indian Association at the preliminary meeting in April 1911, under the coordination of Ohio State University sociology professor and SAI enthusiast Fayette Avery McKenzie, the association adopted a preliminary platform and an executive committee and sent out invitations for the first national conference.

64. Maddox, *Citizen Indians*, 14.

65. Coolidge, presidential address, "The Indian American," 20.

66. Special provisions for aliens of foreign birth to acquire US citizenship were made through the Act of July 19, 1919; Indian men who enlisted to fight in the war (and were not US citizens) were naturalized four months later through the Act of November 6, 1919. See Felix S. Cohen, *Handbook of Federal Indian Law* (Charlottesville: Michie, 1982), 154.

67. The Dawes Allotment Act of 1887 held that Indian allottees would become citizens of the United States and of the state in which they resided if they adopted "the habits of civilized life," for which they received "certificates of citizenship." Other citizenship provisions of the Allotment Act included after 1906 the granting of a patent in fee simple to Indians deemed "competent"; Native children born to citizen parents in the United States were citizens through special acts of Congress; after Indian soldiers served in World War I, a congressional act in 1919 provided that Native soldiers and sailors could become citizens in "courts of competent jurisdiction" (over ten thousand Indian soldiers fought in World War I).

68. David Martinez, *Dakota Philosopher: Charles Eastman and American Indian Thought* (Minneapolis: Minnesota Historical Society Press, 2009), 106.

69. I refer here to the title of Frederick Hoxie's edited collection, *Talking Back to Civilization: Indian Voices of the Progressive Era* (Boston: Bedford / St. Martin's, 2001).

70. Fayette Avery McKenzie, *The Indian and Citizenship* (Washington, DC: The Society of American Indians, 1912), 4, 10.

71. Quoted in Maddox, *Citizen Indians*, 110.

72. Arthur C. Parker to Charles D. Carter, March 12, 1918, reel 1, SAI Papers.

73. Fred'k E. Parker, "The Indian as a Citizen," *Quarterly Journal* 1, no. 2 (April–June 1913): 131–34, quote on 133.

74. Gabe E. Parker, "The Great End: American Citizenship for the Indian," *Quarterly Journal* 2, no. 1 (January–March 1914): 60–63, quote on 60.

75. This talk was later reprinted in the *Quarterly Journal*. See Carlos

Montezuma, "The Reservation—Fatal to the Development of Citizenship," *Quarterly Journal* 2, no. 1 (January—March 1914): 69—73.

76. Hertzberg, *The Search,* 184.

77. R. H. Pratt, "Why Most of Our Indians Are Dependent and Non-citizens," *Quarterly Journal* 2, no. 3 (July—September 1914): 219—23, 223, emphasis in the original.

78. Although this section is limited to the arguments for citizenship in the SAI journal, it is worth mentioning that Charles Eastman published the article "The Indian as Citizen" in *Lippincott's* in 1915, where he engaged with an earlier scheme of citizenship proposed by Fayette McKenzie: tribal ward, allotted ward, citizen ward, and full citizen. Instead, Eastman argued for citizenship and its privileges for Native people without the erasure of Native cultures.

79. *American Indian Magazine* 4, no. 4 (October—December 1916): 326.

80. Lawrence Hauptman, "Governor Theodore Roosevelt and the Indians of New York State," *Proceedings of the American Philosophical Society* 119, no. 1 (February 1975): 1—7, 1. See also Gary Gerstle's assessment of Roosevelt's legacy as "a contradictory man" with an intransigent stand against the "savage Indians" ("Theodore Roosevelt and the Divided Character of American Nationalism," *Journal of American History* 86, no. 3 [December 1999]: 1280—1307, esp. 1280).

81. Arthur C. Parker to Gertrude Bonnin, July 5, 1917, reel 1, SAI Papers.

82. Pratt, "The Indian? No Problem," paper read at the Women's New Century Club, Philadelphia, January 10, 1896, 7. See also Pratt, "Education for Indians," n.d., presented at the Library Company, Philadelphia.

83. Reverend Coolidge made the motion to adopt Pratt at the SAI second meeting, held also in Columbus, Ohio; the motion was seconded by Thomas Sloan. Arthur Parker interjected that "we do not need to adopt Gen. Pratt as an Indian, he is already one—none better" and moved on to the business agenda. See *Quarterly Journal* 1, no. 2 (April—June 1913): 136, 137.

84. *American Indian Magazine* 6, no. 4 (Winter 1919): 160.

85. "Proceedings of the Second Annual Conference," quote on 137—38.

86. Quoted in Russel Lawrence Barsh, "Progressive-Era Bureaucrats and the Unity of Twentieth-Century Indian Policy," *American Indian Quarterly* 15, no. 1 (Winter 1991): 1—17, 6; Robert G. Valentine, "Making Good Indians," *Sunset* 24, no. 6 (1910): 599—611, 611.

87. Fred E. Parker, "The Indian as a Citizen," in "Proceedings of the Second Annual Conference," 138.

88. In the 1930s Commissioner of Indian Affairs John Collier formed the Division of the Civilian Conservation Corps (CCC), which created jobs for Native men. On Collier's strategic use of *Indians at Work* to advance his Indian educational policies, see John J. Laukaitis, "*Indians at Work* and John Collier's Campaign for Progressive Educational Reform, 1933—1945," *American Educational History Journal* 33, no. 2 (2006): 97—105.

89. Her report on "figures" includes the following: "There are altogether 357 government schools; 70 of these reservation boarding schools, 35 non-reservation boarding schools, and 223 day schools. The enrollment in these

schools totals 24,500 children. Besides these, there are 4,300 children in the mission schools and 11,000 in public, of the 11,000, the Five Civilized Tribes of Oklahoma have 6,900. The number of the children of the race in school in the country then is 39,800. The last report shows an increase of nearly 2,000 in attendance over the year before" (quoted in Ackley and Stanciu, *Laura Cornelius Kellogg*, 159).

90. Most SAI members used the term "the Indian" most frequently, but they often referred to "the Indian race" or "the race," as Hertzberg observes. Besides these designations, SAI members and Indian public intellectuals used the phrases "our people" and "the Indian people," with the words "people" and "tribe" being synonymous occasionally. See Hertzberg, *The Search*, 71.

91. Laura Cornelius [Kellogg], "Some Facts and Figures on Indian Education," in Ackley and Stanciu, *Laura Cornelius Kellogg*, 154–66.

92. Ibid., 163.

93. Immigration Act of 1907, section 2, https://www.loc.gov/law/help /statutes-at-large/59th-congress/session-2/c59s2ch1134.pdf, emphasis added.

94. Kraut's term "medicalized nativism" is quoted in Priscilla Wald, "Communicable Americanism: Contagion, Geographic Fictions, and the Sociological Legacy of Robert E. Park," *American Literary History* 14, no. 4 (Winter 2002): 653–85, 654; Alan M. Kraut, *Silent Travelers: Germs, Genes, and the "Immigrant Menace"* (New York: Basic Books, 1994), 4. See also Brenda Child, *Boarding School Seasons: American Indian Families, 1900–1940* (Lincoln: University of Nebraska Press, 1998), 55–58. According to David W. Adams, "By the turn of the 20th century it was clear that the boarding school itself was a major contributor to the spread of disease. . . . By 1910 the campaign to improve Indian health moved into high gear. At a few locations sanatoriums and eye hospitals were built" (*Education for Extinction: American Indians and the Boarding School Experience, 1875–1928* [Lawrence: University Press of Kansas, 1995], 133–34).

95. Arthur C. Parker, "The Editor's Viewpoint: What Makes the Indian a Problem?," *Quarterly Journal* 1, no. 2 (1913): 105.

96. William P. Dillingham, *Reports of the U.S. Immigration Commission, 1907–1910: Abstracts of the Reports of the Immigration Commission*, 2 vols. (Washington, DC: Government Printing Office, 1911), quote from 1:14. See also King, *Making Americans*.

97. The report is from 1876, reprinted on the title page in *The Indian before the Law* by Henry S. Pancoast (1884).

98. Mirel, *Patriotic Pluralism*, 37–44.

99. Arthur C. Parker, "The White Aryan and the Red American," *American Indian Magazine* 4, no. 2 (April–June 1916): 121–26, quotes on 124, 126. See also Joseph P. Widney, *Race Life of the Aryan Peoples*, 2 vols. (New York: Funk & Wagnalls, 1907).

100. Parker, "What Makes the Indian a Problem?," 106, 105, 104.

101. Parker, "Problems of Race Assimilation," 285, 299, 290.

102. Ibid., 303.

103. On the legal construction of race in the United States, see Ian Lopez, *White by Law: The Legal Construction of Race* (New York: NYU Press, 1996).

104. Gertrude Bonnin, "Editorial Comment," *American Indian Magazine* 7, no. 2 (Summer 1919): 63, emphasis added.

105. Parker, "What Makes the Indian a Problem?," 105; Barsh, "Progressive-Era Bureaucrats," 2—3.

106. Bonnin, "Editorial Comment." Toward the end of the editorial, Bonnin reverts to the immigrant analogy: "As they believe in Americanizing the foreigner so should they desire the privileges of American citizenship for the native, the aborigine!" (63).

107. Bonnin, *Americanize the First American*. The cover sheet of the pamphlet included a picture of Bonnin framed by a number of American flags. Papers of Mary Walden, Special Collections, Newberry Library, Chicago.

108. P. Jane Hafen, introduction to *Dreams of Thunder: Stories, Poems, and the Sun Dance Opera by Zitkala-Sa* (Lincoln: University of Nebraska Press, 2001), xxi, xvii.

109. Congress selected "The Star-Spangled Banner" as the national anthem in 1931. On the cultural history of the song, see Robert J. Branham and Stephen J. Hartnett, *Sweet Freedom's Song: "My Country 'Tis of Thee" and Democracy in America* (Oxford: Oxford University Press, 2002), 14—34.

110. W. E. B. Du Bois, "My Country 'Tis of Thee," Poetry Foundation, https://www.poetryfoundation.org/poems/43026/my-country-tis-of-thee.

111. Samuel Francis Smith, "America" / "My Country 'Tis of Thee," first performed on July 4, 1831, in Boston. See https://www.loc.gov/item/ihas.200000012/.

112. Bonnin, "The Red Man's America," *American Indian Magazine* 5, no. 1 (January—March 1917): 64.

113. For accounts of Indian men's participation in World War I, see Thomas A. Britten, *American Indians in World War I: At Home and at War* (Albuquerque: University of New Mexico Press, 1997) and Susan A. Krouse, *North American Indians in the Great War* (Lincoln: University of Nebraska Press, 2007).

With this issue, we introduce a new occasional feature in the journal that opens up space for extended consideration of noteworthy new works. Audra Simpson contributes a close examination of how Susan Hill's prize-winning book (NAISA Best First Book, Canadian Historical Association Aboriginal History Group Book Prize, and Ontario Clio Prize, all 2018) constitutes a field-change intervention in Haudenosaunee and Indigenous studies. Matthew Cohen reviews Lisa Brooks's new book by way of an interview with the author about her groundbreaking methodology.

Jean M. O'Brien and Robert Warrior

AUDRA SIMPSON

Reading for Land: Susan Hill's *The Clay We Are Made Of: Haudenosaunee Land Tenure on the Grand River*

SUSAN HILL'S PRIZE-WINNING BOOK *The Clay We Are Made Of: Haudenosaunee Land Tenure on the Grand River* (2017) offers a comprehensive history of land and governance that is rare in its framing, its focus, and its execution, rendering it one of the most important studies to emerge on Haudenosaunee history to date.[1] In this book Hill documents the relationships that Haudenosaunee had with lands, peoples, and waters in what is now the North American "Northeast." She moves us through the vicissitudes of the Revolutionary War, documenting Haudenosaunee movement up into the northern points of their hunting territory and their relocation and negotiations with Mississaugas at what would become Six Nations of the Grand River. On the way we run into some of the usual protagonists of Six Nations history: Joseph Brant (Thayendenaga), William Johnson, and John A. MacDonald. Brant's sister and Johnson's wife, Molly Brant, appears briefly, and one of the most chronicled Indigenous women in North America, Pauline Johnson, notably does *not* make an appearance. These are not ellipses or oversights, as Hill's approach is far from hagiographic; thus, there are very different players in this story. The central concern or protagonist is not a person or an event but a set of ethics. The ethics of *land* are the central protagonists in this study, and this makes for a very different kind of history than we have been taught about Six Nations.[2]

These ethics of land speak through the archives that Hill works with: speeches and letters, council minutes, Indian agent correspondence, and arguments and negotiations. Through Hill's readings we see the process of treaty, of deliberation and decision making regarding property and inheritance in colonial contexts laid bare for us, and it is the burning question—the question of the contradiction between ethics and practice in the teeth of settler-colonial constraint and imperative—that orients her analysis. She asks specifically of this material, "If our relationship to the earth and to land is central why would we negotiate land sharing deals, treaties and, leases and direct sales?" (4). These negotiations over land are in seeming *contradiction* to Haudenosaunee philosophy and belief. We see how chiefs, clan mothers, and councils tried to *maintain* land and territory through policy, land tenure practice, and inheritance decisions in the face of rapid and unrelenting attempts to divest them of land and (annuity) money. Gone is the emphasis on militarism, decline and defeat, and then cultural salvage that has marked much of the literature on the Iroquois. Not only is this a sort of story different from the one we have been told, but this is also a model study of how to read archives for Indigenous history, theory, and principle.

Hill offers a robust account of the Haudenosaunee eighteenth-century alliance with the British, a relationship based on mutual recognition, on equality. This alliance with the British, however, extends the principles of the earlier seventeenth-century Kaswentha ("Two Row Wampum") Treaty between the Dutch and the Haudenosaunee and transposes it onto relations with the British. But eighteenth-century Haudenosaunee not only treated with British, they maintained their relationships to others in the Confederacy and those in the shadow of the Confederacy. As such, they brought with them protectorate nations like the Nanticokes and Tutelos when they moved to what is now Ontario, but they also brought with them their obligations to people and land. Hill demonstrates how these obligations and relationships with other political orders were (and still are) *animated by their own* stories and understandings of land and cultural history (2). *The Clay We Are Made Of* moves through two hundred years of those relationships to others, to land as well as the decisions based on their governing principles and governance structure of fifty chiefs and clan mothers. We see two important thematics emerge: Haudenosaunee trying to keep land, settler regimes trying to take it, to allot it, to use it, to profit from it. But these two thematics are colored with gray areas, with confounding moments of imperfect decisions and sometimes contradiction.

The goal always was and perhaps still is maintaining land and perpetuating the knowledge systems that will allow for this. We learn about this philosophical and governmental commitment from the groundbreaking history dissertation of Deborah Doxtator (1996), as well as recent Six Nations literature.[3] For example, in *In Divided Unity: Haudenosaunee Reclamation at Grand River* (2016), Theresa McCarthy documents the reclamation efforts of Haudenosaunee of the near-contemporary aftermath of all that Hill documents, of misinterpretations of the Haldimand Tract of 1784 in the 2000s, and the legacy of striving not only for correct interpretation of treaty and land grant arrangements but the commitment as well to "collective land ownership" (210) that Hill documents throughout the past two hundred years. As well we see in Rick Monture's literary history, *We Share Our Matters: Two Centuries of Writing and Resistance at Six Nations of the Grand River* (2015), the commitment to land and to this philosophical and political system of governance and political conduct and reasoning supports the maintenance of Haudenosaunee governance and justice. To this end Hill not only assembles evidence for her readers but also performs what some might view as an Indigenous and specifically Haudenosaunee hermeneutics as she reads these documents, much in the way that we would understand subaltern reading practices, or queer reading practices, "red viewing" practices as exposited by Michelle Herman Raheja (2011), where we read or look for the other story, in this case for the agency of this animating belief and commitment to land even in the clutches of colonial imperative and design. Gone then is the version of Six Nations history as literal Loyalists to the British Crown who broke the Confederacy in their forced geographic removal of sorts to what is now Ontario after the Revolutionary War—enter over two hundred years of the microphysics of maintaining and caring for land in people in the eyes of several storms.

Six Nations as a reserve is narrated first as Six Nations as a people. This earlier group of Haudenosaunee, the ascendants of the present Six Nations reserve, were the Haudenosaunee of the eighteenth, nineteenth, and twentieth centuries. This history documents their endurance through tremendous "land grabs" in the eighteenth-century Mohawk Valley, as well as the sustained and legalized infractions on land when they moved to what was then Upper Canada in the form of white squatters, wrongful annuity allocations, land cessions, and consolidations. Hill documents the ways in which these different forms of "grab" on land and violations of land were contrived and also were resisted. She offers detailed accounts of the colonial machinations and characters behind these moves to take land (and money) away from Six Nations once they were on a reserve and the short- and long-term consequences for decision making within the community, upon governance, and later in the courts. So, for example, even where there was a provincial imperative to privatize or allot land at Six Nations in the 1840s, they continued to hold land communally. But even when supposedly succumbing to pressure to allot land, they did so regardless of gender or age, so that *everyone* was given land, not just heads of households (174). There are gendered valences of this decision that will not be lost on scholars of American allotment history and the allocation land in the Dawes Act (1887) to "heads of households" (men and widowed women). Six Nations title holders—those whose responsibilities were translated as "chiefs"— would not in cases of property disputes divide land further if they surmised that the land would not go to their children, even in the cases of "mixed" marriages. Their concern was always that children, whether or not they were clan holders, maintain land. Hill's documentation goes from the grand scale of the nation and negotiations and insistent pushing on matters of justice to the smaller unit of governmental decision making.

In the process of narrating this land-based history of who and what is now Six Nations of the Grand River, Hill also offers us several crucial and yet subtle revisions to the way Six Nations history has been told. One is the now staid and presumed disconnection of Six Nations from land ethics and into the ambit of failure—even where land, water, and sky are central to every ceremony, every opening that Haudenosaunee do. It is as if these discursive and philosophical orientations are not manifest in political life after the Revolution, or in the case of so-called mission Indians like those from Kahnawà:ke, not a matter of culture or political decision making at all. Hill intervenes in the anthropologization and fetishization of Iroquois culture through this meticulous attention to the archives (colonial archives even!), as well as the Haudenosaunee hermeneutic that she brings to those documents. As with McCarthy (2016), Simpson (2014), Parmenter (2010), and Jordan (2008), this book documents vigorously against the "declension" narrative that has been central to the paradigm of Iroquois studies since Morgan (1851). With this central premise, Haudenosaunee are imagined as "slums in the forest," failures of a sort at culture, at politics, readied for white civilization (and citizenship) when moved out of military significance. Hill's second intervention is to read gender in a language-based and revisionary way. Here the book intervenes (see chapter 2) against the tired axioms of "mothers of the nation," which suggests not only matrilineal descent but superiority of women. Hill offers a concise history of ideas governing this fixation in part of the literature (back to Lafitau) but uses language to demonstrate not only the equality of men and women but the role of women not as property owners but as property givers in *relation* to others. Hill nuances this role and responsibility as "carriers" (60). The book then offers one of the most robust accounts of women as faith keepers and mediators to date (see all of chapter 2). Third, *The Clay We Are Made Of* offers a very close examination of Joseph Brant and his various roles in Confederacy politics. Hill does a very careful and exhaustive job of exploring his role (not abstracted at all out of context) in several land dealings in an even-handed way (chapter 3). Joseph Brant has long been controversial within the broader Confederacy and within Six Nations. He was responsible in part for encouraging the aforementioned Haldimand Proclamation of 1784 that "granted" Six Nations their land in what is now Ontario as "faithful allies to the British." But he is also known as "the man that split the Confederacy" in other communities, and a supposed "pine tree chief," or appointed negotiator on behalf of the Confederacy, because of his skill in dealing with white matters. With her eye trained on the archives Hill offers a very nuanced account of Brant *not* as a pine tree chief. The documents suggest he may appear to be a spokesman for the Confederacy, "but there is no evidence that he was given that authority" (158). Hill demonstrates the moves he made not only to guarantee land for Haudenosaunee people but especially so for himself and his family (160), the ways in which he was also overstepping what authority he was given by the Confederacy chiefs. Hill compares what he was, for example, *authorized* to sell and what he did sell in 1796, a difference of 14 percent more than he was authorized to let go of (161). By 1801 he had been released of his spokesman duties and replaced with twelve *royaner* (title holders or chiefs) to negotiate for Six Nations. This attention to detail connects the dots for Haudenosaunee of the eighteenth century and moves Six Nations back to the land and its losses and gains. We have here the macro- and microphysics of how lands were not only granted to Six Nations in conversation and collaboration with Mississaugas but then were consolidated and then leased and alienated through sale to other Indians but also to whites, to failing "enterprises," with effects that continue well into to the present (McCarthy 2016). Hill's stark annexing of census data and a two-page itinerary of claims filed with the specific claims branch of Indian Affairs (with acreage noted) is a stark representation of what this looks like in other terms and into the present day.

One can only hope that a study of this detail and care will not only revise the way that we understand Six Nations of the Grand River but also prompt others to take up courses of historical inquiry that take not only documentary cues but also analytical and hermeneutical cues from this work. What will it mean to take the ethics of land or water or animals to be the central protagonist in a study of governance through time among other Indigenous or subaltern peoples? What will it mean to use philosophical and political traditions—"creation stories"—to guide our analysis and our reading of the archives? One can see a clear flight line again for more work on gender. The chapter on women and the Confederacy introduces thematics that are remarked upon continuously by outsiders doing work on this community and taken up in different ways by Monture and McCarthy. We are starting to see a very robust, interlocking account of literary and governance history, of the hermeneutics of individual lives in political and material contexts. Both Rick Monture's and Mishuana Goeman's (2013) work with Pauline Johnson's writing and Monture's work on her life and history at Grand River are examples of these deeper accounts of intellectual and political lives of Six Nations people. McCarthy's (2016) ethnography of the reclamation site in Caledonia is in some ways an ethnography of and with women, although not objectified as such, as her concern too was land.

Hill's work also readies us for a study of settler-colonial, specifically "Indian affairs," type accounting practices—of the forensics of colonial dispossession. Here one can imagine studies of land grabs at the level of financial "appropriations," of transfers, of nonconsensual, shoddy investments, and all that communities and people did (and still do) to manage, to minimize the damage, or to resist these practices full stop. More specifically, the misappropriation of Six Nations funds comes up again and again in this study, with Six Nations *royaner* resisting and petitioning again and again the movements of their monies. One can imagine after Hill a robust and close forensic analysis of their annuities and what happened to them—what, for example, the nonconsensual investment in the Grand River Navigation Company (GRNC) meant for their finances, but also where that money went beyond GRNC. Annuities from Six Nations were transferred in the mid-nineteenth century to a then-gasping McGill University to keep it afloat. That money was never returned to Six Nations.[4] In an American story on the life of money, we see that profits from armaments used in the Indian Wars made for the largesse of families that endowed Ivy League universities like Columbia University (Ramage 2017). These financial circuits and the interconnected profits and losses they engendered for land, for lives would add to our understanding of social inequality and wealth today. Hill's meticulous, philosophically grounded, and crucial study not only revises the way we understand the Haudenosaunee past, it lays the groundwork for just that kind of work, and so much more.

AUDRA SIMPSON is a Kahnawake Mohawk and professor of anthropology at Columbia University.

Notes

1. Winner of the 2018 Best First Book in Native American and Indigenous Studies from the Native American and Indigenous Studies Association, the Aboriginal History Group Book Prize from the Canadian Historical Association, and the Ontario Clio Prize from the Canadian Historical Association. The book was also nominated for the Sir John A. MacDonald Prize (recently renamed the CHA Prize for Best Scholarly Book in Canadian History) from the Canadian Historical Association in 2018.

2. Hill's is a history of Six Nations of the Grand River, now a legally demarcated space of a reserve or reservation made up of Canada's largest (reserve) population of Indians (25,660 on their band list or "roll," with 12,271 living on reserve). Six Nations of the Grand River are made up of Six Nations (Tuscarora, Seneca, Cayuga, Onondaga, Oneida, Mohawk) understood as Haudenosaunee (People of the Longhouse), who were known most commonly in ethnographic literature as the Iroquois. At Six Nations of the Grand River there are also protectorate nations that came under the Great Tree of Peace and joined these Haudenosaunee in their journey north. Although Hill's study is focused on the life of Six Nations of the Grand River, the story of this "reserve" community is historically rooted in a broader matrix of Haudenosaunee history and as Indigenous people in a settler society. As such, the work speaks to the historical and political experiences of Indigenous people beyond the boundaries of their reserve. In this brief review essay I speak of the Haudenosaunee with these four designations: Six Nations of the Grand River, Six Nations, Haudenosaunee, Iroquois to mark their different designations through time, but also in the terms with which they are known by others and to themselves. For recent population data on Six Nations of the Grand River, see http://www.sixnations .ca/CommunityProfile.htm.

3. The Tyendinaga historian Deborah Doxtator passed on before her dissertation could be worked into a book.

4. This money was taken from the Six Nations Trust Fund by what was then the Executive Council of the Crown of the Province of Canada in 1860. According to one account, in *The Two Row Times*, in 1881 McGill paid back the loan to the borrowers, but the borrowers never returned the funds to Six Nations. See https://tworowtimes.com/historical/six-nations-funded-colleges -universities-never-repaid/ for an account. According to this piece by the Aboriginal Peoples Television Network reporter Tom Fennario there is no evidence of the payment: http://aptnnews.ca/2015/11/19/first-nation-claims -unpaid-loan-to-mcgill-university-in-1860-now-worth-1−7b/.

Works Cited

Doxtator, Deborah. 1996. "What Happened to the Iroquois Clans? A Study of Clans in Three Nineteenth Century Rotinonhsyonni Communities." Ph.D. diss., University of Western Ontario.

Goeman, Mishuana. 2013. *Mark My Words: Native American Women Writing Our Nations*. Minneapolis: University of Minnesota Press.

Hill, Susan. 2017. *The Clay We Are Made Of: Haudenosaunee Land Tenure on the Grand River*. Winnipeg: University of Manitoba Press.

Jordan, Kurt. 2008. *The Seneca Restoration, 1715–1754: An Iroquois Local Political Economy*. Gainesville: University of Florida Press.

McCarthy, Theresa. 2016. *In Divided Unity: Haudenosaunee Reclamation at Grand River*. Tucson: University of Arizona Press.

Monture, Rick. 2015. *We Share Our Matters: Two Centuries of Writing and Resistance at Six Nations of the Grand River*. Winnipeg: University of Manitoba Press.

Parmenter, Jon. 2010. *At the Edge of the Woods: Iroquoia, 1534–1701*. East Lansing: Michigan State University Press.

Raheja, Michelle H. 2011. *Reservation Realism: Redfacing, Visual Sovereignty, and Representations of Native Americans in Film*. Lincoln: University of Nebraska Press.

Ramage, Noah. 2017. "In the Arms of a Settler: Marcellus Hartley's Market for Genocide." Undergraduate thesis, Columbia University.

Simpson, Audra. 2014. *Mohawk Interruptus: Political Life across the Borders of Settler States*. Durham, NC: Duke University Press.

MATT COHEN

A Conversation with Lisa Brooks
about *Our Beloved Kin*

MATT COHEN: Thank you very much for being willing to do this. I'm going to just appreciate for a moment, because this is a beautiful and disturbing book that obviously took a lot of heart, energy, persistence, patience, and time to write. But it's also a personal joy for me to talk with you because, like so many other people, I have learned so much from your work, and from your way of being in this profession, if I can put it that way. I'm grateful to you.

Your first book, *The Common Pot,* was hugely provocative for lots of us in its gesture of simultaneously recovering the centrality of writing and literacy to Indigenous resistance in the Northeast and modeling a new approach to literary history. *Our Beloved Kin,* I feel, continues its strong thread of regarding, paying respect to, and telling stories about the landscape of the Northeast. It alters the metaphorical landscape of our imaginative and, I think a lot of people would say, sacred connection to the past.

Now, this new book is, on the one hand, a new history of King Philip's War: it uncovers new information about the motives of the settlers; the motives of Natives and Native communities leading up to the war; new understandings of the action, the scope, the impact, the duration of the war. It also offers an unprecedented picture of Indigenous experience of the war. I mean unprecedented in the sense of scope, but also its willingness to follow people down difficult and what seem like contradictory paths.

LISA BROOKS: That's such a great way of putting it. You're describing a lot of my experience while writing it.

MC: There's also an underlying argument about how the historiography of the war from the 1670s until now has itself been colonialist, with a few important exceptions. This is even the case when the historian has every intention of doing justice to Native people, then and now, affected by the conflict. But it still happens, and it has something to do with the storytelling. The other thing I find amazing is that the book—because it takes its stance as an act of remembering and of decolonizing a major story about American history—is itself a diplomatic event.

LB: That is so true.

MC: So maybe I should start by asking, what are, at the broadest level, the revisions of the war or of the telling of the war you wanted readers to come away with or to confront? And then, how did this other way of telling and this other kind of gesture of the book as linking people today come together?

LB: That's a great question, and a big question, and it's amazing to hear you talk about it in this way, because I feel like at this point, even though I'm a short remove from the writing process, I had a similar experience of being taught by it. I was learning from the process of researching and writing it and teaching various aspects of that and not just seeing things through my own lenses, but also so many other people's lenses through that process; I learned so much from it. And it's like it has its own life, really.

So I think the questions that you're asking speak to the process, as well as the final product that it became. I've said this at several talks already: I didn't set out to write a book on King Philip's War. That wasn't my goal. And it's not actually a goal I would recommend to anybody, right? [Laughs.] It's not something I would say: "Hey, you know what you really need to do is write a book about King Philip's War." It's been written about so much, but also it's a traumatic violence to live with for a number of years, even if going back through the history is nothing compared to what it was like for the people who lived through it.

So often people have tried to rein in the war and make it more orderly. I think what I did from the very beginning is surrender to the chaos of it. That's what I saw everywhere, even as I just started to begin to untangle some of the threads related to the main figures that I was tracking, like [Wampanoag saunkskwa] Weetamoo and James Printer, and things that came up from looking more deeply into Mary Rowlandson's narrative. The chaos was so evident everywhere, and the fractures of kinship networks and networks of communication and alliance. Like the networks you write about in your book; this war is so much about the tearing apart of networks and the attempt to try to rebuild networks in the midst of all this chaos.[1]

I think researching it was one thing, because I could get into the nitty gritty, trying to reconstruct some of these strands and how they connected to each other. But I think the writing was an entirely different process, because sometimes that became about trying not to capture or contain but to express the chaos of the war. Initially I was really interested in the recovery of James Printer's story; that was one of the first motivations. I was really interested in the role of Native women leaders throughout the Northeast and the way that their stories become sublimated in both the history of the war and these larger pictures of New England history and American literature.

But also I was just struck by how often when we teach Mary Rowlandson's narrative—whether it's students or fellow professors—the immediate turn is to Rowlandson and her plight. And there are these remarkable and significant Native people that she's traveling with, as well as Native places that she travels through, that we're kind of blending together into this sense of an "Indian wilderness." Of course, her narrative does that work, but the way that it's been read over centuries also does that work. So it became really important for me to be able to offer something that would allow readers of all kinds to be able to name and place those Native people and those Native spaces.

MC: I've found your renarrativization of the part of the war covered by Rowlandson's narrative extraordinary and challenging in a lot of ways. Let me follow up on something you mentioned. It sounds like this sort of more *emerged* as a project than *began*, per se. Could you say a little more about the process of researching and writing this book? Stylistically—I mean, there's a poem in here, one that's devastating but also shows a difficult moment in which the kinds of choices that Weetamoo has to make seem only expressible in a form that defies the linearity and causality not just of history telling in the Western sense but of storytelling itself.

LB: Absolutely. That poem was certainly something that emerged, right? It definitely wasn't anything I planned. I didn't say, "Yeah, I'm going to write this historical book and then I'm going to suddenly put a poem in." [Laughs.]

But I remember very distinctly, I was in the midst of either writing or revising that whole section and having a conversation with Christine DeLucia, who wrote *Memory Lands,* which is focused on the memory of the war and the places of memory of the war and also has a long temporal trajectory, up to the contemporary moment now. She was doing a lot more research on the Great Swamp Massacre, which is the moment in the book when that poem emerges, thinking about Weetamoo's experience in the massacre. And I remember having this conversation with her about the importance of *not* writing about things—of the silences, of the things that you choose not to write about in detail or maybe sometimes not even to write about at all.

There were whole sections that could have been written and that I scrapped because it's things you needed to understand but you don't necessarily need to put out there into the world as a public document. I knew that I had to deal with Great Swamp just because Weetamoo was so involved in it. And there was an outline of the book that lasted for a long time, that was going to follow Mary Rowlandson's narrative and go chapter through chapter of her removes, then extend out from the removes. But Weetamoo and James Printer's stories and the research on their networks really took over the book, as you can see, right? The longest chapter is on Weetamoo and it's before the war! It changed because of finding things like that: that the desire to capture Weetamoo, her relatives, but also her land was a major motivation for an event in the war that almost all historians of the war write about—and yet they rarely mention her.

There were a lot of moments like that, where things appeared in the documents that made it seem obvious that there had been stories that were left out. But then there's the question of how to tell those stories, and I didn't want to reconstruct the Great Swamp Massacre. I knew that. I didn't want to belabor the numbers of people. Some historians go with the numbers because there are so many English documents that focus on how many people were killed. Christine writes beautifully about that, thinking about the obsession with numbers and what that's about. There was a lot that I didn't want to write about and that I didn't feel it was appropriate for me to write about, but I also had to somehow capture what it meant to be a mother and a leader trying to enable other people to survive something that seems unsurvivable.

And the medium that ended up making me able to do that was poetry. I don't ever want to think about whether it's a good poem or anything like that [laughs], but it enabled me to try to capture what I imagined to be that experience and what I could glean from the documents I had, as well as other accountings of what it is like to experience something that traumatic—not just for you as an embodied person but for all of the people around you.

MC: That is really compelling. It struck me as another of the strengths of the book, though, that you don't ever really let the reader rest in a certain kind of sympathy, if that makes sense. How did you imagine an attitude toward the people or the events that would allow you not to do that? Not to repeat the historian's error, but with sympathy on the other side? Or even outside either of these, since the other danger is to say, "Oh no, I'm above the fray and I'm not invested in any of these people, so I'm just going to call it like I see it in the documents."

LB: Right. That's such a great question and I've seriously thought about the "how" of that. I mean, I was always feeling that empathy was an important piece of this. It really started when I was at Harvard, and we did this major symposium that was focused on the legacy of the Harvard Indian College.

I was not an organizer of it; I had just recently arrived there. There were phenomenal people organizing it, and my main job was to talk about James Printer, the Harvard Indian College, and that history.

The empathy that I felt for him and his brothers and the different ways that they were pulled apart and pulled into a war that none of them wanted—that was a story that really pulled me in, and it pulled me in because of its complexity. It wasn't a story that was easily captured in a simplistic framework. You had to sit with the complexity. You had to sit with the difficulty of living during this time and all the things that they had to grapple with. Empathy was really important because, for me, for this story, the opposite of empathy would have been judgment, right? To sit where we are now and look at some of the people like James Printer and his family, it would be easy to sit in judgment of them, you know? But I think that would be the wrong approach. When you're dealing with something like the epidemics or this war—the distance thing wasn't something that I could do. I think it also meant I felt really responsible not just to the people who I was writing about but the descendant community.

When the symposium happened, the descendants of James Printer were there; the descendants of the Wampanoag students who'd gone to the Indian College; the descendants of other people who had been impacted by the war. They were all there, and they were there throughout the time I was writing this, thinking about responsibility to them and trying to hold myself, whether I achieved it or not, to a high level of integrity, because these people suffered a great deal but also adapted, many of them adapted and survived. I didn't want to disrespect them by writing something that would somehow create a sentimental narrative, and I didn't want to make up stuff that wouldn't be true.

It was really a challenge. I think some of it was just a matter of really listening as best I could to the people—to the ways that I could listen to the people I was writing about, but also the people who are descendants of those people. Sometimes that empathy also had to extend to some of the characters involved that were people that I wouldn't automatically identify with. That was an important move, too, and for me even getting into some of the colonial kinship networks, as I know you are well aware of. And it's why it takes so long to write a book like this, because you can't anticipate the connections you're going to see. Once you start teasing out those relationships and connections, you have to follow them—at least, I feel like I have to follow them—because you can't just cut them off and say, "Well, we'll look at that another day." I think that leads to a whole different understanding.

MC: Let me ask you this, then. This book is directed at historians, and it certainly is also making this gesture across groups of people whose inheritance of kinship and a shared experience has partly been shaped by this war and writing about it. But I also feel like there's a way this book is speaking to Native American studies folks more broadly. Could you say a little bit about that and what kinds of reading you're encouraging that might speak to the ways folks are trying to think about, write about, argue about the Indigenous past?

LB: Wow, that's a big question. I don't think this book, for me, would have happened without the incredible twenty-first-century network of Indigenous studies. I feel like, more than speaking to Indigenous studies, it emerges from them, that the work has been enabled by this incredible group of people coming together and validating each other's work—and also validating approaches that are not just interdisciplinary but discipline-challenging. I don't feel like a lot of us necessarily set out to challenge these particular disciplines. It's just that doing things differently, sometimes even perceiving things differently, you're going to challenge, to have integrity about saying, "No, I'm not going to change that in order to fit a certain box." I think that's common in Indigenous studies, and I think that's why Indigenous studies has become kind of a home for so many people who see things differently and want to see things and do things differently.

And so I feel mostly that I hope that this, then, can become another kind of block on which people who are coming up in the field: people who are undergraduate students, or graduate students, or junior scholars, or people who are my peers who are just trying to do something similar, that this could be another shoring up of that kind of work in the same way that I've felt shored up by so many, so many people. And also for those people who are working outside academia, working on these histories in tribal communities and in other community-based projects, that it can be that for them likewise. I feel like it's coming up from within that network and hopefully can help to shore up that network as well.

MC: I really like that, that feeling that you described of not a self-conscious interdisciplinariness but a kind of space responding to the way disciplines attach to certain kinds of storytelling and do not produce the story you need, do not produce the story that is needed. That's what I felt all along: this double gesture of acknowledging uncertainty, on the one hand, and then saying, "You know what, this book can nonetheless be an occasion for bringing together people and the acknowledgment of and the creation of new networks today."

LB: Yeah, and I think that to me has been the remarkable thing about watching the book make its way into the world, is seeing those networks emerge from the discussions about it. And it's been so good to see people then talking with each other—whatever it is they're taking out of the book, whichever piece of it or overarching idea they're taking out of it—the ability to generate discussions around places and history and kinship and responsibilities. I wouldn't take any credit for that, but it's been pretty incredible to be able to participate in that, and it's been regenerative in a way to see that happening.

Yeah, and I like what you're saying; I do feel that one of the things that I'm always trying to do in my work is to center different places and also to decentralize some of the spaces, events, and themes that have been centered previously. This war really was a colonial attempt to insert a center, right? And the resistance against that kind of centering and containment is all over the documents.

I think what's ironic is that it's that very desire for control, it's that very desire for containment, that actually creates the chaos and the violence. That is what *creates* it. And that's a vitally important realization for us to contemplate today as we see movements toward centralization and toward containment and control affecting so many of our lives and so many people's lives around us. Understanding how core that is to the nation-state and understanding that those structures, in the time period we're talking about, those colonial structures were not yet set. Settlers were still attempting to create them.

MC: Now I don't want to take up too much of your time. But I want to say that what this conversation has shown me that I was not seeing before is the degree to which shifting that desire that you talked about, that is really at the core. It is the desire that, ultimately running against its circumstance, can produce violence so often. Changing that desire, shifting the direction of desire is one of the things storytelling does. This book tackles that problem at the heart of storytelling; it is suggesting that as historians we have this power, as literary scholars we have this power, not just to tell the new story but to shift desire, and I like thinking about it that way.

LB: Yeah, that's fantastic. And I'm just reminded of, I'm not going to quote her well, but I remember my sister and me having a long conversation about Joy Harjo's poetry and saying that desire is the most powerful force in the universe. And that's not something you can contain; I think storytelling—same thing. I'm thinking of Thomas King's statement that "the truth about stories is, that's all we are." So then it's about understanding the power of storytelling, not turning away from it. I think we have an impulse—it's one of those things that I think is true among human beings—we have an impulse for telling stories. Isn't it ironic that in academia and even sometimes in English departments, where we value storytelling and literature so much, that in our scholarship we would be asked to turn away from that power? I think you're right, and that's so at the core of what I think a lot of us are trying to do in Indigenous studies.

MC: Absolutely. Well, thank you, Lisa. I am so grateful, once again, and I'm really looking forward to our next conversation.

LB: This has been so great, to hear about how you're thinking about the book. It means so much to me to hear you articulate this and also just to be able to have this exchange back and forth.

Notes

Our Beloved Kin: A New History of King Philip's War (Cambridge, MA: Harvard University Press, 2018). This conversation was initially transcribed by Ashlyn Stewart from a digital audio recording made on August 28, 2018.

1. See Matt Cohen, *The Networked Wilderness: Communicating in Early New England* (Minneapolis: University of Minnesota Press, 2009).

RITA M. PALACIOS

Recovering Lost Footprints, Volume 1: Contemporary Maya Narratives
by Arturo Arias
State University of New York Press, 2017

ARTURO ARIAS'S *Recovering Lost Footprints, Volume 1: Contemporary Maya Narratives* is the first of three volumes focusing on Indigenous narrative, specifically novel, short story, and *testimonio,* from the mid-twentieth century to the present in Abya Yala (the Kuna name for Land in Its Full Maturity, used to refer to the Americas). Arias's study of Maya literature is important given that we find ourselves before an emerging field. One of the study's most valuable contributions lies in its thorough contextualization of the works and their authors in Guatemala, particularly as they pertain to a thirty-six-year-long civil war. Arias's decolonial stance is also notable because it reflects recent developments in Indigenous studies that seek to decenter Western thought and to privilege the voices of Indigenous peoples above all. This is no easy task, but it is one that other critics similarly face, given that we continue employing defined categories of literary inquiry to understand the work of Maya authors that in many cases challenges or simply refuses to play by the rules established by the Western academy.

In the introduction, Arias offers a discussion of issues that will prove useful to those unfamiliar with the field, starting with the development of Latin American studies and, later, Indigenous studies; delving into what it means to work within a decolonial framework, including the use of concepts such as Abya Yala or Iximuleu to talk about Guatemala in the latter case; and, lastly, defining a Maya literature. Chapter 1 then traces the emergence of a Maya literature in Iximuleu, highlighting the major players, the sociopolitical landscape, and issues of language. Chapter 2 takes on the work of Luis de Lión, whom Arias considers a pioneer of decolonial Maya literature and whose short stories and novel showcase a "racialized subalternity" that is deployed to rearticulate Maya subjectivities and generate agency (87–88).

Chapter 3 looks at "manifest affect and grieving" in Gaspar Pedro González's work "as calls to knowledge and as the means to grapple with the brutal racism and genocide experienced by Iximuleu's Mayas during the last three decades of the twentieth century" (131). The author's discussion of translation issues is interesting and gives us much to think about, particularly as we are confronted with languages in which, in many cases, we lack fluency. Finally, chapter 4 looks at Victor Montejo's work, focusing on narrative, though Arias also includes a narrative poem, *El Q'anil: Man of Lightning*, which was first published in English in 1982 in Pittsboro, North Carolina. Curiously, he labels *El Q'anil* a novella, though Montejo himself calls it an "epic poem of the Jalkaltek people" (Víctor Montejo, *El Q'anil: Man of Lightning* [Tucson: University of Arizona Press, 2001], xxviii–xxix). Arias's approach reveals what he labels a "Maya ethics" that is sustained through its own cosmovision (182). In this section, Arias's analysis of *Brevísima relación testimonial de la destrucción del Mayab'* is noteworthy as he deftly shows Montejo's testing and rewriting of the *testimonio* genre.

Overall, this study of major Maya narrative from Guatemala comes at an important time, when the field is expanding and other contributions are not far off. In 2019 we can expect to see Arias's *Recovering Lost Footprints, Volume 2*; Gloria Chacón's *Indigenous Cosmolectics: Kab'awil and the Making of Maya and Zapotec Literatures*; the critical collection *Indigenous Interfaces: Spaces, Technology, and Social Networks in Mexico and Central America*, edited by Jennifer Gomez and Gloria Chacón; and Paul Worley and Rita Palacios's *Unwriting Maya Literature: Ts'íib as Recorded Knowledge*. Perhaps the study's only limitation lies in the scope itself: though Arias is quite clear in what he sets out to do, when he restricts *Recovering Lost Footprints* to the study of narrative, he leaves out poetry, the one area in which Maya authors, particularly women, are most active. In general, Arias recognizes the complexity of the decolonial task at hand, acknowledging in his conclusion the need for different approaches and methodologies. This is perhaps what is most illuminating about *Recovering Lost Footprints*: it marks an important point in the development of the study of Maya literature, signaling a movement toward innovative decolonial approaches that set out to not only understand but also engage more fully with Maya authors and their work. The study also raises two important questions to keep at the forefront of our inquiries: How do we "read" Indigenous literatures? And how do we work with them if the categories for their analysis simply "do not exist," as Arias claims (224)?

RITA M. PALACIOS is professor of liberal studies at Conestoga College Institute of Technology and Advanced Learning in Kitchener, Ontario.

PAUL MCKENZIE-JONES

From Daniel Boone to Captain America: Playing Indian in American
Popular Culture
by Chad A. Barbour
University Press of Mississippi, 2016

CHAD BARBOUR'S *From Daniel Boone to Captain America* is an exhaustive examination of (mis)representations of American Indian identity in American popular culture from the founding era of the settler nation to the present day. Barbour focuses exclusively upon interpretations and appropriations of American Indian masculinity in his work, exposing an iteration of toxic white masculinity that has been present in American identity since the colonial era.

Within the work, Barbour analyzes and exposes the depth of the American subconscious desire to "be" American Indian, which has also been a focus of Indigenous critique and scholarship through recent controversies about passing for and claiming indigeneity where there is none and the fallacy of the DNA industry's attempts to pander to this subconscious desire among the American populace. Rather than focus upon the more commonly discussed aspects of American pop culture interactions with American Indian stereotypes, Barbour focuses upon a journey through the American imagination from early frontier mythology via early twentieth-century comic books to more recent trends in superhero fiction. In each of these, the desire to play Indian to access a form of hypermasculinity and thus a hyper-Americanness is artfully argued by Barbour. As such, the mythology of the American comic book and frontier mythology share a lot with sports mascot imagery and red face in early American westerns. This commonality helps strengthen Barbour's argument that playing Indian is a ubiquitous component of American identity.

Utilizing a wider array of resources, Barbour's work is part psychological exposé of white American male desires to be other than they are and part literary critique of the works in question. From the much-examined Chingachgook and Hawkeye in James Fenimore Cooper's *The Last of the Mohicans* to the less widely known *Tomahawk* cartoon of the 1970s, imagined American Indian men sit next to fictional Americans who embody their (assigned) best characteristics—from Daniel Boone, who was at one with and capable of taming the wilderness around him, to David Brown, a white man who was trained in the arts of "being" Indian and who was capable of transforming into the Golden Warrior. Barbour explores their literary significance next to their nationalistic significance, highlighting trends in national eras, from the celebration of westward expansion to the anxiety of the Cold War.

Within this framework, both Daniel Boone and Captain America, the two chronological bookends of this study, are the significant heroic ideals of American masculinity and patriotism. They borrowed the very essence of their masculinity from imagined ideals of virulent and threatening American Indian manhood. Here, American Indian men are ahistorical "others" who can be rhetorically (r)emasculated into white American heroes. Barbour highlights this process as yet another aspect of the dispossession of Indigenous sovereignty through which white America can write its own stories, a wild landscape to be cleared and rebuilt, much as the mythology of the pre-American landscape has been reimagined.

Chad Barbour's *From Daniel Boone to Captain America* is a wonderfully detailed critique of the many complexities of identity, community, territory, and cultural connectivity, all entwined in race, gender, and nationalism, that constitutes the United States' imagined American Indian landscape. It details the sometimes subconscious, often overt, sometimes well-meaning, other times insulting, racism that extracts the objectified hypermasculinity of American Indian manhood for the (mis)use of American whiteness. It offers a timely reminder of the work to be done within the wider culture to educate them/ourselves about American Indian masculinity rather than imagine and appropriate it for their/our own benefit. However, as Barbour shows, such is the depth to which playing Indian is embedded in American culture, and American white gendered identity, that this work may always be "in progress."

PAUL McKENZIE-JONES is assistant professor of Indigenous studies at the University of Lethbridge.

KEVIN BRUYNEEL

Native Land Talk: Indigenous and Arrivant Rights Theories
by Yael Ben-zvi
University Press of New England, 2018

YAEL BEN-ZVI'S *Native Land Talk* refuses to isolate the study of the political history of Indigenous people from that of Black people in the United States. Looking at the 1760–1840 time period, Ben-zvi analyzes the effort of arrivants (the term coined by Kamau Brathwaite and elaborated upon by Jodi Byrd to refer to people forced to the Americas) to secure rights and freedom in and of the land called the United States, as well as Indigenous peoples' efforts to challenge settler-colonial mappings in order to assure freedom on their territories, *not* as part of the United States. *Native Land Talk* confronts the reader with the triangularity of claims for settlement, resettlement, and unsettlement articulated by, respectively, settler, arrivant, and Indigenous peoples, all of whom ground their notion of freedom in a claim to Native status via their particular meaning and practices of inhabitation. However, the refusal to isolate Indigenous and Black/arrivant narratives in the US context does not mean constructing harmonious ones.

As Ben-zvi shows, arrivant claims to belonging through a discourse of resettlement can thereby affirm the status of settler claims to territory, whereas Indigenous claims to historical Native status and sovereignty can deny the status and agency of slaves and their descendants on the land. We see this in chapters on Mohegan and Cherokee efforts to resist removal in ways that demonstrate their strategy and rights theorization against settler-state impositions but that also did not recognize arrivants as legitimate inhabitants. On the other hand, efforts by Olaudah Equiano to construct an Indigenous African claim, while the best example in the book of an effort at conceiving of Indigenous and arrivant solidarity, worked with rather than against imperialist logics, and Black resistance to the African colonization movement affirmed the settler geopolitical mapping as a means to gaining rights within it. This is just a sample of the way in which Ben-zvi has successfully achieved the task of engaging in a complex analysis of anti-settler-statist theories of rights and freedoms generated by Indigenous and arrivant political actors while not being blind to how these efforts can conflict.

We see this complexity in chapter 3, "Spaces of Slavery and Freedom," a sublime comparison of settler notions of freedom based in movement across lands and arrivant claims premised upon spatialized stability. One discerns in Ben-zvi's narrative the way in which white settler masculine freedom is driven by anxiety about a rooted, interdependent relationship to land, an anxiety that solidifies a liberal bourgeois notion of negative *freedom from* attachments and interference. In comparison, connection to land, belonging, and community form the bases of arrivant rights claims. Similarly, the brilliant chapter 5, "Ancestral Blood," followed by the "Blood and Graves" interlude and chapter 6, "Ancestral Graves," explores the differential arrivant/Indigenous relationship to land and nativity discernible in the politics of memory regarding the blood and bones of their ancestors. For arrivants, in a Lockean twist, the blood of enslaved ancestors mixes with the soil to establish positive birthright status, whereas the ancestral graves of Indigenous peoples unsettles the colonial mapping of this regime by asserting the precolonial temporal persistence of Indigenous relationships to the land on their own terms.

In all, *Native Land Talk* is a needed intervention that shows the fruitlessness of efforts to split off a deeply interwoven, fraught history of settler colonialism and enslavement and thus of Indigenous and Black political agency. Ben-zvi also reveals how Indigenous and Black claims that undermine each other reproduce the mutual exclusivity of the Native/settler and Black/white binaries. At the same time, by my reading, *Native Land Talk* shows how the Native/settler and Black/white binaries are contained within each other, as one binary cannot exist without the other in the US context. With this in mind, we can consider the way in which whiteness is an inherently settler positionality and political identity in US settler society as in other settler societies. The tragedy of Indigenous and arrivant claims that undermine one another only further underscores the need for solidarity, such as in Maroon communities historically and as we see today in the mutual support and solidarity between the Black Lives Matter and Standing Rock movements, both of which mobilize against white settler-statist institutions and practices as composite forms of domination. This is just one of the possible insights Ben-zvi's book inspires. *Native Land Talk* should be read by scholars in Indigenous studies, Black studies, US history, and political theory.

KEVIN BRUYNEEL is a professor of politics at Babson College in Wellesley, Massachusetts.

NATHANIEL F. HOLLY

The Indian World of George Washington: The First President, the First
    Americans, and the Birth of a Nation
by Colin G. Calloway
Oxford University Press, 2018

THE MOST RECENT BOUNTY of Colin Calloway's particularly fruitful intellectual orchard is well worth a read for scholars concerned with indigenizing early America's master narrative. By focusing on the experiences and policies of Conotocarious, the town destroyer, Calloway illuminates how Indigenous people "shaped the life of the man who shaped the nation" (15). In so doing, the author hopes to provide a more complete telling of what he calls "America's story" (14). Divided into three parts, this study describes the constantly evolving Indigenous world Washington lived, fought, and negotiated in. It follows the first president from his days as a sixteen-year-old surveyor in the spring of 1748, to his ill-conceived forays into Indian Country at the head of an invading force, to his seemingly more detached role as president of the United States. Yet while the resulting narrative certainly includes more Indigenous actors, actions, and anxieties than its biographical predecessors, its larger contours and perspectives will be familiar to most scholars.

While part 1 begins with a sketch of Indigenous Virginia prior to Washington's early work as a surveyor, most of the opening seven chapters chart the early stages of Washington's education in Indian affairs. Unsurprisingly, perhaps, his learning curve depended heavily on Indigenous knowledge. As a twenty-year-old, for example, Washington carried some correspondence to a French commander deep in Indian Country at the behest of Robert Dinwiddie. In order to make that trek, Washington relied on a Seneca named Tanaghrisson to teach him how to navigate the "slow and deliberate process" of Indigenous diplomacy required to safely cross a variety of Indigenous lands. Even if he was traveling to a French fort, Washington quickly learned that he was crossing "Tanaghrisson's World." But that did not stop the future land speculator in chief from commenting on the "Several extensive and very rich Meadows" he encountered that might be good for future colonization (75).

The bulk of part 1 and virtually all of part 2 emphasize Washington's martial encounters with the Indigenous residents of the eastern woodlands. After describing how the young colonel "consistently misread the motives and actions of the Ohio Indians" as being pro-French rather than pro-Delaware, Calloway guides the reader into the wilderness of Washington's years as general of the Continental Army (96). By examining these historiographically well-trod years with an emphasis on Indigenous peoples, Calloway highlights the contradictions inherent in Washington's views of his Native neighbors. While he knew that "Indians could have a critical impact on the war" as allies, he also thought that the safety of his fledgling country depended upon offensive wars to "Root out these nefarious Wretches, from the face of the Earth" (221, 245).

The sorts of military actions he advocated for were necessary to make a legitimate claim on western lands that he had long hungered for. Part 3 explores the first president's efforts to use his public position to seize as many Indigenous lands as he could while simultaneously treating with these same peoples as sovereign nations. Though Washington willingly entertained visiting diplomats in Philadelphia as a means to secure lands as peacefully as he could, he was not averse to more bellicose solutions. Indeed, Washington's Indian policy was essentially an ultimatum: "civilization or death" (387). But as Calloway points out, Conotocarious "saw his policies as setting Indians on the road to survival, not destruction" (484–85).

As Calloway promises in his introduction, this is a book that expertly describes the relationship between the first president and the first Americans. On several occasions, however, Calloway concedes that this half century has a "different cast viewed from Indian country" (217). But aside from a few allusions to these Indigenous perspectives—the United States as "Thirteen Councils" or the Seven Years' War as a "war of independence"— Native views of Washington's world are lacking (306, 114). While there is nothing wrong with providing a view of Indian Country from the perspective of Washington—where Indigenous people shaped Washington, his world, and the historical narrative—readers are left wondering what Indians might have thought of Conotocarious. What might George Washington in an Indian world have looked like? Even still, with this sophisticated study Calloway provides the foundation necessary to rewrite the master narrative from an Indigenous perspective.

NATHANIEL F. HOLLY is a Ph.D. candidate in the Lyon G. Tyler Department of History at the College of William & Mary.

CHRISTOPHER PERREIRA

Monuments to Absence: Cherokee Removal and the Contest over Southern Memory
  by Andrew Denson
University of North Carolina Press, 2017

IN *MONUMENTS TO ABSENCE*, Andrew Denson analyzes memorialization, heritage work, and a century of tourism focused on the public memory of Cherokee removal and the Trail of Tears in the US South. Broadly, the book explores public commemoration in tourism across the twentieth century, specifically in relation to its embrace of Cherokee history. *Monuments* covers the "romantic story" of the Eastern Band Cherokee origins (popularized in the 1920s and 1930s), removal commemoration after World War II, and regional and national efforts to remember the Trail of Tears as part of an exceptional narrative of the United States. For Denson, memorials invite rethinking what indigeneity, race, and US colonialism continue to mean for visitors, tourists, and heritage workers. As a comparative project, this study points to dominant narratives of Indian removal as central for understanding how the US South emerged along multiple axes of race and settler frameworks.

Comprised of an introduction, seven chapters, and an epilogue, *Monuments* begins with the 1960s construction of Georgia's New Echota and the establishment of the 1987 National Historic Trail. Through the promotion of tourism in the region, Cherokee removal represents the most infamous form of Native dispossession—and an enduring narrative for "sympathetic white Americans" (3). The author seeks, in part, to highlight contradictions in US South memory studies, particularly its reliance on Black/white racial paradigms. Tourism popularized Cherokee history as a public discourse and at the same time sustained a "conception of a biracial contemporary South and, with it, the idea of Indian disappearance" (8). This comparative approach offers useful ways to understand how the story of Cherokee people in North Carolina has been consistently narrated as the past.

Chapter 1 traces earlier histories of long-standing preoccupations in early American politics that strategically dispossessed Indian nations' lands. It outlines US policies intended to "civilize Indians" as part of the eighteenth and nineteenth centuries' imperial expansion project, tracing the emergence of treaties as the tool the United States leveraged to expand its borders. Along with the 1827 Constitution, the chapter looks to print culture in the 1820s (such as the bilingual *Cherokee Phoenix* newspaper) as a platform for challenging policies. Chapter 2 shifts to auto-industry tourism in the Great Smoky Mountains National Park of Tennessee and North Carolina. As automobile production surged during the 1920s and 1930s, tourism literature promoted the region by recounting "episodes from the Cherokee past" (focused on the Eastern Band and the Trail of Tears), encouraging tourists to "bask in Cherokee history when they visited" (53–54). A performance of Cherokee identity developed out of this increase of white tourists, and pageants provided one public platform. Booster tourism enabled promoters to incorporate a sense of history to advertise "Cherokee distinctiveness," promising intimate contact with "a premodern way of life." The chapter traces an in-transit Trail of Tears discourse across North Carolina, Tennessee, Missouri, and Kansas through memorials, plays, and pageants.

Chapter 4 examines 1950s memorials in Georgia and the restoration of several Cherokee public buildings at New Echota. Memorialization of Cherokee removal in Georgia garnered state support, yet Black civil rights activism met intense resistance and violent suppression. Civil rights made remembering Cherokee removal more desirable for public memory, and acknowledging Native dispossession, Denson argues, allowed some white southerners a "politically safe way to consider their region's heritage of racial oppression" (112–13). Chapter 5 reads *Unto These Hills*—a play debuted in 1950 in North Carolina on the Qualla Boundary depicting Cherokee history from European contact through removal—as an underexamined cultural event. Viewed by over one hundred thousand people in its first season, the play offers a lens for reading debates surrounding American Indian affairs and termination at mid-twentieth century. As Denson notes, the drama "celebrated Cherokee assimilation, employing language that strongly echoed that of termination advocates" (136). The play re-presents an enduring narrative that writes Indians out of time, but it also demonstrates how tourism development shaped economic and social life in other ways. Tourism, for example, launched unexpected conversations about economic sovereignty and Cherokee-owned businesses.

The book's final chapter, "The National Trail," focuses on the longer reaches of the Trail of Tears in southern memory, considering how much of the current wave of heritage work continues to ignore critical scholarship. Closing with a discussion of Cherokee art and activism, Denson ends with reflection on what Eastern Band artist Jeff Marley calls the "finality" of official memorials in public memory (221–23). *Monuments* poses rich questions about the ways public memory holds sway over social life in the US South, providing critical frameworks for examining how Cherokee history became useable in the tourism industry. More broadly, the book provides researchers and students in Native and Indigenous studies and in memory studies useful comparative entry points into these fields.

CHRISTOPHER PERREIRA is an assistant professor in the Department of American Studies at the University of Kansas.

CLYDE ELLIS

Recovering Native American Writings in the Boarding School Press
edited by Jacqueline Emery
University of Nebraska Press, 2017

IF EVER THERE WAS A PLACE where we would expect Native voices to be muted, surely that place would be a boarding school newspaper. In thrall to the coercive assimilation agenda for which they were invented, boarding schools intended to erase Native voices and repackage them based on white middle-class models of comportment and gender. School administrators confidently relied on cheery newspaper stories and essays to push assimilation forward by touting the merits of hard work, discipline, and success. But as with so many other boarding school programs, the plan often went off the rails when students dutifully learned their craft but then employed their new skills to write and publish essays and commentaries celebrating Native histories and cultures and defending Native interests and needs. In this important new book, Jacqueline Emery argues that far from obliterating Native voices, student authors "gained control over their self-representations and revised what it meant to be educated Indians" (23).

Emery's selections reflect a wide array of stances on everything from religion to work to education, and they highlight the complex mix of attitudes and opinions that shaped Native identities in the late nineteenth and early twentieth centuries. Importantly, the sources challenge "the assumption that Native Americans voiced static or homogenous perspectives on issues like assimilation, citizenship, and education; indeed, these issues were widely debated in Native writings" (13). Thus the book juxtaposes John Milton Oskison's ardent praise for the pragmatism and goodwill of the Sherman Institute's founders against Charles Eastman's unbridled celebration of traditional cultures. Angel De Cora lauded the reemergence of Native art at Carlisle, but Arthur Parker lamented that "the Indian cannot always remain an Indian" (287). Henry Roe Cloud, no sentimentalist he, asked Native people to rely on "Almighty God" (307), and Carlos Montezuma decried the "gross injustice" (194) of allowing Indian people to dance. Samuel Townsend, the Pawnee editor of Carlisle's *School News*, called on Indian families everywhere to "send all their children to school" (57) so that they could learn the skills necessary to prevent whites from controlling them, while Gertrude Bonnin bitterly remembered feeling like "one of many little animals driven by a herder" (257).

Many students used the newspapers to convey their versions of traditional stories, subtly reminding readers that the lessons and values in those narratives continued to have deep resonance. Others heaped praise on their reservations. Alonso Lee (Eastern Band Cherokee), for example, lauded his people as "peaceful, law abiding citizens" (88) who were models of comportment for their white neighbors, and he took delight in describing the reservation as a beloved homeland. Other writers celebrated their enduring friendships with students from far-flung communities. In an especially endearing commentary, four authors from four different nations collaborated on an 1892 editorial in Hampton's *Talks and Thoughts* and noted that although writing in the English language helped "our readers . . . get our thoughts," this did not mean they were ignoring their native tongues. "We do not mean that we can lay aside our Indian language in which we have grown up," they wrote, "but we wish you to know that we realize the need of the English language, and that we are trying very hard to master it" (62).

This important and revealing collection of documents reminds us that Native people were negotiating modernity in ways that simultaneously confounded and pleased critics and friends alike by revealing complex notions about ethnicity and identity. If some modern-day readers are discomfited by the proassimilationist leanings of Arthur Parker and John Milton Oskison, it is well to remember that they were forcefully asserting that it was Native people, not outsiders, who would determine what it meant to be a Native person. In doing so, these authors also remind us of the many ways to express Indigenous sensibilities and identities.

CLYDE ELLIS is a professor of history and university distinguished scholar at Elon University.

FERNANDA VIEIRA

Indigenous Cities: Urban Indian Fiction and the Histories of Relocation
by Laura M. Furlan
University of Nebraska Press, 2017

IN *INDIGENOUS CITIES: Urban Indian Fiction and the Histories of Relocation*, Laura M. Furlan demonstrates that contemporary indigeneity is traversed by the urban experience and its narratives. Dealing with contemporary theories of diaspora, transnationalism, and cosmopolitism, Furlan articulates the transportability of cultural identities, affiliations, and ideas, situating Native identity through the urban stories written by Janet Campbell Hale, Sherman Alexie, Louise Erdrich, and Susan Power alongside other Native artists and filmmakers. Furlan disassembles outdated theories that state that authentic Native writing should come only from the reservations, debunking the narrative elaborated and maintained by coloniality that affirms that Indigenous peoples cannot live in the cities and that they do not belong to urban centers, which strengthens the ghettoization of the First Nations to the confined spaces determined by coloniality. Thus, considering the persistent mindset of coloniality, which deprives Indigenous peoples of urban landscapes, the reservation could be understood not only as a place of resistance but also as the only "authorized space" for Indigenous survival.

Laura M. Furlan holds a B.A. in American studies from the University of Iowa, an M.A. in English from San Diego State University, and a Ph.D. in English from the University of California, Santa Barbara. In *Indigenous Cities* she exposes how urban Indian literature provides a fuller imaginary of the Indigenous peoples of North America, as stated by the author. Furlan broadens how urban Native literature explores the tension between local and global culture, between traditional knowledge and the cosmopolitan world. Urban Indigenous texts formulate a new tribal consciousness, uncovering a cosmopolitan Indigenous past and reminding us that Indigenous peoples' places are all places and not only those designated by the forcible removal of Native peoples. Considering the vast subject of Indigenous literature, Furlan's work provides a good and up-to-date viewpoint on urban Indigenous artistic production, especially literature. Moreover, she does not colonize Native epistemologies and art by applying outdated theories still embedded by coloniality.

Indigenous Cities presents a significant overview of urban Indigenous artistic production and how dislocated subjects explore different senses of rootedness or rootlessness regarding their geographies of home, nation, place, and space. Furlan's work relates to epistemologies being produced in Latin America, such as the decolonial turn, working toward a decolonizing viewpoint and the production of new epistemologies. Throughout Furlan's examinations and theorizations about Native citizenship and identity, she does not paternalize Native identities and experiences or romanticize an ideal Native America that could reinforce stereotypes that must be questioned.

Indigenous Cities is a groundbreaking study on the literary production of Native writers and their representation of indigeneity in urban spaces. In a world still sunk in coloniality, Furlan depicts Native identities as complex as they are, highlighting how their cosmopolitan identities do not invalidate their Native selves. Indigenous dislocation and relocation lead to the constant interlacing of the notions of space, place, home, belonging, nonbelonging, in-betweenness, and nationhood, subjects that are posed as issues in contemporaneity but that have not yet been solved. By providing a thorough analysis of urban Native literature, Furlan works toward the deconstruction of the marginalization of intertribal relations and urban lives, exposing how Native American literature was pervaded not only by the reflexes of relocation and Indigenous diaspora but also by a strong sense of reclaiming and reshaping Indigenous identities. Furthermore, considering that the majority of American Indigenous populations does not inhabit reservations, urban spaces usually permeate the literary production of Native authors, nourishing discussions about Native belonging and identity.

In summary, *Indigenous Cities: Urban Indian Fiction and the Histories of Relocation* by Laura M. Furlan provides a decolonial and contemporary study of the literary representation of Native peoples in urban spaces. It breaks with the commonplace theoretical and literary analyses of Indigenous authors' productions in an urban context. Furlan goes beyond the outmoded understandings of Native identities as restricted to reservations, trespassing the ghettoization and marginalization of urban Indigenous identities. Her work provides a deep reflection on Native American literature for scholars, especially the ones working with a decolonial approach. By demonstrating how Native writers build the understanding that all spaces are Native spaces, Furlan secures the city as Indigenous land as much as the reservation, reminding us that Native peoples have always been cosmopolitan.

FERNANDA VIEIRA (*Mestiça*/Mixed-blood) is a doctoral student at the Rio de Janeiro State University.

CAROLINE FIDAN TYLER DOENMEZ

Violence against Indigenous Women: Literature, Activism, Resistance
by Allison Hargreaves
Wilfrid Laurier University Press, 2017

FAMILIES OF MISSING and murdered Indigenous women were countering violence and commemorating their loved ones long before their suffering gained widespread attention. It is only in recent years that the crisis has been publicly acknowledged by politicians, human rights organizations, and the media. Whose stories are heard or privileged in the midst of this increased focus on Indigenous women who have been stolen on stolen land? How are these narratives crafted and consumed, and to what ends? Allison Hargreaves's book emerges in a timely moment when the questions of public remembrance, knowledge making, and justice for missing and murdered Indigenous women are circulating intensely.

Drawing on Indigenous feminist theorists to guide her analysis, Hargreaves sets out to develop three main claims: that the disappearance of Indigenous women is a systemic and ongoing product of colonialism; that words and storytelling can play vital roles in countering this crisis beyond mere description; and that Indigenous women's literature engenders new possibilities for imagining and enacting resistance to violence. Each of her four chapters compares an official response to violence with an example of Indigenous women's literary interventions, including documentary film, poetry, memoir, theater, and a revenge-drama. Hargreaves emphasizes that through these comparisons, she is seeking to explore how literature "can imagine resistance differently" (22) and how it can highlight the constraints or blind spots of antiviolence activism. Through this method, one of Hargreaves's main themes emerges: looking to Eve Tuck and K. Wayne Yang's theorization of an "ethic of incommensurability" (4), she draws attention to the ways in which Indigenous women's insights and analyses cannot be aligned with certain presumptions undergirding recognition-based approaches. For example, it becomes clear that many initiatives are circumscribed by their failure to analyze colonial violence as structurally produced and proliferating into the present.

Hargreaves is also concerned with the consumption of the stories of missing and murdered Indigenous women. She carefully considers which values and paradigms are deployed in shaping their narratives, highlighting how certain modes of telling and listening—despite being extractive, exclusionary, or depoliticizing—are often uncritically assumed to be sufficient. This troubles the notion that increased visibility will automatically lead to change. She observes dynamics within human rights and mainstream feminist frameworks, in which confessional modes of personal testimony by women of color are often mobilized to shore up the benevolence of white feminists, liberal institutions, and the settler state; their stories are construed as "'catharsis' rather than critique" (113). Subsequently, a major target of her incisive analysis is the construction of the white, liberal, conscientious citizen for whom "Indigenous death is sometimes a necessary condition of their absolution and goodness" (151). Hargreaves's work is concerned with the broader context of Canada's "culture of redress," in which a performative array of apologies, acknowledgments, and inquiries attempt to subsume Indigenous life and sovereignty into a multicultural, supposedly postcolonial present. Hargreaves is issuing a challenge to non-Indigenous readers to refuse the fantasy of easy absolution or closure. She also crafts a critical discussion of how a hierarchy of worthy life is established through the telling of specific women's stories, while others are either marginalized or vilified: Whose lives are considered worthy of mourning, and whose deaths are rendered inevitable?

This text could have been strengthened by a more pronounced focus on the critical role of family members in shaping the memories and stories of their missing and murdered loved ones. Although not explicitly an aim of the book, it is critical to center those who are on the front lines doing the hard work of memory keeping, care taking, knowledge making, and envisioning otherwise.

Hargreaves's book ultimately underscores what is at stake in how we commemorate missing and murdered Indigenous women, how non-Indigenous people must confront the dynamics that would maintain their claim to innocence, and how we must unequivocally center Indigenous women's writing and knowledge as we work against violence. Moreover, her conclusion engages the question of what justice outside of the state might look like; justice that is rooted in Indigenous women looking to each other. This attentiveness to the power of relationships in thinking through stories and survival is one of the greatest strengths of the text. On some level, this book is about how we refuse to disappear the missing and murdered Indigenous women yet again in our narrative and listening practices, nothing less than how we might remember better, and remember with more care. As she writes, "*How* we remember might be as, or more, important than the fact of remembrance itself" (167).

CAROLINE FIDAN TYLER DOENMEZ is a doctoral student in the Department of Anthropology at the University of Minnesota.

FREDERICK E. HOXIE

American Indian History on Trial: Historical Expertise in Tribal Litigation
by E. Richard Hart
University of Utah Press, 2018

RICHARD HART has done the historical profession and the Indian law community an enormous service. This book—a combination memoir and litigation history—spans Hart's forty-year career as an expert witness on behalf of American Indian tribes. It is an excellent summary of four major cases, three of which examine federal intent with regard to reservation status and boundaries and one involving tribal recognition. A fifth section contains a brief overview of western water rights litigation featuring his work on this issue at Zuni and Klamath.

The bulk of *American Indian History on Trial* contains compelling and clearly presented descriptions of the specific historical questions Hart was assigned to answer by attorneys representing four tribes. The clarity of those questions and the precision of his answers are instructive. Tribal litigation turns on defining the central issue of the case and then—if historical evidence is to play a significant role in resolving the dispute—framing a question that will support a responsive narrative. For example, in 1832 in *Cherokee Nation* John Marshall asked, "Do the Cherokees constitute a foreign state?" Were he present, Hart might have been charged by the attorneys with responding to this historical question: "When, if ever, have the Cherokees acted as a foreign state?" Answers to historical questions do not determine outcomes—as *Cherokee* illustrates—but they do force judges to respond to reality rather than misguided cultural assumptions.

The four questions at the heart of Hart's narrative are:

1. Did the 1873 executive order creating the Coeur d'Alene reservation convey to the tribe an interest in the "beds and banks" of Coeur d'Alene Lake?
2. When the Wenatchi tribe signed the Yakama Treaty of 1855, did it obtain the Wenatshapam Fishery on the Wenatchi River?
3. Are the Amah Mutsun people of San Juan Bautista, California, an Indian group worthy of recognition by the United States as a federal tribe?
4. Did the executive order signed by President Chester A. Arthur in 1883 creating the modern Hualapai reservation extinguish the tribe's title to land west and southwest of the borders described in

that document? (The tribe viewed those lands as part of its aboriginal homeland.)

Hart masterfully explains the broad legal context for each of these questions. By doing so he demonstrates that resolutions of *big* issues of justice and equity usually rest on clear and well-documented answers to *small* historical questions. He also makes clear that this type of historical research is slow and (because it is created for each dispute) expensive. Most of the cases remained unresolved for years, even decades. Tribes without resources or knowledgeable legal teams suffer the fate of most poor people who enter courtrooms: they lose. And, Hart notes, precise historical answers do not necessarily resolve cases. The Wenatchi could only win a right to fish; they did not win title to the fishery itself. The Amah Mutsun community remains unrecognized after decades of struggle. Nevertheless, the message of Hart's narrative is that documenting tribal experiences is essential if the legal process—however flawed—is to move forward.

Anyone considering work as an expert witness should read this book, even if the tribes and issues involved do not overlap with the cases discussed here. Hart "shows" rather than tells us how to be an expert. His narrative demonstrates that experts must rely on archival sources rather than secondary "experts" or historical theory. He shows that historians must be prepared to use all possible sources: material culture, baptismal records, cartographic information, and oral testimony. And by identifying the questions that drove his work, he illustrates that successful experts do not argue. Instead, they impress the court with their credibility—a credibility earned through thoroughness and by acknowledging and discussing contradictory evidence and opposing arguments. As flawed as they are, courts view themselves as fair-minded and neutral. Experts must adapt themselves to that environment.

There is probably another volume to be written about the occasions when experts have been forced to answer unproductive questions or when their well-documented answers have been ignored. No doubt Hart has seen his share of unscrupulous attorneys and "hired gun" experts who will testify to whatever their clients desire. Indian law has no shortage of either. We will wait for that book. For now, we have this excellent tour of recent litigation combined with a fulsome profile of a model expert witness.

FREDERICK E. HOXIE is professor emeritus at University of Illinois, Urbana–Champaign.

BARRY JUDD

The Critical Surf Studies Reader
edited by Dexter Zavalza Hough-Snee and Alexander Sotelo Eastman
Duke University Press, 2017

HOUGH-SNEE AND EASTMAN bring together a high-quality collection of eighteen essays that not only succeeds in introducing the reader to the world of surfing but also digs deep into the complex histories, politics, and economics that shape and influence what has become a significant world sporting subculture. The *Critical Surf Studies Reader* demonstrates the interdisciplinary nature of surf studies as an emergent field of scholarship with the collected essays characterized by the disparate and diverse range of topics, issues, and geographies they discuss. While the reader is underpinned by a rich diversity, essays collected here all find a certain degree of unity through a shared commitment to critical analysis and reflexivity that marks each as a serious intellectual engagement with the world of surfing. Unity is further achieved by the editorial decision to evenly group essays contained in *The Critical Surf Studies Reader* according to a number of overarching themes.

Part 1 of the reader commences with the theme of coloniality and decolonization. Here the relationship between contemporary world surfing and its capitalist domination by California and East Coast Australia is critically explored against a history of cultural appropriation from Indigenous Hawaiians and the perpetuation of colonial discourse through surf tourism that sees surfers from the affluent Global North "discovering" the "pristine" waves of the Global South with little thought, reflection, or empathy for the local populations whose everyday experience is one of overwhelming poverty and/or political oppression. In "*Kai Ea*: Rising Waves of National and Ethnic Hawaiian Identities" Isaiah Helekunihi Walker demonstrates how surfing is much more than a sport to *kānaka maoli* who regard it as an important cultural artifact, a symbol of both historical achievement and contemporary identity.

Part 2 of the reader addresses the themes of race, ethnicity, and identity and explores issues including cultural appropriation, the marginalization of groups based on race and ethnicity, and the importance that surfing might play for contemporary Indigenous and nonwhite political struggles. Contributions by Kevin Dawson and Colleen McGloin point to the marginalized histories of surfing among Indigenous peoples beyond Hawaii. In "Surfing Beyond Racial and Colonial Imperatives in Early Modern Atlantic

Africa and Oceania," Dawson reminds us that surfing practices developed independently in numerous coastal places around the world by recalling the rich surf-based cultures and practices that emerged in Atlantic Africa. The theme of racial marginalization and exclusion from the surf by white invaders is investigated further by Belinda Wheaton in "Space Invaders in Surfing's White Tribe: Exploring Surfing, Race and Identity." Through a study of Black surfers in southern California, Wheaton finds that surfers who inhabit Black bodies continue to face discrimination. Wheaton shows that the surf zone (and contemporary market-driven surfing) remains a designated "white space."

Part 3, "Feminist Critical Geography," contains the fewest essays, but in many ways these contributions are the most important. Bringing complexities associated with intersectionality together with detailed analysis associated with geographic specificity, these essays draw attention to surfing in unexpected places. Questioning persistent capitalist forms that narrowly define surfing, Krista Comer outlines how feminism in surf can be transformative by bringing together feminist theorists with surf activists to change the narrative about the role of women, sex, and sexualities, among other things, in the sport. This possibility is demonstrated by reference to the Institute for Women Surfers (IWS) as a mechanism to shift the narrative beyond the mere inclusion of women. Limitations in the inherent representation of women surfers as heteronormative, feminine, white, middle-class "surfer girls" who exist as accessories to the normative white male surfer are contrasted with the work of IWS members, including that of Farhana Huq and her alternative reality of the Brown Girl Surf.

Part 4 concludes the reader, addressing the theme of capitalism, economics, and the commodification of surf culture. Adopting an economic analysis to the world of surfing, these contributions grapple with the ever-present tension between the ideal of surfing as a counterculture leisure activity pursued for its spiritual dimensions and the reality of the sport as a global industry in which profit and market share have become key drivers.

The breadth of material contained in *The Critical Surf Studies Reader* makes adequate summary in this review difficult, with many fine essays not discussed. High-quality scholarship and insightful critical analysis make this a worthy addition to other works in the field of Indigenous studies.

BARRY JUDD is a professor of Indigenous social research at Charles Darwin University, Alice Springs, Australia.

MELANIE BOEHI

Steeped in Heritage: The Racial Politics of South African Rooibos Tea
by Sarah Ives
Duke University Press, 2017

THROUGHOUT THE FIRST HALF OF 2018, the question "who belongs in South Africa?" was fiercely debated in the South African public sphere. Some commentators argued that understanding the politics of race and belonging in their historical and contemporary makings was crucial for countering the lasting apartheid legacies of racialized divisions. This makes the recent publication of *Steeped in Heritage: The Racial Politics of South African Rooibos Tea* timely. In the book, a detailed ethnographic account of the social worlds of rooibos, Sarah Ives analyzes how residents in the rooibos-growing region in the Cederberg area in South Africa's Western Cape and Northern Cape provinces negotiate the politics of race, land, indigeneity, and belonging in the context of economic, political, and, increasingly, ecological uncertainties.

Ives aims to provide an understanding of the world through the commodity of rooibos tea. What makes rooibos such a compelling subject is that it is embedded in assemblages of people, plants, and land that constantly blur perceived boundaries between nature and culture, the Indigenous and the alien, or the wild and the cultivated. Her focus on a plant commodity and human-plant relationships breaks new ground for understanding multispecies formations of race and belonging.

Over the past hundred years, rooibos evolved from a plant harvested in the wild for local consumption into a commodity consumed by tea aficionados worldwide. Marketers characterize rooibos as extraordinarily healthy, natural, and deeply rooted in its habitat. Rooibos's value largely derives from its status as being indigenous to the Cederberg area. While the plant's indigeneity in the region is undisputed, the people who grow it do not smoothly fit into this category. The two dominant groups of rooibos cultivators are Afrikaans farmers and coloured farmers and farm workers (Ives uses the term "coloured" in the way people self-identified). Afrikaans farmers are white descendants of European settlers and to this day own most of the rooibos-producing land. Coloured farmers and farm workers are descendants of Indigenous people, slaves brought from elsewhere, and white settlers. They mostly don't own land, and their livelihoods are made precarious by the lasting apartheid legacies of racism, violence, and poverty. Neither Afrikaans nor coloured people claimed belonging primarily in terms of indigeneity; instead, they claim a sense of belonging to the land in which rooibos is central. Rooibos is part of people's everyday practices and mediates people's belonging to the land. Ives writes that residents relate to rooibos "as a commodity, as an indigenous plant, and even as an extension of the self."

Throughout the book's five chapters, Ives approaches the question of how people in the rooibos-growing region claimed belonging from various angles. Contextualizing the findings of her ethnographic fieldwork in a historical perspective, Ives provides a detailed account of how people negotiate their identity and belonging in a way that was always precarious, uncertain, and relational. An analysis of the material and symbolic aspects of rooibos cultivation shows how narratives that framed rooibos as a wild plant concealed the labor of coloured and African farm workers and thus further alienated their belonging and naturalized Afrikaans farmers' landownership. In a discussion of the discourses around alien plants and alien people, Ives shows how Afrikaans and coloured residents perceived an invasion of seasonal African migrant laborers and alien plants as a threat to indigeneity and belonging, though not generally, but rather when they appeared to be out of their control. Taking rumor and gossip seriously as data, Ives shows that storytelling about rooibos was an important aspect of narrators' struggles over history, meanings, and relations. Focusing on anxieties, Ives discusses how people negotiate claims to belonging in place in times of increasing ecological uncertainties as climate change threatens to shift the rooibos ecosystem southward. While some residents hoped that technology or adapted wild plants might come to their rescue, the shift of rooted plants and their ecosystem caused them to question their own identities and emplacements.

The vivid descriptions of fieldwork encounters and their contextualization in current debates in commodity studies and multispecies ethnography make this book a fascinating and enjoyable read. The focus on a relatively small region enables Ives to write a comprehensive account. At times, this makes the narrative dense, and some chapters are divided into numerous short subsections. However, Ives convincingly connects the diverse threads and perspectives on politics of race and belonging in the rooibos region. The book is an important contribution to studies of South African history and anthropology, as well as to the fields of commodity studies and multispecies ethnography.

MELANIE BOEHI is a postdoctoral fellow in the History Department, University of the Witwatersrand.

DAVID DRY

Seven Myths of Native American History
by Paul Jentz
Hackett Publishing Company, 2018

MYTHS ABOUT AND STEREOTYPES OF American Indians abound in American culture. Although the myths examined in *Seven Myths of Native American History* will likely already be familiar to many readers, Jentz looks at less well acknowledged aspects of popular myths: the history behind their formation, the reasons for their endurance over centuries, and the pernicious ramifications they have had on Indian communities. Jentz considers in depth seven of the most familiar and long-lasting caricatures of American Indians and argues that they were fashioned to meet specific needs of white settler-colonial society and adapted over centuries to cater to the shifting appetites of mainstream American culture. For each myth, Jentz begins with its origins, connecting its emergence to that period in American history and US government Indian policies, and then proceeds to trace the various configurations of the myth in the popular imagination to the twenty-first century. In Jentz's analysis, myths are far from static—they continually adapt to compartmentalize and limit Indian people in service of the dominant culture.

Each of the seven myths gets its own chapter. In chapter 1, Jentz examines the myth of the noble savage, a romantic image of primitive and idealized Indians that emerged in part as a tool by white authors to critique their own society. Jentz underscores its detrimental effects in labeling Indians as incompatible with modernity. Chapter 2 explores the myth of the "ignoble savage," which labels Indians as objects of scorn, as savages, fools, and drunkards, and was unleashed to justify wars of conquest and extermination. Jentz describes these two myths as "foundation myths," and the remaining five myths are viewed as subsets of these broader positive and negative classifications. Two myths that Jentz links strongly to nineteenth-century government policies include the myth of the wilderness, which seeks to erase Native people from the lands they occupied and was an extension of Manifest Destiny, and the myth of the vanishing Indian, which was based in notions of racial inferiority and used to justify removal, forced assimilation, and boarding schools. The last three myths find their fullest expressions in the twentieth century and include the myth of the authentic Indian, which confines Indians to traditional roles and was circulated on stage and screen; the myth of the ecological Indian, which classifies Indians as innocent and primitive devotees of nature; and the myth of the mystical Indian, which turns Indian spiritual practices into a commodity to be bought and sold.

Every chapter opens with a primary source document that is subject to scrutiny, and the book is littered with additional primary source examples, ranging from letters and administrative documents to artistic and literary works. Jentz takes on many well-known depictions of American Indians, from the earliest European accounts into the twenty-first century. From the world of literature and poetry, excerpts from Henry David Thoreau, Mark Twain, Charles Sprague, and Francis Hopkinson are examined in some detail. Visual culture is examined through the works of artists such as George Catlin, Thomas Moran, and John Gast, with black-and-white images accompanying the text. Notable movies from the silent film era to the present find a place in Jentz's work, as do public figures such as Brooke Medicine Eagle and Chief Buffalo Child Long Lance. Jentz also draws upon numerous less well known examples, and even a student of American Indian studies will find new examples in Jentz's work.

Jentz is not the first to attempt to correct erroneous generalizations regarding American Indians; however, he is more effective than most in exposing the historical genesis of these constructed depictions. One limitation of his approach is its Euro-American focus. Although Jentz does take pains to dispel each myth by highlighting the complexity of Indian societies, Indians' agency in their responses and resistance to the imposition of myths does not always fall within the purview of his analysis. The book is successful in being accessible to the undergraduate and general audiences Hackett Publishing intended for its Seven Myths book series, and Jentz, a longtime community college instructor, has written a useful companion text for undergraduate survey courses in American history. The book also avoids the temptation to critique seemingly all popular depictions of American Indians, and Jentz closes on a positive note by providing examples of more complex portrayals of and by American Indians to which readers can turn.

DAVID DRY is a doctoral student in history at the University of North Carolina at Chapel Hill and examines the history of the Ottawa Tribe of Oklahoma.

WASKAR T. ARI-CHACHAKI

Now Peru Is Mine: The Life and Times of a Campesino Activist
by Manuel Llamojha Mitma and Jaymie Patricia Heilman
Duke University Press, 2016

THIS BOOK IS A HANDSOME CONTRIBUTION to scholarship on Indigenous activists, their historical context, and the activist intellectual role in the Andes. It shows the trajectory of *campesino,* or peasant, identity, with this term, highlighting the limitations Indigenous identity has in Peru.

This book is almost unique, because Manuel Llamojha and Jaymie Heilman worked through methodological boundaries to create a testimonial biography based in oral history and archival research. Llamojha is also a crucial actor in this narrative. His last name, Llamojha or *llamaxa*, meaning "my llamas," comes from Aymara, and his region of birth, Ayacucho, has a lot of toponyms originally from the Aymara language that predate Quechua and Inca dominance in the region. Heilman, a specialist in radical history, is a professor at the University of Alberta. The big contribution of this book is that, through Llamojha's story, it illuminates the specific historical conditions previous to the emergence of the Shining Path, a guerrilla movement that shook Peruvian society in the 1980s, and the oppressive historical conditions that the Shining Path would later exploit and amplify.

The first section addresses the era prior to the agrarian reform of 1962, during which Llamojha was a strong organizer against the power of *gamonales* (bossism or powerful *hacendados*). Because he is from a region of extreme abuse against Indigenous people by *gamonales* and where the state had little presence, Llamojha felt ostracized in his own country, and only when he went to complete military service did he feel as if he belonged to his country. This amalgamation, in symbolic terms, between Peru's and Llamojha's goals leads him to assert the sense of appropriation that he uses in the title of the book: *Now Peru Is Mine.* This need to claim his own country leads to his idea of becoming president of Peru as the way to incarnate his dream of being part of a neglected group that actually represents the majority of Peru: people of Indigenous background. His most crucial achievement was to recuperate land for his community of Concepción from the Ayrabamba hacienda. His activism was possible because of his linguistic and writing skills. This case confirms how important the production and consumption of documents is to Indigenous struggles in the Andes.

The second section focuses on the era after the agrarian reform. Llamojha was general secretary, the highest post of the Confederación de Campesinos del Peru (CCP), one of the most representative Indigenous peasant organizations in twentieth-century Peru. In this role, he traveled extensively in rural Peru. Activists like him were attacked as *comunistas* during this era whether or not they were associated with the Communist Party because this was a way to denigrate them and undermine their credibility. Although Llamojha worked for an extended period with liberal and populist parties such as the Alianza Popular Revolucionaria Americana (APRA), Fernando Belaúnde de Terry's Acción Popular, and Juan Velasco Alvarado's military regime, during this time he also was a candidate for a seat in Congress. As they did in other parts of Latin America during the Cold War, activists from Indigenous peasant and working-class backgrounds only found ways to participate in democracy through leftist organizations, in this case, the Communist Party of Peru.

The last section is about Llamojha in the era of the Shining Path. Llamojha is no longer an influential leader; instead, he has been silenced by the repression and violence that reached his family. His community of Concepción and the region of Vilcashuamán became later on the area where the Shining Path begins its history. Shining Path carried out an attack and killings in the hacienda of Ayrabamba, and the Peruvian Army then created a countersubversive unit in Quyllur Cancha in 1983. Llamojha's son was killed, and he went into hiding in Lima with the rest of his family.

This well-written work provides not only an approachable view of Indigenous intellectuals in the Andes and the Americas but also shows the trajectory and nature of Indigenous peasant organizations. The book is an excellent piece to teach Modern Latin America and other courses on Indigenous peoples' history in the Americas. For this reason, it will be an excellent addition to graduate and undergraduate courses in Latin American studies, Native American studies, radical history, and labor history of the Americas.

WASKAR T. ARI-CHACHAKI is an associate professor of history and ethnic studies/ Latin American studies at the University of Nebraska—Lincoln.

MELANIE VASSELIN

*Sovereign Acts: Contesting Colonialism across Indigenous Nations
    and Latinx America*
edited by Frances Negron-Muntaner
University of Arizona Press, 2017

SOVEREIGN ACTS: *Contesting Colonialism across Indigenous Nations and Latinx America* offers a refreshingly interdisciplinary critical exploration of the concept of sovereignty. This book brings together in twelve chapters the viewpoints of a variety of authors writing on diverse subjects and places that are united by the common theme of sovereignty. While at first glance the link of sovereignty may appear tenuous between such distinct topics as the sartorial aesthetics of a Puerto Rican political activist group, explored in Frances Negron-Muntaner's piece, and the tensions in the Native Hawaiian struggles for sovereignty amid US racial politics, explored in Davianna Pomaika'i McGregor's chapter, there is an abundance of common threads running throughout the book.

These unifying features take the form of authors and key themes primarily related to decolonization and sovereignty. Glen Coulthard's chapter on Indigenous peoples and the politics of recognition provides an in-depth exploration of Frantz Fanon's writings on the psychological effects of colonization and is a key text in the field, influencing many of the other pieces, such as Pomaika'i McGregor's on Hawaii. Coulthard's chapter also links to others that refer directly to Fanon in their pieces, such as Michael Lujan Bevacqua's chapter on decolonization processes in Guam and Negron-Muntaner and Yasmin Ramirez's chapter on the artist Jean-Michel Basquiat. Along with the cross-fertilization of ideas between the chapters' authors, *Sovereign Acts* is also tied together by the various explorations in different chapters of key thinkers on recurring themes such as the political theory of sovereignty with Wendy Brown and Giorgio Agamben and decolonization and Indigenous sovereignty with Taiaiake Alfred. Mark Rifkin's chapter, "Indigenizing Agamben," offers a rich exploration of Agamben's state of exception from an Indigenous perspective, with Rifkin convincingly arguing that Agamben crucially omitted geopolitical considerations from his biopolitics theory.

The diversity of areas explored in this book and the necessity of providing a historical backdrop and context to each chapter do not result in a superficial analysis. The authors provide context through their examples, with their engaging arguments accompanied by enough context for a reader unfamiliar with the particular case study or region to learn of both the context and the content of the argument. While the national context is largely restricted to the United States and the various Indigenous, sovereign, or semisovereign entities within its jurisdiction (with the exception of Coulthard's chapter, written in a Canadian context), the diversity of these entities, from Hawaii to Puerto Rico, Guam to American Samoa, along with several Native American communities, offers the reader a culturally, politically, and geographically diverse exploration of this theme. The restriction to a mostly American context highlights the abundance of different semisovereign arrangements existing within that single nation-state and the distinct ways in which communities navigate and contest their relationship to the US government, as well as offering diverse perspectives on the possibilities for the future—and their limitations.

The authors in this book do not shy away from challenging politically and ethically contentious topics. Jennifer Nez Denetdale's chapter offers a nuanced critique of gender politics within the Navajo Nation, neither dismissing cultural practices nor hesitating to highlight the strategic use of "tradition" in some instances to uphold patriarchal structures. Stephanie Nohelani Teves also explores gender and Native politics through her analysis of Hawaiian hip hop rapper Krystilez's melding of Indigenous Hawaiian musical performance tradition and hip hop culture with its attendant misogyny. Jessica A. F. Harkins similarly explores the contested use of tradition on both sides of the debate over same-sex marriage in the Cherokee Nation, emphasizing the instrumentalization of culture in these instances and the dangers of defining such debates in terms of mainstream liberalism.

In addition to exploring the politics of gender and sexuality in Native American communities, Brian Klopotek's chapter offers a nuanced, forthright investigation of antiblack racism among Native communities in the American South. Klopotek carefully delves into the phenomenon of racism upheld by Native communities, contextualizing it in relation to federal recognition scheme requirements and highlighting the common foundation of both racism and colonialism: white supremacy. Madeline Roman also tackles the difficult question of whether sovereignty ought to be struggled for; through a deconstruction of sovereignty in terms of both the nation-state and the individual, she suggests that contemporary struggles for sovereignty may be misdirected in light of the current political and social environment.

The critical engagements with ethically and politically difficult topics in this book make for a frank and nuanced exploration of struggles for sovereignty, their various manifestations, and their limitations.

MELANIE VASSELIN works in human rights law, specializing in refugee law, and has a strong interest in Indigenous rights.

KEITH RICHOTTE JR.

Crime and Social Justice in Indian Country
edited by Marianne O. Nielsen and Karen Jarratt-Snider
University of Arizona Press, 2018

BEAUTY, AS THE OLD ADAGE GOES, is in the eye of the beholder. So it is with *Crime and Social Justice in Indian Country.* The utility of the edited volume will depend on a reader's expectations before engaging with the text.

First explaining what the volume does not do is the most useful way of then engaging with the successes of the work. Unsurprisingly, in a book titled *Crime and Social Justice in Indian Country,* there are a number of passing allusions to the legal framework that makes crime and social justice in Indian Country different from anywhere else in the United States. And yet, very surprisingly, there is no serious attempt to describe that framework or give the reader any sense of the context in which crime and social justice operate in Indian Country. There is no workable description of how the federal government came to be deeply involved in criminal law in Indian Country (e.g., the Major Crimes Act), how certain states became more involved in criminal law in Indian Country (e.g., Public Law 280), or the various constraints on the criminal law and punishments that tribal nations can proscribe (e.g., *Oliphant*). Many of the critical cases and statutes that shape how crime is treated in Indian Country do receive some explicit mention—*Oliphant*, perhaps the most important Indian law case in the last half-century, is eventually mentioned by name on page 187—but often in a manner that, at best, assumes that the reader already has a level of knowledge about the material.

Lacking this critical grounding, the volume can sometimes feel as if it is missing a true sense of purpose. What is this work trying to accomplish, since it does not provide the context to most fully engage with the questions it raises? For example, Alisse Ali-Joseph's chapter on Native athletic participation on the collegiate level is a fine piece of scholarship that asks some useful questions about the role that sports have played and do play in Native America. Yet it takes a lot of imagination to understand it as fitting within the category of either crime or social justice.

This lack of critical grounding also leads to some deeper problems. At a minimum, opportunities are missed. For example, on page 6 the editors of the volume offer the shocking statistic that while Natives only account for approximately 2 percent of the American population, they account for 16 percent of the federal prison population. Within the text, this statistic is used merely to note the overrepresentation of Native people in the criminal justice system. In fact, the problems of crime within Indian Country—as the volume frames it—never rise above the general notion of colonialism. As stated by the editors on page 3, "Indigenous Americans are a population with a unique political and legal status, whose justice issues—and solution—are rooted in colonialism." Had the text established the critical grounding that shapes issues of crime for Native America, the editors could have made the much more direct and powerful argument that this overrepresentation is caused, in large part, by the federal government both under- and overenforcing criminal law in Indian Country as a result of the structure of federal Indian law.

These drawbacks make it impossible to recommend this volume as a primary text for a scholar or class that wants a global view of crime and social justice in Indian Country. Nonetheless, individual chapters are provocative and would be useful secondary readings for a scholar or class seeking to seriously engage with this subject matter. As with any edited volume, there is a varying degree of helpfulness among the chapters. But of the volume's three units, the third, "Community Responses," is the standout. Anne Luna-Gordinier's chapter is a very nice description of the Tribal Law and Order Act and the Violence Against Women Act and how they could be most useful for Indian Country. Danielle V. Hiraldo's chapter on the efforts of state-recognized tribal nations to engage in legislation similar to the Indian Child Welfare Act at the state level is a tremendous reminder of the varied political landscapes that tribal nations have to negotiate. And the final chapter in the unit is a helpful piece that demonstrates the utility of rethinking the purposes and methods of punishment for Indigenous youth by comparing the experiences of Native child offenders in Arizona and New Zealand. The volume's concentration on gender disparities under the law, specifically how Native women are particularly victimized, is critical as well.

KEITH RICHOTTE JR. is a citizen of the Turtle Mountain Band of Chippewa Indians, an assistant professor at the University of North Carolina—Chapel Hill, and an associate justice on the Turtle Mountain Tribal Court of Appeals.

JESSICA LANDAU

Unsettled
by JoAnne Northrup
University of Chicago Press, 2017

FROM THE MOMENT YOU OPEN THE BOOK, the very nature of its construction will unsettle you. Instead of a book bound at the spine and packaged neatly between two covers that open right to left, *Unsettled*'s binding is exposed, and the spine that faces you is a false one—the book is wrapped in its cover, and you must open two flaps in order to get inside. In this manner, this large format becomes even larger. It is not a book to casually flip through—the materials themselves force you to sit down with the images and text at a table and spend some time with them.

Unsettled is primarily an exhibition catalog and conference publication. Curated by JoAnne Northrup in consultation with the artist Ed Ruscha, the exhibition features works by artists both living and dead, yet all grappling with, in some way, issues about indigeneity and the environment. The travel exhibition has three hosts: the Nevada Museum of Art (August 26, 2017—January 21, 2018), the Anchorage Museum, Alaska (April 6—September 9, 2018), and the Palm Springs Art Museum, California (October 27, 2018—February 18, 2019). Sprinkled throughout the often large-format illustrations are limited text and twitter poems by Allison Warden.

Northrup calls *Unsettled* "a dialogue across time and space," positioning the exhibition as a sort of ongoing practice featuring artworks that tell stories of the North American West. They are organized into five thematic areas: "Shifting Ground," "Colliding Cultures," "Colonizing Resources," "The Sublime Open," and "Experimental Diversity." While the exhibition highlights the work of a diverse group of artists, many contemporary, others older, the work of LA artist Ed Ruscha features prominently and is included within each theme, often serving as a touchstone for the overall exhibition and thematic layout. In fact, Ruscha's bold use of color and suggestive text, combined with what Northrup describes as his "insightful yet dispassionate vision of our world," seem to even serve as graphic inspiration for the catalog itself.

Ruscha's work is a perfect place to begin this discussion because it is never attached to singular meanings—and as the catalog itself does, his paintings unsettle the viewer, not allowing them to be grounded in the American West they are so often attached to. His work is evocative, never descriptive. Because of this starting point, the West pictured in this catalog not only is the West of the American "frontier" but also connects to the Arctic Circle, the Bikini Atoll, and Australia's Great Victoria Desert, among other places. It feels at many points like the West is not only a shifting ground but also essentially ungrounded—and this is certainly a strength of this catalog.

This wide berth and nonspecific point of departure allow the curators to cover an impressive range of material, juxtaposing artists as far apart thematically and chronologically as Brian Jungen and Emily Carr and including pottery from Mexico dated 100 BC—AD 250 alongside performance and video art. These combinations are far from obvious, and while they are interesting, readers are sometimes at the mercy of the catalog essays to begin to form a meaningful interpretation. Worded differently, what can be said is that these curatorial choices are tricky: the works illustrated are often opaque, they require the viewer to work hard in order to arrive at meaning, and the comparisons offered by the curators require even more effort. But this is by no means a bad thing—viewers of art should be asked to work hard. Cultural meaning is not easy, especially concerning topics as complex as sovereignty, environmentalism, indigeneity, and settler colonialism. And while the catalog essays help elucidate meaning in these juxtapositions to some extent, they are in no way didactic. They encourage readers to flip back to illustrations and think harder. In many places, the authors raise more questions than they answer, making this catalog and exhibition an excellent tool for the study and teaching of art history, contemporary art, Indigenous critical theory, and the legacy of settler colonialism. I look forward to adding it, in pieces and in whole, to my syllabi as an early career scholar.

JESSICA LANDAU is a PhD candidate in art history at the University of Illinois at Urbana—Champaign and the executive director of the Midwest Museum of Natural History.

MELONIE ANCHETA

Corey Village and the Cayuga World: Implications from Archaeology and Beyond
by Jack Rossen
Syracuse University Press, 2015

IN 1779 GEORGE WASHINGTON ordered a scorched-earth campaign against the Iroquois Confederacy (also known as the Haudenosaunee Confederacy) with the intent of total annihilation. He sent almost one-third of the Continental Army into central New York State, and what is called the Sullivan Campaign left the Cayuga Tribe, one of the original five tribes in the Confederacy, with no home territory or resources and a history rewritten. *Corey Village and the Cayuga World* presents evidence and a view of Cayuga life in the last half of the sixteenth century, just prior to European contact and up to the American Revolution that may help restore the true Cayuga history.

In *Corey Village and the Cayuga World*, Ithaca College professor Jack Rossen and his students explore two large questions: "Were the Cayuga part of the factions warring against the colonists?" and "Just how old is the Iroquois Confederacy?" They also investigate questions about the sociopolitical and cultural organization and practices of the Cayuga people.

Examination of the Corey Village site along with neighboring village sites overturns the common narrative that these villages were at war against the colonists. The types of artifacts found, overwhelming evidence of a thriving agriculture that also served as an economic resource, the composition of the villages themselves, lack of projectile points, and no fortifications, all indicate that the inhabitants were not living defensively or actively participating in warfare.

Rossen discusses how mounting evidence demonstrates that sites being chosen for villages were proximal to a specific soil type that is rare in the region but extremely fertile and perfect for the agricultural practices of the Cayuga. He points out agricultural lands such as Peachtown, with an orchard of fifteen hundred peach trees (which were not indigenous and had to be introduced and cultivated), were deliberately chosen for specific microclimates suitable for specific crops.

A variety of cultigens such as beans, squash, corn, sunflowers, and gourds (many cultigen seeds present evidence of long-range travel, trade, and exchange), along with the remains of stone hoe blades, offer images of well-tended fields of nutritious crops that not only supplemented foraging but could have been the primary vegetable resource. Evidence of genetic manipulation is clear in plants like sunflowers that were bred to increase the size of the kernels. This indicates a firm understanding of the principles of how to increase crop yields and adds evidence to other findings of the Cayuga being agrarian people with specific sites dedicated not only to crops but also to the harvesting, processing, economic trade, and celebration of those crops.

Along with his team of field students from Ithaca and Wells Colleges, Rossen implemented what is called "Indigenous archaeology" and worked cooperatively with Cayuga elders, medicine people, and tribal members in 2002 and 2003 to integrate Cayuga cosmological values, political consider- ations, and oral history into the archaeological examination of Corey Village and neighboring Cayuga village sites located in central New York State.

Corey Village and the Cayuga World focuses on interpreting the implica- tions of the particular types of lithics found, village placements, evidence of occupational specialties, soil types, local flora, and site-specific activities in a more cohesive narrative more closely resembling the actual oral history of the Cayuga people.

In his examination of the types of lithics found at Corey Village, such as nonprojectile points (projectile points are commonly found in great num- bers in villages engaging in war), unifacial stone tools such as scrapers, cut- ting tools, and stone palettes, Rossen suggests they are indicative of spe- cific types of activities related to healing practices. This artifactual evidence at Corey Village, along with an abundant variety of medicinal plants, both indigenous and introduced, gives strong testimony to Corey Village being a "hospital" or "clinic" village dedicated to healing.

Corey Village and the Cayuga World is laid out in a series of essays writ- ten by Rossen and eight students. These chapters focus specifically on topics such as describing site locations, comparing the characteristics of ceramic materials and decoration, analyzing stone tools and raw materials, and fau- nal and botanical remains.

The epilogue is dedicated to Rossen, explaining his thoughts and position on "dominant archaeological narratives of the Haudenosaunee" explicat- ing some of those narratives, and challenging them with a less constrictive approach to interpreting archaeological findings.

Questions about who the Cayuga were, their role in the American Revo- lution, their traditional territories, how they lived, and their actual history have been examined and, perhaps, partially answered. The evidence collated through the study of artifacts from Corey Village and neighboring villages, as well as the implications of the manner of living, all speak to the Cayuga as a much more peaceful, agrarian, and neutral culture than American history has portrayed them. The oral history they have carried down through the past two hundred years may well be validated through the archaeological evidence found by Rossen and his students, and through the practices and beliefs of archaeologists and scholars like Jack Rossen and those working with him.

MELONIE ANCHETA is a recognized authority on color use and the pigment and paint technology of Northwest Coast Native Americans and is founder, owner, and head researcher at Native Paint Revealed (www.nativepaint revealed.com).

RAYMOND D. AUSTIN

Claiming Turtle Mountain's Constitution: The History, Legacy, and Future
   of a Tribal Nation's Founding Documents
by Keith Richotte Jr.
University of North Carolina Press, 2017

DR. KEITH RICHOTTE'S well-researched and well-written book tells a story that is all too familiar to the American Indian people. Whether it be the Plains Ojibwe, the Metis, the Sioux, or the Navajo, the story follows a familiar pattern: in spite of the federal government's promise to protect American Indian nations and their members—a duty of protection recognized in Indian treaties and United States Supreme Court decisions—the federal government established laws and policies resulting in Indian removals, theft of treaty-promised lands, allotment of Indian lands, termination of Indian nations, and excessive federal control over the lives of the Indian people on reservations. The overarching theme of this book, and of federal Indian laws and policies for over two hundred years, is the federal government's practice of doing justice for white settlers while simultaneously doing injustice to its treaty partner, the American Indian nations.

Give the American Indian people credit for surviving—physically, mentally, culturally, spiritually, and as nations—the federal government's outright destructive Indian policies and laws. Challenged by obstacles erected by federal Indian policies, the Plains Ojibwe and the Metis, just like other American Indian nations of the second half of the nineteenth century, struggled to forge a political identity that the federal government would recognize as legitimate and capable of a nation-to-nation relationship. Richotte, using federal documents, newspaper clippings, letters of the day, and some between-the-lines reading, has woven a clear narrative in the style of traditional Indian storytelling of how the Indian nation now known as the Turtle Mountain Chippewa used the constitutional process to pursue and eventually establish its political identity. One might even say that the leaders of this Indian nation had foresight because they strategized development of a constitution long before the 1934 Indian Organization Act was enacted.

Central to the Turtle Mountain Chippewa's drive for a constitution was its desire to file a claim against the United States for wrongs the United States committed, including the taking of the Chippewa's ancestral lands without just compensation. The problem was that an Indian nation could not file a claim against the United States without its consent made in a duly enacted law. The leaders of the Turtle Mountain Chippewa believed that the best strategy would be to solidify the nation's political identity through a constitution. The federal government would then recognize the Plains Ojibwe and the Metis as a single political unit, the Turtle Mountain Chippewa. Congress would then enact legislation allowing the Chippewa to file a land claim, and the president would sign it into law.

One can argue that the federal government should have recognized the Turtle Mountain Chippewa as a sovereign nation, even without a written constitution, pursuant to established legal doctrines established in the early Cherokee cases *Cherokee Nation v. Georgia* (30 U.S. [5 Pet.] 1 [1831]) and *Worcester v. Georgia* (31 U.S. [6 Pet.] 515 [1832]). However, federal policy and the rules of the day would not permit it. In the late 1800s, Indian people were considered uncivilized "wards of the federal government," and the federal government had "plenary power" over them. Thus, the federal government's pervasive control of Indian nations and the lives of Indian people left no room in giving effect to already established legal doctrines that would have recognized the political status of the Turtle Mountain Chippewa.

The Turtle Mountain Chippewa voted on and passed a constitution in October 1932. It was heavily influenced by the federal government and had many faults. Nonetheless, it was an instrument that provided another step on the road to a claim against the United States. Unfortunately, the adoption of the constitution did not lead to the filing of the long-anticipated claim. The Turtle Mountain Chippewa had to wait until Congress established the Indian Claims Commission in 1946 to pursue its claim. The claim was finally filed in 1951. Judgment was awarded in 1978, but the money was not released until 1984.

This is a story of loss, desperation, frustration, victory, and sadness. Yet it advances a valuable lesson for the Indian nations and their leaders today. The diverse social, economic, and educational problems that we see in Indian Country have roots in the destructive federal Indian policies and laws of the past. One can better understand these problems by looking at the history of the Indian nation itself and its historical relationship with the federal government. Richotte used this approach and gave us a richly informative narrative that is easy to understand.

RAYMOND D. AUSTIN (Navajo) is a professor with the Applied Indigenous Studies Department at Northern Arizona University, Flagstaff.

ELIZABETH HOOVER

A Land Not Forgotten: Indigenous Food Security and Land-Based Practices in Northern Ontario
edited by Michael A. Robidoux and Courtney W. Mason
University of Manitoba Press, 2017

IN *A LAND NOT FORGOTTEN*: *Indigenous Food Security & Land-Based Practices in Northern Ontario*, researchers affiliated with the multidisciplinary Indigenous Health Research Group (IHRG) at the University of Ottawa describe their collaborative work with First Nations in northwestern Ontario, seeking to address issues of public health and food security. The communities working with IHRG are isolated, with access only to expensive food and goods; they lack many public services; and they face high rates of chronic disease, suicide, and unemployment. The goal of the book is not to dwell on these negative statistics but rather to describe their complex history and to demonstrate community-created, land-based cultural practices being used as an avenue to wellness.

The book opens with a conversation with Wawakapewin elder Simon Frogg, who shares stories about the origins of land-based foods and describes the impact of colonization on his community. Giving Frogg the first word in this book sets the tone for the message the authors are aiming to drive home: the importance of including community voices in project design and implementation.

In the introduction, Mason and Robidoux describe how academics have consumed millions of dollars of research funding to determine that Indigenous Canadians suffer from food insecurity and high rates of chronic illnesses. Yet despite this research, those rates are increasing. The authors humbly recognize their role in this type of research and then offer examples of how they have moved to a more community-derived and community-driven approach to respond to the complexities of Indigenous health and food systems in an effort to "build resiliency in ecosystem and communities" (9).

Chapter 1, by Joseph LeBlanc and Kristen Burnett, lays out the colonial conditions that have directly contributed to contemporary food insecurity and that must be taken into consideration to address these issues. While food is connected to many different systems—social, sacred, economic, cultural—the current market system puts control of food economics in the hands of remote entities driven by profit margins. Thus the solutions to food insecurity cannot emerge from the existing paradigm. In the second chapter, François Haman, Bénédicte Fontaine-Bisson, Shinjini Pilon, Benoît Lamarche, and Michael A. Robidoux problematize the idea of genetic determinism to explain the disproportionate rates of chronic disease in Indigenous communities, citing other complicating factors and presenting research on the role played by foods in promoting or preventing disease. In chapter 3 Robidoux describes three of the community projects IHRG has engaged with, giving an honest assessment of the successes and challenges within each project and summarizing outcomes in a series of helpful charts that include activities, supplies needed, teachings, yields, and outcomes.

The fourth chapter, by Desirée Streit and Courtney W. Mason, lays out the history of how Western assimilationist education programs removed Native youth from their culture, homes, language, food systems, and the land. To combat the ensuing social and physical health impacts, some communities are reclaiming control through land-based curriculum development. The chapter includes a curriculum model to demonstrate how community needs can be met while also satisfying provincial curriculum standards. In the fifth chapter, Cindy Gaudet emphasizes the critical role of women in the development of land-based programs and notes that reconnecting to the land does more than increase food access for these communities; it also awakens cultural practices and knowledge expressed and embodied in the land, language, and stories. *A Land Not Forgotten* concludes with examples of productive collaborations between Indigenous communities and non-Indigenous organizations to improve health and cultural continuity. Mason and Robidoux highlight the need for researchers to support community-based solutions, because without addressing larger health and social issues alongside food security challenges, efforts to improve dietary practices will have little impact.

The only thing that might have improved this book would have been to hear directly from the community members with whom these researchers were collaborating. In each chapter, university-based researchers reflect on their experiences in discovering the importance of land-based education. While they include direct quotes from interviewees, the book would have benefited from either an entire chapter or at least a segment of one written from the perspective of one of the participating communities. While the opening interview with Simon Frogg brings in important cultural context, he does not directly address any of the studies or programs that comprise the rest of the book.

A Land Not Forgotten does an admirable job highlighting both the vulnerability and the resiliency of remote Indigenous communities. It would be useful in college courses in public health or research methods; for health professionals, especially those working in Indigenous communities; and for Indigenous communities seeking to establish relationships with university researchers or even looking for examples of food sovereignty projects to implement on their own.

ELIZABETH HOOVER is Manning Assistant Professor of American Studies at Brown University and a board member of the Native American Food Sovereignty Alliance (NAFSA).

JESSICA LESLIE ARNETT

The Tanana Chiefs: Native Rights and Western Law
by William Schneider, with contributions from Kevin Illingworth,
    Will Mayo, Natasha Singh, and Thomas Alton
University of Alaska Press, 2018

IN HIS BOOK *The Tanana Chiefs: Native Rights and Western Law*, historian William Schneider chronicles a little-known though vastly important meeting between Interior Alaska Athabascan leaders and representatives of the US government. Gathered in a library in Fairbanks, Alaska, in 1915, representatives from several Tanana Valley villages interrogated territorial officials about white encroachment on Indigenous lands and made requests for access to wage labor, education, and medical care. While neither side achieved their immediate goals, Schneider's book rightfully contextualizes the meeting in the long genealogy of Alaska Native assertions of sovereignty in response to US colonialism.

The book is organized into five chapters, a postscript, and four appendices. The first two chapters, authored by Schneider, examine the history of white encroachment into Native lands from the late nineteenth-century fur trade to the early twentieth-century gold rushes. Chapter 3, contributed by Alaska historian Thomas Alton, provides details about the 1915 meeting and the responses of the Tanana leaders to their choice between proposed Indian reservations or individual 160-acre allotments to prevent white settlers from completely dispossessing them of their land. Chapter 4 is a rich analysis of the transcript of the meeting by past Tanana Chiefs Conference president Will Mayo. In chapter 5 Schneider contextualizes the meeting within the long history of Alaska Native land rights activism. Appendix 1 consists of an introduction to the transcript of the meeting, and the second appendix contains the transcript in its entirety. Appendix 3, arguably the most significant part of the book, is the transcript of a 2015 interview conducted by Schneider with Will Mayo; Kevin Illingworth, associate professor with the University of Alaska Tribal Management Program; and Natasha Singh, a Koyukon Athabascan activist, lawyer, and tribal member of Stevens Village. Appendix 4 is a timeline of important events impacting tribal governments in Alaska.

This book aims to bring long-overdue attention to this historic meeting; however, the bulk of its contents dances precariously on the edge of familiar tropes that frame Indigenous people as unwilling or unable to adapt to the changes wrought by US territorial expansion. While pointing out the often-derogatory attitudes of settlers and federal officials toward Alaska Natives and the hardships Native people endured under assimilative policies, Schneider's and Alton's essays fail to account for these events within the larger processes of settler colonialism and Indigenous dispossession. Rather, they argue that the United States was "caught off guard" and "unsure how to respond to the impact of . . . settlers on the Natives and their way of life" (27, 32) while contending that the Tanana chiefs were simply "not ready to consider the choices the white men laid before them" regarding land (74). In addition to treating white ownership of Alaska as a foregone conclusion, neither Schneider nor Alton mentions Native sovereignty as fundamental to these conflicts over land, instead deferring to the language of "use" and "occupation" as the basis for establishing Native land rights. Framing Indigenous-US relations in territorial Alaska in this way portrays settler colonialism as passive and inevitable while naturalizing Indigenous dispossession. This is perhaps reflective of Schneider's and Alton's failure to meaningfully engage contemporary Indigenous studies scholarship, which would have contributed immensely to their analysis of this meeting and its historical significance.

The most compelling component of the text is buried in the back of the book. In the third appendix, Natasha Singh offers a powerful rebuke to US claims over Alaska Native lands following the 1867 purchase, testifying to the Tanana chiefs' assertions of sovereignty at the 1915 meeting and the persistence of that sovereignty "despite any recognition from anyone" (121). Schneider's and Alton's accounts of the Tanana meeting imply that the chiefs' failure to negotiate with federal officials on land ultimately led to their dispossession. Singh argues against that framing by linking the chiefs' actions to the survival of tribal governments that "have persisted, throughout backdoor termination, through missionaries raping our children, and now throughout our own Alaska Native people," who "still, with no legal jurisdiction over their own lands, seek to be stewards of the land" (129). Her redirection of the conversation aptly situates the Tanana chiefs' meeting in a historical and contemporary context.

Indigenous-US relations in interior Alaska remain an understudied topic, and this book draws attention to an important event in that relationship. However, these objectives are undermined by the author's failure to foreground Indigenous voices, draw on the rich field of Indigenous studies in his analysis, and consider Indigenous sovereignty and US settler colonialism as integral to the nature and outcome of this historic meeting.

JESSICA LESLIE ARNETT is a lecturer in the Department of History at the University of Minnesota.

DAVID A. CHANG

The Power of the Steel-Tipped Pen: Reconstructing Native Hawaiian
    Intellectual History
by Noenoe K. Silva
Duke University Press, 2017

IN THIS MUCH-ANTICIPATED WORK, Noenoe K. Silva builds a methodological and theoretical foundation for the reconstruction of Native Hawaiian intellectual history. Through a study of the Hawaiian-language works of Joseph Hoʻonaʻauao Kānepuʻu and Joseph Mokuʻōhai Poepoe, two writers active in the late nineteenth and early twentieth centuries, Silva traces an intellectual practice of using the Hawaiian past to speak to the present and future needs of the Hawaiian people (Kānaka ʻŌiwi). Moreover, she demonstrates the power of this practice by enacting it herself. The result is a compelling and erudite book whose linguistic and methodological range demonstrates that dedication to Indigenous futures is deeply rooted in Native Hawaiian intellectual history.

In her path-breaking 2004 study, *Aloha Betrayed: Native Hawaiian Resistance to American Colonialism,* Silva directed scholars to the rich archive of Hawaiian-language newspapers. It was in these newspapers that Kānepuʻu, Poepoe, and other intellectuals published their work. In the new book, Silva wisely eschews a broad overview of Native Hawaiian intellectuals through time. Instead, Silva chooses depth, and readers will be glad she did.

Writing about Kānepuʻu and Poepoe, Silva both describes and enacts what she calls "moʻokūʻauhau consciousness" (4). Moʻokūʻauhau is a term commonly glossed as "genealogy." The consciousness she describes relates it to another key term in Hawaiian life and Hawaiian studies, kuleana, which encompasses the English-language concepts of right, responsibility, role, and duty. Silva describes moʻokūʻauhau consciousness as "a certain mode of thought and action" in which writers "drew on their ancestral knowledge and accepted and carried out the kuleana to record it" for Native Hawaiians of their own time and "in the distant future" (6).

Silva tells us that Kānepuʻu and Poepoe were teachers in the broadest sense. Kānepuʻu was a classroom teacher in the Hawaiian Kingdom's schools, and over his career Poepoe was a classroom teacher, lawyer, newspaper publisher and editor, and legislative representative in the kingdom. At a time when missionization and foreign-style schooling had largely displaced the learning of mele (songs) and moʻolelo (stories), Kānepuʻu, Poepoe, and other Hawaiian intellectuals preserved this literature and taught Kānaka the interpretive and critical skills needed to engage with it. Silva emphasizes that they foresaw that future generations of Kānaka (including those of our own day and beyond) would need this knowledge.

Following an introduction, Silva dedicates a three-chapter section to each of the authors. She begins with Kānepuʻu. Born around 1824 on Molokaʻi, he "was among the first generation to take the oral traditions and create literature from them" (22). Silva focuses on Kānepuʻu's works from the 1860s and 1870s. Through analyses of the literary devices he deploys, Silva demonstrates how Kānepuʻu skillfully taught his readers and also instructs her own readers in the skill of reading such texts. Silva dedicates a chapter to Kānepuʻu's extensive serialized geography of the world, an 1877 work that critically commented on the political economy of late nineteenth-century Hawaiʻi, where haole (white Americans and Europeans) were coming to command land, wealth, and power. Here, she develops a theme that runs through the book: the centrality to the Hawaiian intellectual tradition of aloha ʻāina, "a complex concept that includes recognizing that we are an integral part of the ʻāina (land) and the ʻāina is an integral part of us" (4).

Silva then examines Poepoe's life and work and the way that his expressions of aloha ʻāina changed due to changed circumstances. Poepoe was more than a generation younger than Kānepuʻu. Born in 1852 on the island of Hawaiʻi, he faced the full onslaught of American colonialism and had to navigate the troubled waters of the politics of annexation. Silva's tracing of his political engagements is fascinating, nuanced, and needed by historians. Most impressive is her careful discussion of how Kānepuʻu came reluctantly to endorse American annexation and thus looked for ways to express aloha ʻāina in the context of ongoing American power in Hawaiʻi. It is important for Kānaka today to understand the reactions of Kānaka to the colonial onslaught in all their diversity. Silva dedicates a chapter to the examination of Poepoe's published mele and a chapter to the moʻolelo he published.

Throughout the book, she reads the authors' work with attention to the nuances of allusion and kaona (roughly, "multiple meanings") that enrich Hawaiian oral and written literature. The work powerfully brings together close readings, biographical study, and historical contextualization. Silva has produced a major work that demands the attention of all readers committed to Hawaiian history, Hawaiian literature, and Hawaiian studies.

DAVID A. CHANG is professor of history and American Indian studies at the University of Minnesota.

AMY GORE

The Specter of the Indian: Race, Gender, and Ghosts in American Séances, 1848–1890
by Kathryn Troy
State University of New York Press, 2017

AMID THE PLETHORA OF SCHOLARSHIP on Indian ghosts, Kathryn Troy contributes a new approach that looks specifically at the appearances of Indian specters within the Spiritualist movement during the second half of the nineteenth century. Because Spiritualists rebelled against authoritarian structures and lacked organization, they remain difficult to define, as Troy and other scholars note, yet participants in the movement commonly believed that the "spirits of the dead could communicate with the living," most often through séances and mediums (1). While most scholarship on the Spiritualist movement in America ties it politically to the promotion of women's rights and abolition, Troy instead cites the movement as inextricably tied to federal Indian policy and claims that it asserted the continuing presence of ghostly Indians to challenge the prevailing rhetoric of the vanishing Indian. Through extensive research in primary documents, including the foremost Spiritualist journal, the *Banner of Light,* Troy examines the function of the Indian specter within a religious organization that included an estimated millions of members and enhances the psychological complexity of the Indian ghost in American society outside of literature.

Troy avoids a repetition of the nearly exhausted topic of Indian ghosts in American literature, as well as the historical significance of the Indian image made in many other works of scholarship, including Phil Deloria's *Playing Indian* (1998). Rather, she examines what she calls the literal haunting rather than the literary haunting of Americans and unexpectedly builds upon Deloria's work when she calls for a greater attention to the particularities of Indian images and hauntings according to gender and to individual Indian "celebrities" such as Black Hawk (xvii, xix). In addition, rather than comment on the authenticity of Indian ghosts and their messages, Troy more productively matches the supernatural manifestations to unfolding federal Indian policy and the complexities of public opinion. Her introduction contains a clear delineation of her project, and her first chapter provides a helpful overview of the Spiritualist movement through the lens of their Indian politics. Troy returns to the political platform of the Spiritualists in her equally strong fifth chapter, "Race and Reform Among Spiritualists," in which she details and problematizes their push for "an absence of racial difference" and quickly points out the "catastrophic consequences of such policies for Indian peoples" despite the best of intentions (145).

Troy's best contribution comes from an examination of specific Indian images in regard to individuals and gender. For example, Troy's second chapter looks exclusively at the frequent appearances of Black Hawk during Spiritualist séances, arguing that his celebrity status speaks to the ways in which Spiritualists "sought to define ideal manhood and womanhood" (22). Her third chapter focuses on the political function of the Indian chief apparition, which she argues stood for "a specific model of manhood to be admired and mimicked by their white male spectators" and ultimately encouraged the spiritual progress of forgiveness and political advocacy (55). As yet another angle, the fourth chapter specifically examines the apparitions of "Indian maidens" in Spiritualist séances and scrutinizes the gender differences that they reinforced (91). Each chapter draws forth the insights to be gained by a greater attention to such particularities, and though the arguments in these middle chapters do not resound with the clarity of her beginning and ending chapters, Troy's strongest chapters would serve as beneficial readings in courses on the popular appropriations and the cultural impact of the Indian image, on the Indigenous or American Gothic, or on race and religion.

As painful as the racialized images and cultural appropriations are, the world of the Spiritualist movement marks a fascinating and understudied moment in American history and demonstrates the persistence and mutability of Indian images across all aspects of American history. Her book successfully balances the delicate walk between racial stereotypes and religious beliefs, and Troy maintains an admirable professionalism when describing Spiritualist beliefs and activities while also making its iterations of racism and sexism clear. While *The Specter of the Indian* contributes more significantly to nineteenth-century American studies than Indigenous studies, as Troy's research minimally incorporates Native voices or perspectives, her research benefits Native studies by evincing the perniciousness of Indian images, even into antiestablishment religious groups such as the Spiritualists.

AMY GORE is a doctoral candidate in American literary studies at the University of New Mexico.

CARTER MELAND

Indian Horse: A Novel
by Richard Wagamese
Milkweed Editions, 2018

RICHARD WAGAMESE'S *Indian Horse* is a brilliantly layered and moving novel that tells a story about the healing power of hockey. We need to understand hockey the way our protagonist, Saul Indian Horse, understands it, though. Saul is a seer, a gift he inherited from his great-grandfather, a skill that his beloved Ojibway grandma recognizes in the boy. Hockey, as Saul lives it in the first half of the book, is not a sport; instead, it is an embodiment of the same sort of life force that moves through the universe. It is the creative energy of controlled chaos; bodies speeding over the ice are meteorites burning through the sky; the puck squirting out from a scrum of players spins "like a small planet in a universe of white" (69); body pounding into body are stars exploding in space; and time only stops "when the puck is in the net" (149). Like all things in the universe, time does not really stop, though. It is ceremonially restarted with the face-off when the creative power of chaos is once again unloosed.

Saul sees through the chaos on the ice, sees the energy of the bodies in motion in ways that allow him to anticipate where the puck or a teammate will be and how to best get the puck in the net. A scout for the pros tells Saul that the great players "can harness that lightning. They're the conjurers. They become one with the game and it lifts them up and out of their lives too." The scout then asks, "That's what happens to you, isn't it?" (150).

The game lifts Saul out of his life at a Canadian residential school in the mid-twentieth century. He rises from grooming the ice to skating with the older boys under the tutelage of the humorous and kind Father Leboutilier. While the villain of the book, the school is not Saul's foundational experience of life; rather, the life he lived in the bush under the care of his grandmother before he is removed to the school sets his foundation. Saul is grounded in the Ojibway way of seeing, which informs his knowledge of the game. As his talent lifts him toward the pros, though, the game stops lifting him and instead becomes a site where the cutting racism of the Zhaunagush (the English/whites) drives Saul to become the stereotype the Zhaunagush want. The game stops being about creative energy, and Saul quits, turning down the destructive path of alcohol abuse.

From the first pages of the book we know we are reading the words Saul is writing while in rehab. We know, in other words, that Saul is working on getting back to that good way of living his grandmother taught him about, the way that lives in knowledge of that chaotic energy that is the creative force of the living universe, that lives in knowledge of the world the ancestors lived in and made for him. He recalls the story of his great-grandfather Shabogeesick, bringing the first horse to their community—the horse from which his family got their name, Indian Horse. Shabogeesick tells his community that many changes are coming with the Zhaunagush, "ways of thinking that will crash like thunder in our hearts and minds. But we must," he counsels, "learn to ride each of these horses of change" (7). Implicit in Shabogeesick's words is that we must learn to ride them in light of Ojibway teachings, not those of the Zhaunagush. Saul's narrative of his life arcs toward this realization, toward recovery of those teachings and healing from the losses in his personal life and the traumas endured at the residential school—and on the ice.

Before I was even halfway through *Indian Horse* I knew I'd be teaching it in my Native literature class this coming year (and likely for many years to come). In a powerful series of images, visions, and epiphanies, Wagamese draws the many strands of this powerful book together at the end in devastatingly moving ways. I was smiling through my tears as Saul makes his way back to the rink at the school and finds what he thought he'd lost waiting there for him. And, once again, the game lifts him out of the life he'd fallen into.

CARTER MELAND is a senior lecturer in the Department of American Indian Studies at the University of Minnesota. His novel, *Stories for a Lost Child*, was a finalist for the 2018 Minnesota Book Awards.

NEW BOOKS FROM **DUKE UNIVERSITY PRESS**

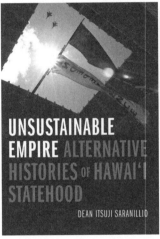

**Ethnographies
of U.S. Empire**
**CAROLE MCGRANAHAN and
JOHN F. COLLINS, editors**

Mapping Modernisms
Art, Indigeneity, Colonialism
**ELIZABETH HARNEY and
RUTH B. PHILLIPS, editors**
Objects/Histories

**Paradoxes of
Hawaiian Sovereignty**
Land, Sex, and the Colonial
Politics of State Nationalism
J. KEHAULANI KAUANUI

Unsustainable Empire
Alternative Histories of
Hawaiʻi Statehood
DEAN ITSUJI SARANILLIO

A World of Many Worlds
**MARISOL DE LA CADENA
and MARIO BLASER, editors**

dukeupress.edu

DUKE
UNIVERSITY
PRESS

NEW FROM MINNESOTA

MINNESOTA

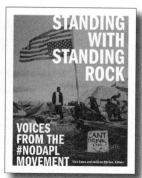

Standing with Standing Rock
Voices from the #NoDAPL Movement
Nick Estes and Jaskiran Dhillon, editors

Dispatches of radical political engagement from people taking a stand against the Dakota Access Pipeline, reflecting on Indigenous history and politics and on the Standing Rock movement's significance.

$24.95 paperback | 496 pages | Indigenous Americas Series

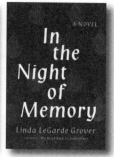
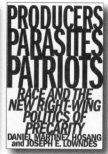
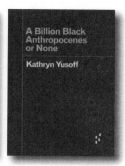

Translated Nation
Rewriting the Dakhóta Oyáte
Christopher Pexa

How authors rendered Dakhóta philosophy by literary means to encode ethical and political connectedness and sovereign life within a settler surveillance state

$25.00 paperback | 304 pages

In the Night of Memory
A Novel
Linda LeGarde Grover

"Riding on the wave of this poignant novel are some of the most important issues affecting American Indians today, including the loss of family and heritage and the destruction and disappearance of American Indian women. A remarkable achievement." —**David Treuer**

$22.95 hardcover | 224 pages

Producers, Parasites, Patriots
Race and the New Right-Wing Politics of Precarity
Daniel Martinez HoSang and Joseph E. Lowndes

"A powerful analysis of white precarity embedded in an anti-racist critique of white supremacy in multicultural times." —**Cristina Beltrán**, New York University

$19.95 paperback | 224 pages

A Billion Black Anthropocenes or None
Kathryn Yusoff

Rewriting the "origin stories" of the Anthropocene

$7.95 paperback | 130 pages
Forerunners: Ideas First Series

University of Minnesota Press | www.upress.umn.edu | 800-621-2736

NEW FROM UNC PRESS

 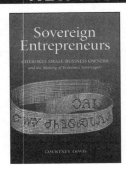  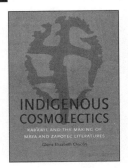

THE LUMBEE INDIANS
An American Struggle

Malinda Maynor Lowery

"This book is nothing less than a retelling of American history itself, a story marked not just by violence and betrayal but also by kindness, tenacity, and a deep sense of belonging. Lowery is a fine writer with a splendid narrative flair."
—**Elizabeth Fenn**, author of
Encounters at the Heart of the World
328 pages $30.00

SOVEREIGN ENTREPRENEURS
Cherokee Small-Business Owners and the Making of Economic Sovereignty

Courtney Lewis

"In this well-written, ethnographically interesting, and insightful book, Lewis takes readers to the heart of how individuals constitute Indigenous economies, not only via governmental institutions but also via private enterprise."
—**Jessica Cattelino**, University of California, Los Angeles
304 pages $32.95 paper

INDIANS ON THE MOVE
Native American Mobility and Urbanization in the Twentieth Century

Douglas K. Miller

"Miller's impressively researched new history of Native urban migration privileges Indigenous experience that can't be reduced to the vagaries of federal Indian policy."
—**Colleen O'Neill**, Utah State University
280 pages $29.95 paper

CRAFTING AN INDIGENOUS NATION
Kiowa Expressive Culture in the Progressive Era

Jenny Tone-Pah-Hote

"This book reminds us of the importance of understanding Native Americans as distinctly modern people who survived assimilation's assaults by aggressively navigating their way through this era."
—**Clyde Ellis**, Elon University
162 pages $29.95 paper

CAGING BORDERS AND CARCERAL STATES
Incarcerations, Immigration Detentions, and Resistance

Edited by Robert T. Chase

"This cutting-edge and extremely compelling interdisciplinary volume provides a sociohistorical overview of the development and execution of racialized punitive practices and the making of the carceral state."
—**Victor Rios**, University of California, Santa Barbara
400 pages $29.95 paper

MONUMENTAL MOBILITY
The Memory Work of Massasoit

Lisa Blee and Jean M. O'Brien

"This engaging book draws readers into a fascinating story that will help them make sense of collective narratives regarding nature, nationalism, 'Indians,' and the role of monuments. It is a truly enjoyable read, a book that provokes curiosity and a desire to unpack and understand."
—**Lisa Brooks**, Amherst College
282 pages $29.95 paper

INDIGENOUS COSMOLECTICS
Kab'awil and the Making of Maya and Zapotec Literatures

Gloria Elizabeth Chacón

"A meaningful contribution to the study of Indigenous cultural production, and particularly to the understanding of Indigenous literatures across Mesoamerica."
—**Tracy Devine Guzmán**, University of Miami
260 pages $32.95 paper

LITERARY INDIANS
Aesthetics and Encounter in American Literature to 1920

Angela Calcaterra

"By asking what it meant to be literary in early America, Angela Calcaterra finds intriguing, likely controversial connections that bind Native and Euro-American literary practices together. A significant new way to look at nineteenth-century American literature."
—**Phillip H. Round**, author of *Removable Type*
246 pages $29.95 paper

ALLEGORIES OF ENCOUNTER
Colonial Literacy and Indian Captivities

Andrew Newman

"In this fascinating study, Andrew Newman explores how captives ranging from Mary Rowlandson to John Marrant drew meaning from literacy and literature as they reflected on their own experiences and used citations and allusions to interpret those experiences for a broader audience. Historians will be intrigued by Newman's insightful new take on an essential topic in early American studies."
—**Christina Snyder**, Pennsylvania State University
Published by the Omohundro Institute of Early American History and Culture
236 pages $24.95 paper

**Shop our American History sale –
save 40 percent and free shipping for orders
over $75.00!**

 THE UNIVERSITY *of* NORTH CAROLINA PRESS
at bookstores or 800-848-6224 · uncpress.org · uncpressblog.com